Ameri MW00413781

Perish
Stella Fawn Ragsdale

The Hour of Feeling
Mona Mansour

Bethany
Laura Marks

Neighbors
Branden Jacobs-Jenkins

Methuen Drama

Published by Methuen Drama 2012

Methuen Drama, an imprint of Bloomsbury Publishing Plc

1 3 5 7 9 10 8 6 4 2

Methuen Drama
Bloomsbury Publishing Plc
50 Bedford Square
London WC1B 3DP
www.methuendrama.com

Perish © Stella Fawn Ragsdale 2012
The Hour of Feeling © Mona Mansour 2012
Bethany © Laura Marks 2012
Neighbors © Branden Jacob-Jenkins 2012

Cover image © Rob Drummer

ISBN 978 1 408 17307 7

A CIP catalogue record for this book is available from the British Library

Available in the USA from Bloomsbury Academic & Professional,
175 Fifth Avenue/3rd Floor, New York, NY 10010.
www.BloomsburyAcademicUSA.com

Typeset by Country Setting, Kingsdown, Kent CT14 8ES
Printed and bound in Great Britain by CPI Group (UK) Ltd,
Croydon CR0 4YY

This book is produced using paper that is made from wood grown in
managed, sustainable forests. It is natural, renewable and recyclable.
The logging and manufacturing processes conform to the environmental
regulations of the country of origin.

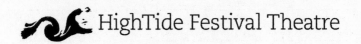 HighTide Festival Theatre

HighTide Festival Theatre in partnership with
The Public Theater Emerging Writers Group present

American Next Wave

Four Contemporary Plays from
HighTide Festival Theatre

Perish
Stella Fawn Ragsdale

The Hour of Feeling
Mona Mansour

Bethany
Laura Marks

Neighbors
Branden Jacobs-Jenkins

HighTide Festival Theatre in partnership with
The Public Theater Emerging Writers Group present

American Next Wave

Four Contemporary Plays
from HighTide Festival Theatre

A HighTide Festival Theatre production in partnership
with The Public Theater Emerging Writers Group

Writers

Stella Fawn Ragsdale
Mona Mansour
Laura Marks
Branden Jacobs-Jenkins

Cast

(in alphabetical order)

Emma Beattie	Georgia Maguire
Ishia Bennison	Stuart Martin
Geoffrey Breton	Lynne MIller
Jack Cosgrove	Marcel Miller
Frank Fitzpatrick	Miles Mitchell
Robert Gilbert	Clare Perkins
Edward Halsted	Jessica Pidsley
Elizabeth Healey	Gemma Stone
Louis Hilyer	Joseph Strouzer
Elisabeth Hopper	Sofia Stuart
Phillip James	Abi Titmuss
Nicole Lecky	Olivia Vinall
Jonathan Livingstone	William Byrd Wilkins
Pearl Mackie	

 HighTide Festival Theatre

Creative Team

Directors
Steven Atkinson, Rob Drummer,
Richard Fitch, Melanie Spencer

Set Designer
Clem Garrity

Design Assistant
Holly Hooper

Lighting
Matt Prentice

Sound
Neil Sowerby

Casting
Philippa Wilkinson

American Next Wave
Four Contemporary Plays
from HighTide Festival Theatre
were produced in partnership with
The Public Theater Emerging Writers Group, New York

All four plays received their first staged readings
in the UK at the HighTide Festival, Halesworth, Suffolk,
on the 5th, 6th, 12th and 13th May 2012

American Next Wave was generously supported by IdeasTap

www.hightide.org.uk
www.publictheater.org
www.ideastap.com

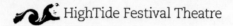 HighTide Festival Theatre

New Theatre For Adventurous Audiences

'Sharp, irreverent and fresh.' Daily Telegraph

HighTide Festival Theatre is a national theatre company and engine room for the discovery, development and production of exceptional new playwrights.

Under Artistic Director Steven Atkinson, the annual HighTide Festival in Suffolk has become one of the UK's leading theatre events, and in 2012 we are excited to premiere 18 new works. HighTide's productions then transfer nationally and internationally in partnerships that have included: the Bush Theatre (2008 & 2009), National Theatre (2009), Old Vic Theatre (2010), Ambassador Theatre Group / West End (2011), to the Edinburgh Festival (2008, 2010 & 2011) and internationally to the Australian National Play Festival (2010).

HighTide receives, considers and produces new plays from all around the world, every play is read and the festival is an eclectic mix of theatre across several venues in Halesworth, Suffolk. Our artistic team and Literary Department are proud to develop all the work we produce and we offer bespoke development opportunities for playwrights throughout the year.

HighTide Festival Theatre is a National Portfolio Organisation of Arts Council England.

A Brief History

The Sixth HighTide Festival in 2012

Luke Barnes, Jon Barton, Ollie Birch, Mike Daisey, Joe Douglas, Vickie Donoghue, Tom Eccleshare, Kenny Emson, Berri George, Karis Halsall, Nancy Harris, Ella Hickson, Branden Jacobs-Jenkins, Mona Mansour, Laura Marks, Ian McHugh, Jon McLeod, Shiona Morton Laura Poliakoff, Mahlon Prince, Stella Fawn Ragsdale, Stephanie Street, Philip Wells, Nicola Werenowska, Alexandra Wood

The sixth HighTide Festival in 2012 will premiere eighteen plays in world and European premiere productions in partnerships with emerging companies and leading theatres including: Bad Physics, curious directive, Escalator East to Edinburgh, Headlong, Halesworth Middle School, Latitude Festival, Lucy Jackson, macrobert, nabokov, The Nuffield Southampton, The Public Theater, Soho Theatre, Utter.

Ella Hickson's *Boys* will transfer to The Nuffield Theatre, Southampton and Soho Theatre in a co-production with the Nuffield Theatre, Southampton and Headlong.

Luke Barnes' *Eisteddfod* will transfer to the 2012 Latitude Festival.

Joe Douglas' *Educating Ronnie* will transfer to the 2012 Edinburgh Festival produced in association with macrobert and Utter.

Luke Barnes' *Bottleneck* will premiere at the 2012 Edinburgh Festival.

Charitable Support
HighTide is a registered charity (6326484) and we are grateful to the many organisations and individuals who support our work, including Arts Council England and Suffolk County Council.

Trusts and Foundations
The Bulldog Arts Fund, The Chivers Charitable Trust, The Coutts Charitable Trust, The DC Horn Foundation, The Eranda Foundation, The Ernest Cook Charitable Trust, Esmée Fairbairn Foundation, The Foyle Foundation, The Garrick Charitable Trust, The Genesis Foundation, IdeasTap, Jerwood Charitable Foundation, The Leche Trust, The Mackintosh Foundation, The Peggy Ramsay Foundation, Scarfe Charitable Trust, The Suffolk Foundation, SOLT/Stage One Bursary for New Producers, Harold Hyam Wingate Foundation, subsidised rehearsal space provided by Jerwood Space.

Business Sponsorship
ACTIV, AEM International, Ingenious Media Plc, Lansons Communications, Plain English.

Major Donors
Peter Fincham, Nick Giles, Bill and Stephanie Knight, Clare Parsons and Tony Langham, Tony Mackintosh and Criona Palmer, Albert Scardino, Peter Wilson MBE.

With thanks to all our Friends of the Festival

HighTide Festival Theatre, 24a St John Street, London, EC1M 4AY
HighTide Writers' Centre, The Cut, Halesworth, Suffolk, IP19 8BY

0207 566 9765
hello@hightide.org.uk
www.hightide.org.uk

Contents

Introduction

We think a lot about waves at HighTide Festival Theatre, not least because the metaphor best encapsulates our energy for seeing new playwrights crash against the establishment, and the vitality in their plays sweep across our cultural landscape. This same vitality, which fills the HighTide Festival programme year after year, best captures a generation of writers with a collective enthusiasm for writing. There is a commitment to storytelling among a generation who are living through rapid change, political upheaval and the levelling, or renegotiation of democratic ideals.

Around the world, cities have been occupied, students have protested, our news outlets overwhelmed and political platforms challenged. Notions of how the collective conscience is plugged into a network of viral news, video, online social political forums, Twitter and Facebook are evolving. This planet fundamentally is smaller or perhaps, in its rapid population expansion, feels smaller as shared voices are heard, experience is offered up and the codes of online, democratic space are in conflict with the everyday reality.

Playwrights have been grouped in the past, considered alongside their peers to suggest a trend; after all there is safety in numbers and something useful in considering new work against a zeitgeist, a movement, a manifesto. As readers of new plays we of course notice those writers who feel part of the same frustration, with a shared urgency. Their plays are vital, their message bold, clear.

The festival this year is the product of reading such plays and realising we are riding the crest of a wave, where the establishment that hands down opportunities must accommodate the emerging voices and the very notion of a top-down industry is bending under strain. We feel privileged to produce the work of peers, to give soapbox to storyteller and productions to playwrights.

This wave is not restricted to HighTide, it is not focused on the UK, but it is global and if our international submissions are anything to go by we must consider a generation across land and water, and work hard to defeat censorship, bring down walls and discover the most distinct voice under the most obscure rock. This search is ongoing but most recently took us to New York, where we first encountered the plays that make up this volume and were presented at the HighTide Festival.

All four of these playwrights and all four of these plays are from the Public Theater in New York, a powerhouse and a home for exceptional voices. The Public, through their Emerging Writers' Group, part of a wide programme of support for playwrights, champion and support, in much the same way as we do, ambitious writers and their bold stories.

What all four of these plays represent is the vanguard of exceptional talent, writers who are championed in America but have yet to find a home in the UK. We are their first home and also a platform as we proudly share their stories with our audiences and an industry that will want to listen. Having met Stella, Mona, Laura and Branden we can vouch for their determined, focused enthusiasm for words, for storytelling, for pushing an audience and sharing a world that is theirs for the taking.

Each play is of course unique, but also, when seen together or read here, they paint the most contemporary portrait of America and by extension of this world we all share. *Perish*, claustrophobic and poetic is inspired by family lore and Appalachian roots. Stella exposes the plight of women in rural America, and in the play's eloquent language evokes a world eroding, somehow timeless but diminishing.

The Hour of Feeling sets a newlywed couple against academic ambition and the changing map of the Middle East in 1967, while through the lens of history the play reconciles what it is to possess culture, how we mitigate love, honour and ambition when fighting against uncontrollable forces.

With Laura Marks's play *Bethany* it is the image that resonates strongly, the image of foreclosure, empty streets, abandoned homes, suburbs lacking community. Crystal, a young saleswoman, struggles to sell one last car to Charlie, a motivational speaker – but the paranoid squatter she lives with has other plans. Soon, Crystal discovers how far she'll have to go in order to survive.

Finally, *Neighbors* – quite simply one of the boldest new plays we have read at HighTide – is ferocious in its repositioning of an image, that of the minstrel. In its writer Branden Jacobs-Jenkins's non-intention to shock, but rather to 'put these ideas into constellation', it completes our American wave of bold voices and vital stories.

What we hope we have captured here in 2012 is a bold statement of intent to champion those playwrights who have something to say and the audacity to say it. These writers through the words on the page and the productions of their plays are the future of theatre and have, through their stories here told, staked a claim on the establishment.

If we can do anything further it is simply to say these four playwrights give us the best hope in that wave crashing down and with force giving voice to a generation energised and ready to effect change. These plays, these writers are more than a step in the right direction.

STEVEN ATKINSON & ROB DRUMMER
HighTide Festival Theatre

Stella Fawn Ragsdale

Perish

For my sister, Mindy Leah

With much gratitude to Liz Frankel

Perish received its first UK staged reading at the HighTide Festival, Halesworth, Suffolk, on 5 May 2012, and featured the following cast and creative team:

Porter	Elisabeth Hopper
Hazlitt	Georgia Maguire
James	Frank Fitzpatrick
Shannon	Emma Beattie
Cove	Stuart Martin
Coryden	Gemma Stone
William	Edward Halsted

Director Rob Drummer
Musician Joseph Strouzer

Characters

in order of appearance

Porter, *female, twenty-eight. Stoic, strong-spirited, Irish with Creek Indian blood, olive-skinned.*

Hazlitt, *Porter's sister, thirty. Paler, more dreamy, seems the younger one of the two although she is the elder.*

James, *Shannon's father, Porter and Hazlitt's uncle, fifties. Stubborn, Irish, broad-shouldered and powerful, slow to age, a shock of black hair not yet grayed.*

Shannon, *Porter and Hazlitt's cousin, female, thirty-six. She was both sister and mother to them at times.*

Cove, *a hunter, muscular, shows the years of hard labor and drink.*

Coryden, *childhood friend of Hazlitt's, female, twenties. Something puck-like about her, small and greasy like a kid who has always taken care of herself with varying degrees of surprising success.*

William, *Porter and Hazlitt's father, fifties. At least a quarter Creek Indian, smaller than James, wry, something mean about him.*

Setting

East Tennessee. A front porch of a house surrounded by woods of a few acres. There are other houses within walking distance and probably old forgotten shacks and stills to be found within the bounds of the woods. The girls all know the woods well, having trampled them back and forth through their youth. All action takes place either on the front porch of the house or in the woods.

Scene One

East Tennessee. What was once the most beautiful place on earth. In the distance, the Smoky Mountains cradle the valley, imposing their blue breath and heavy foliage of maples, birch, hickory, chestnut and alder, trees of heaven and the devil's walking stick, not yet bare for winter nor changed by autumn, but faded by late September's light.

A worn but bright turquoise house with a porch sits surrounded by an oak and several tree stumps. The yard gives way to woods.

A single dead magpie hangs from the oak. **Porter** *is on the porch with a suitcase. She is gaunt and dark, her crow-black hair braided. The Creek blood from generations past is revived in her. She looks older than she should.* **Hazlitt,** *her sister, is paler, Irish – the world never seems to sink into her. She watches* **Porter,** *afraid to disturb her reverie.*

Porter It's not like we lived like kings or princes. It's not like we lived on the wind, the way the wind blows there. Denel walked the foreign places as a soldier. I cleaned paint left from the boots of workers in the new houses near base in Idaho. Places I couldn't afford to live. Maybe that was my downfall, cleaning those houses. The ones on the army base don't belong to us. I wanted my own home. I liked the desert out west. I liked hearing the coyotes yell. The sparseness and the lightness of it on my skin. Maybe I missed the mountains of home but the way you miss a done lover. We did alright for a while. But things started slipping. The car broke. Basement flooded. We fought. Denel didn't re-enlist. He couldn't stay in the army anymore than I could stay married to him. He's walking the foreign places for the last time. We got six months slack and that's when Daddy heard about it. I lost the house. Moved to a shitty apartment because by then I couldn't even afford a house on base anymore. Then Daddy showed up one day. Called me unfit. Said I was good for nothing. But said he'd watch Leo while I looked for work. Then I came home one afternoon and he had split with him. Maybe Leo is better off. But I would like to find him. See my son again.

Hazlitt   They're out there?

Porter   Shannon says he's hiding in the woods. You said you'd move back here if I did. You promised. But you won't.

Hazlitt   I'm trying.

Porter   You lived a fancy life in the city and you won't.

Hazlitt   I haven't. Maybe he'll be glad to see you.

Porter   So he can beat my head into the wall. I didn't know he was going to trick me. I wish he'd talk to me.

Hazlitt   It's been a long time since I saw you.

Porter   I know it.

Hazlitt   We're getting old.

Porter   You look the same. Maybe a little older.

Hazlitt   Like Mammaw when she was young. My hands look like hers too.

Porter   It's from working outside.

Hazlitt   Maybe. (*Beat.*) She's been gone twenty-five years. I used to not know what twenty-five years was like. Now I do. When did it happen, when did we get old?

Porter   The year before last. When you lost all your values.

Hazlitt   This isn't the first time we've been broke.

Porter   I suppose it ain't.

Hazlitt   We're likely to be broke again.

Porter   That's the truth.

Hazlitt   What do we do now?

Porter *takes off her boot and tosses it.*

Porter   I don't know. There's things to worry about. What we will get to eat. Where we will live. Who knows if there is any future for us? Just idle wood. (*Beat.*) He said I'm no daughter of his. But he pulls me back. (*Beat.*) You're not really here, are you?

She takes off the other boot.

Hazlitt   No. I suppose not. You're thinking of when I saw you months ago in the desert. It was not so hot. April, maybe. I'm scraping away at the night. Sleeping on some unfamiliar mattress or couch. In a city that is a hundred mazes. I want go back to the mountains where we belong, but there's things keeping me, things I'm looking for. I'm trying to get back to help you. Just a few more dollars and I'll be coming to help you. I swear it.

Porter   Sure.

The light falls and **Hazlitt** *disappears.*

Scene Two

THE ENCHANTED KINGDOM

The occasional laughter and whisper of children. Slowly, the world becomes lighter again and, as it does, their laughter fades into the woods and reveals **Porter**, *wearing a blindfold in the yard and groping in the dark among the trees, playing hide-and-seek, searching for the children, alone.*

A porch light comes on and **James** *steps out of the house, a man in his fifties. He is big-boned and towering. His hair is still mostly that Irish and Cherokee black. He moves as slow as he thinks. His tall shadow falls over* **Porter** *and he carries a large switch. He watches her a moment. Every once and a while the shadow of a magpie swoons behind them.*

James   Porter!

Startled, **Porter** *pushes the blindfold up.*

Porter   Uncle.

James   I'm about to start busting some asses. Where the children?

Porter   Playin'.

James   Well, it's time for them to go in.

Porter   It's still light out.

James   It's nearly dark.

Porter   I hadn't seen my cousins in a long time.

James   I don't care. I thought they'd be in bed when I got home. They've been acting like a bunch of idiots today.

Porter   I guess they take after family.

James   I reckon. Shannon lets 'em stay up all hours when they ought to be in bed. She must be down in the garden. (*Beat.*) How long you here for?

Porter   Long enough to find my son.

James   Then what?

Porter   Don't know.

James   Well, we're glad to see you, we are. I remember when you was just a mean little Indian girl. Just about the meanest thing alive. But I don't want no trouble here, Porter, while you're staying. No men, no drinking, no fighting.

Porter   I never fight.

James   That's right. You're sweet as honeysuckle. I forgot. (*Beat.*) You tell those girls I said they have to go to bed soon.

He exits into the house.

Shannon, *a tall strong woman of thirty-six, comes onto the porch, dishes in her hands. She is the type of woman who by sixty will be worn out but, although we can tell she is the mother of at least four, maybe five children depending on the day, she has not yet lost her youth. Her tallness and breadth, like her father **James**, is almost beyond her, an embarrassment that her humility doesn't know what to do with. When she laughs, she laughs like a child, loud and out of place, spontaneous. Likewise, when she angers, her angers is like a child's, that burns and is forgotten. She is*

mightily self-conscious of her slightly crooked teeth and so, while not so
shy, she also has a habit of cowering like a child.

Shannon   You should get the girls to leave you alone.

Porter   I don't mind it.

Shannon   Well, just tell them to go play by themselves if they start to bother you.

Porter   They ain't seen me in a while.

Shannon   I suppose not. You haven't found him yet?

Porter   Not yet.

Shannon   When he got here two days ago he brought Leo here to see his cousins. So he would know them. I hadn't seen him since.

Porter   He knew I'd be hot on his trail. I ain't got nothing. Spent what there was to get here. Left everything in Idaho. Denel, he's still overseas.

Shannon   Must be rough.

Porter   I feel lighter at least.

Shannon   I bet.

Porter   I know what you think.

Shannon   I don't think nothing.

Porter   Sure you do. What he tell you?

Shannon   Your father told us that when he went up there, your place was a wreck and you were so drunk you couldn't even stand up.

Porter   That's a lie.

Shannon   I just been prayin' about it.

Porter   I looked all day. I've walked those woods to death and back looking for them.

Shannon   He knows these coves like the back of his hands. Even if you hunted him down, he's likely to hurt you.

Porter   Well.

Shannon   I know. (*Beat.*) I was planning on cooking a late dinner. Brown beans, fried squash, corn bread, pickled okra. I been cooking for hours already. Nothing fancy, but if you want to eat –

Porter *notices the dead bird hanging.*

Porter   What's that bird doing there?

Shannon   A warning. The magpies was in my garden this summer. (*Beat.*) My girls are big, ain't they?

Porter   Yeah. Pearl was just a baby last time I saw them.

Shannon   I know I should get them in bed earlier but they won't go, stubborn as poke, sweet as lambsquarter. Sophia. May. Rose. Prudence. And Pearl. My children, they won't never sleep. Sometimes I sit on the porch all night and wait for them to go to sleep.

Porter *listens, but her attention always drifts away toward the woods.*

Porter   All night?

Shannon   Sure. When the stars have set their store for the night, when I have worshed the steel pot and made coffee I sit out here and watch the mountains.

Porter   Your girls wanted to play hide and seek.

Shannon   I figured.

Porter   It took me so long to find 'em. Running between the silver birches. Pale though.

Shannon   I know they're pale. White as ghosts. Or paper. I used to keep them in on account of the yard being full of copperheads. And they sleep late. They sleep deep into summer and don't wake till the moonflowers bloom. I try to feed them good. All they want to eat is sugar cookies. But their lives are untroubled –

Porter   Maybe you ought to let them out more. The girls.

Shannon   I can't keep 'em in. Daddy hates for them to be out late, but I don't see no harm in it.

Porter   They seem like cautious children. When I came here, they all hid at first. I saw Sophia peeking out from behind a tree. She threw an apple at me. (*Beat.*) You'd tell me if you knew where my boy was, wouldn't you?

Porter *stares at* **Shannon** *for a moment.*

Shannon   I would.

The shadow of a bird flies low. **Shannon** *grabs her gun and shoots.*

Porter   Holy shit! You trying to kill us?

Shannon   I want them out of the greens.

Porter   Put that thing away.

Shannon   Fine. (*Beat.*) I keep the garden myself. Daddy got down there one day to try to pull the rocks out for me. It was all he could do to get up off his knees so old was he. I do all the hoeing and weeding and watering. I stake the tomatoes and pole beans. And then I do all the canning too. I look the greens and wash and boil 'em for the winter. I fix the roof, I built that fence there. Hailed out chesser drawers all by myself. I tell you what. I can do it all. Have to. Now night has surely come. Now the wind moves through the maples and alder. There the dragonfly is, when you can see him, with evening dew on his wings. I know how you feel, commed here after making a life. Wondering what was the past. In the day I walk Knoxville, past the old JFG coffee factory, past the railroad tracks, boarded-up buildings, looking for work, wondering what will come.

Porter   There isn't any future for us but there's going to be one for Leo. I even went and saw this guy today. To try to get a loan.

Shannon   Hard to believe.

Porter   Everybody's a whore these days, ain't they? You sleep with men and keep having babies so you can keep your WIC vouchers. Selling pies. Your legs are probably still slick with the juice of the last one. You want me to get you the dish towel?

Shannon   Shut up, Porter. You ain't getting me riled today.

Porter   It doesn't even bother you.

Shannon   My body is temporary. It's my spirit God wants.

Porter   What do I care? I used to pay the boys to go down on me when I was twelve, but now I'd let them pay me if it'd bring my son back. I'm meaner than any one of them. I see the lines and lines. I remember them from when we was kids. Miserable children. Miserable men.

Shannon   My body might be of the world but my spirit is pure.

She gets to looking at the birds again as they swoop. She shoots.

Porter *grabs the gun away from her.*

Porter   Knock it off.

Shannon   When did you ever care about a bird?

Porter   Just leave it alone. Something about it.

Shannon *asserts herself with a nervous confidence.*

Shannon   This is my house. I'll do what I want. Well, if you don't like it you can leave.

Specially if you keep talking like that, that raunchy ass talk a yours.

Porter   You owe me anyhow. I could stick up for myself but Hazlitt was too pathetic and weak.

She sees the row of little girls' shoes lined up.

You don't leave them alone with Uncle, do you?

Shannon   He's fine. Just a little senile. He'd never harm them.

Porter   Do you?

Shannon   I watch my children.

Porter   Stupid.

Shannon   I'm telling you I watch them.

She sees the bird and shoots again. **James** *comes out of the house.*

James   What's going on out here?

Shannon   Nothing.

James   Crows.

Porter   Children.

James   More like it. I can't hardly get around in the kitchen, the mess you made in there.

Shannon   I'll clean it up.

James   Don't even make your money back with those pies.

Porter   Won't you git off her back?

James   Aw, hush, Porter. You always walk around here like you own the place. Seems like you'd come back here with a little humility, losing everything. When I was your age I had me a job.

Porter   What do you want me to do, shit myself a job?

James   That's what a real American would do. Hard to believe.

Shannon   Don't mind him. He just is in a bad mood 'cause he keeps wrecking the truck at work. His vision ain't good.

James (*jokingly*)   My vision is just fine. Won't you come over here and tell me how my fist is doing?

Shannon   Okay.

James   I'm the only one I guess who works.

Shannon   Part-time. Delivering autoparts. You deserve a medal.

James   At least I have a job. Twenty-five years working as a security guard. No thanks or kiss my ass.

Shannon   Won't you go and make yourself useful?

James   A little humility. The both of you. I came out here to tell you that maybe I'd give Porter a hand in the morning.

Porter   Morning's too late. Got to find my son tonight.

James   Not going to be able to find anybody when you can't find the fist in the front of your hands. He could be anywhere in those woods.

Porter   That may be, but I can't sleep till I find him.

James   If I find out any of these folks ain't been telling the truth, not saying where your daddy is, I'll be fierce to deal with. A person like that wouldn't have no decent quality. I've always thought William doesn't have a lick of sense except a selfish one.

Porter *sees the bird again.*

Porter   Hush. There it is. Maybe you hurt it.

Shannon   I aimed to kill it.

Porter   It doesn't look like a magpie. It looks like it has orange feathers or something. Maybe it's a hawk.

Shannon   Well, whatever it is.

Porter   It never bothered anybody. Look how bright it is.

She starts toward the bird.

James   Watch now.

Porter   Now it's going into the woods.

Shannon   What about your son?

Porter   I just want to make sure he's not hurt. Look at him.

James   Particular looking.

Shannon   I'd be careful.

Porter   It'll just take a minute. I'm tired of things getting pushed around.

Shannon   Sophia been seeing the work lanterns of the railroad at night.

Porter   So.

Shannon   They ain't worked on the rails in years. The lights float through her room. Last time she talked about seeing them, someone died. The lanterns move through their room up the hill to the graveyard.

Porter   You're full a' shit. Anyway, I have to see what it is. I'll be back.

Shannon   Suit yourself.

Porter *exits into the woods, searching for the bird.*

James   You know I'd be real upset if someone was keeping things from her.

Shannon   I ain't. I told you.

James   You know God is a watchin you, Shannon. He surely is.

Meanwhile, **Cove**, *who we only see in the shadows, carrying a hunter's bow on his back, hangs a lantern in a far tree, while wandering the woods unseen, then fades back into the rising tides of night.*

Scene Three

THE DARK NIGHT AND THE THRESHOLD

Porter *enters, searching for the beastly bird.*

She walks into the woods and a graveyard filled with modest, sometimes wooden tombstones and petrified statues. Children's clothes hang on the nearby trees. Near the graveyard is a boat on the edge of a pond, which is unseen. The bowers hang low while, above, the silver moon, bright as a high beam, echoes **Porter** *in her companionless hunt, which has grown from a slow to a burning fever, the world an ephemeral hue.*

She senses she is being watched but cannot decipher the direction. The shadow grows at times mountain-high immortal and at other times sloughs little and mean.

From the trees, a voice is heard.

Coryden   Who goes there?

Porter   Hello?

Coryden   I said who goes there?

Porter   Nobody. Who the hell are you?

Coryden   I'm the shepherd of Wear's Valley.

Porter   There ain't no shepherds. Who are you really?

Coryden   It's none of your business.

Porter   Where are you?

Coryden *slips closer.*

Coryden   Move again if you want to die.

Porter   I don't care, living or dying, it's the same to me.

Coryden *comes out of the shadow. She is a girl dressed as a boy, her curls tucked up under her hat fall in wisps around her face, her stature is small and greasy and bright.*

Coryden   Well. you ought to care whether you live or die.

Porter I can't see you.

She tries to go by.

Coryden Watch it.

Porter Get out of my way.

Coryden You try to hop this paw and I'll slam you back so hard your head'll spin.

Porter I've walked these woods almost my whole life.

Coryden I don't let anyone pass.

Porter Who are you? If you don't get out of my way I'll shove my fist down your throat.

Coryden Porter Kidd, is that you?

Porter Who wants to know?

Coryden It's Coryden. I didn't get a good look at you at first but now I recognize your mean streak.

Porter Coryden?

Coryden That's right.

Porter Wipe your face. You look like you been suckin' a cow. What are you doing out here?

Coryden I protect these woods. What are you doing out here?

Porter I followed a bird.

Coryden What kind of bird was it?

Porter I don't know. I don't see it now.

Coryden What are you doing looking for a bird if you can't find your son?

Porter How do you know about that?

Coryden I heard it. In the wind.

Porter I don't know. It was silly, I guess.

Coryden   It's quiet out here. Mostly just me and the stag. How is your sister?

Porter   We ain't talked in a while.

Coryden   Me and her were close.

Porter   I should get going. I have to find my son.

Coryden   Wait. Have you ever hear a strange sound in the woods at night? Drifting up from the trees? Like glass?

Porter   No.

Coryden   Wait. Listen. Do you hear anything?

Porter   I don't hear anything.

Coryden *puts her ear to the earth.*

Coryden   Do you believe in spirits?

Porter   No.

Coryden   You did when you were little. And your mammaw did.

Porter   So.

Coryden   Hazlitt heard them. Always heard things like that. We heard them once together. They came up from the earth. When your father had run her off into the woods, I used to come lay with her till morning. She used to read to me. Some old poems and things. And books on agriculture. And grammar. That's when we did.

Porter   She used to read a lot.

Coryden   It started so quietly at first you could barely hear it. But it came up through the earth and went up into the sky. Chilled me cold. Quiet at first but then deafening, the most beautiful sound you ever heard. It gets lonesome here. I go home to my brothers and sister with their mouths open from morning to night. I keep trying to find it. I don't know why angels would come up from the ground unless they were earthly angels. I get the feeling that they are not invincible, but still hallow. Not even pure. The only thing I think is pure is the stag.

Porter   Aren't there lots of deer in the woods?

Coryden   Not now. He used to have a mate but she was shot last year. Now he just roams the woods looking for her. He's the last. His heart is just a muscle, he loves what he loves. I protect him. You don't know what to say. That's alright. But there's a mystery to things, Hazlitt knew that. Hazlitt is a seeker.

Porter   I have to find my son.

Coryden   I could tell you where to look. I seen your father's truck. If you will help me.

Porter   You saw his truck?

Coryden   Not far from here.

She pulls a book up from the earth.

This is one of the books, papers, she used to hide.

Porter   What do you mean, used to hide?

Coryden   She was made of a gentler rye. You were too. Your father was suspicious of her books. We heard it when she was reading to me.

Porter *takes the book.*

Coryden   I remember when you were just a little girl. Everybody thought you were mean, but you weren't mean. You were lovely and you didn't even know it. You was the wildest and most stubborn-minded girl anybody had ever met.

Porter   I should go back. It was crazy of me to come out here.

Coryden   Will you read a few lines for me? I saw your father's truck. I'll show the way, if you'll help me.

Porter   Just tell me.

Coryden   I won't.

Porter *opens the book.*

Porter   I didn't know she hid things. Why would she do that?

Coryden   Look how small she printed in the margins.

Porter   Here?

Coryden   Yeah.

Porter   My eyes are blurry.

She reads, with effort at first, at about an eighth-grade level, but gains confidence.

'One. The heart. Dioscorides says that the human heart declares that a man can not live more than a hundred and twenty years. That the heart of a one-year-old weighs about two-tenths an ounce, and expands in size by two-tenths an ounce every year until age fifty. But once it reaches the age of fifty it loses about two-tenths an ounce each year. The heart contracts. At age a hundred the heart has returned to its weight when it was a year old and can extend life no further.

They wait. Nothing.

Maybe it ain't the right book.

Coryden   Maybe.

It nearly broke your father's heart when you left. I seen his hair go from black to white. His Indian skin get washed out.

Porter   Show me.

Coryden   I'll point you in the right direction. The deeper woods are haunted. Many have gone and not been able to return when they have descended into the dark night.

Porter   Can't you come with me?

Coryden   You'll have to go yourself. But before you go, you should have a knife at least.

Porter   I don't need a knife.

Coryden *pulls out a handful of knives.* **Porter** *touches one of them.*

Coryden   Don't touch it. It's bad luck if you touch it. Tell me which one.

Porter   I don't need a knife.

Coryden   I told you to pick one.

Porter   That one.

Coryden   That's a good one. Made out of stag bone.

She throws it down onto the earth.

Now pick it up.

Porter   You pick it up.

Coryden   I can't hand it to you. It's bad luck. (*Beat.*) Senseless. I tell you what.

Porter *picks up the knife.*

Coryden   This is as far as I go. You have to see the things you can't see with your eyes. I can't git no further unless I get lost in the dark night.

She leaves **Porter** *abandoned in the woods.* **Porter***, looking around for the devil, fortifies her strength and continues.*

Suddenly she sees or thinks she sees the bird, flap its wings and land in a tree perhaps. She moves toward it but stops when a lower shadow rises and sinks.

It is a beast, a mountain lion. It creeps, encircling her, moving closer.

Porter   Get out of here, beast.

A single apple falls beside her from the tree, then a second. The shadow gets larger and closer.

Prudence? Sophia?

She picks up the apple and throws it at the beast. The shadow first grows larger. She throws the second apple and finally the shadow shrinks and passes.

Hazlitt Porter.

Porter Where did you come from?

Hazlitt Are you drunk?

Porter No.

Hazlitt Then you're imagining me.

Porter Where are you?

Hazlitt In an old apartment in Brooklyn. I'm a moment in our past, which also happens to be our present. I went to the city to seek my fortune and you raised your son. The year is 2010, there has not been any work for years. I'm watching someone's house.

Porter I don't want to talk to you.

Hazlitt You're waiting on me, I know. I'm standing in the kitchen. The tile is yellow cobble. The sun is slant. The window is open. It's still hot, but there's a breeze. Everything I own is stained with dirt.

Porter I don't want to talk to you.

Hazlitt I know when things are wrong. I can feel it. We're connected like that.

Porter If you cared you would already be here.

Hazlitt I told you I am coming. I miss you. I never thought I'd be gone so long. (*Beat.*) I'm dizzy. I haven't slept in days. Last night I slept in this boy's bed and he tried to make moves at night. The idea of liberty. Freedom to live. How's it free for us?

Porter There it is again.

Hazlitt The bird. It's good luck. I have something else to tell you. (*Beat.*) I had a dream about our father. I saw him on the side of the hill on the property we had. He had lost all of the anger that I am used to him having. (*Beat.*) It's true. He looked at me not at first but beyond me, at the sun. The light was pale. He looked like one who had lost the weight of the years. I could see him as a small child.

She stands up as though she sees him. Perhaps she does.

Weightless or like one illuminated by the sunbeam when the clouds depart, leaping over the hillside, shirtless, turned as though waiting for someone. His sisters, perhaps. He looked at me with such a feeling of joy that I was moved beyond words as if to say, 'Look, my sisters are not dead.' The world might be filling with debris and ancient but there is still light in places. We stood in the snow like that. The singing of angels hung around me, the snow in heaps of frozen hope, while the shadow of death hung upon him. The snow surrounded us and to the horizon was deeper. We looked at one another eye to eye as we might have done in the world of the living if fear of his temper had not prevented me. He is our father yet I cannot recall once gazing in his eyes as his daughter. The snow fell. And his expression became sad.

She is still. The light is bright like snow.

And then, without a word, he turned and departed through the drifts and he did something that I had never seen him do before. He looked back to me, like a man not wanting to leave and his gaze stayed on me as he walked. Three, four times he glanced over his shoulder, like a stranger reluctant to leave, like one who knows he is not long for the world. You have to find him. You have to make some peace with him. Porter, things are not well with him.

Porter   Do you think it's true?

Hazlitt   What?

Porter   That I broke his heart?

She turns to **Hazlitt** *but* **Hazlitt** *has disappeared.*

Scene Four

MAGIC CARILLION

Shannon *comes up to the porch, her hands full of four-foot stakes. She ties them into a bundle with string.* **James** *is sitting on the porch.*

While **James** *and* **Shannon** *talk, the following action simultaneously takes place in the woods.*

Porter *follows and catches the glimmer of a shining object half hidden by the ivy and vine. As she comes to it, we see that it is the cab of a rusted '72 Ford truck. Vines push up through its cracks, making it seem an extension of the woods itself. Scattered truck parts litter the ground nearby.*

Porter *runs her hands along its metal, which at times still reflects the light of the moon. She pulls a singular fiery-bright feather from the truck and holds it out, taken with it. Then, continuing her search, moves on through the dark and exits.*

James   You know the trouble with all this, William fighting over Leo, and Porter and Hazlitt being scattered, started a long time ago. William's people were always drifting. A no-luck family, half-Creek sharecroppers from Alabama who came up here to work for the TVA. Most men mark their lives by what they accomplish. William marks his by what he loses. Lost a baby sister from water on the brain when he was a little boy. Lost his baby sister Tammy. The police ruled it a suicide but he knew it was her boyfriend. They had been fighting real big. Lost his mama three days later when she killed herself out of grief. It was my sister Jo who cleaned up the blood. She was nine months pregnant with Hazlitt. Got down on her hands and knees and scrubbed the blood and bits of brain. Hazlitt was born with a shadow over her forehead. Then he lost my sister. He sold our mama's house when she was sick with pneumonia. I think that's what killed her. Sold it from under her and the bit of land. Sold his soul when he did that.

Shannon   I remember a little. But no one ever talked about it.

James *carves bark off the wood.*

James   Well, me and him are old, both of us aren't for long here. Look, I use the natural shape of the wood, leave it curved when I'm making something, where it is knotted and bent. Is it twisted that way because that's the nature of the tree, or was it bent by its environment? By the wind and the rain and the heat? I don't know.

Shannon   I guess he'll die working.

James   What is it you mean by that?

Shannon   He told me he had six thousand saved so he could retire and it's all gone. He gave all of it to Porter. Twice he gived her money to come home on when things was hard. And twice she said at the last minute she wasn't coming.

James   Well, it's hard. Things have changed. Changed a lot. But it's the same ole shit. Times are still hard. That's how times are. I pass by town and see people lined up for work. I'm lucky to be working, but wouldn't take nothing to get laid off. (*Beat.*) It's not right to keep a mother from her child. If I see William I will tell him so. Surely to God. Sick or not. I wonder what my girls are going to do, when I'm gone and when William's gone. Have you thought about that?

Shannon   I think about it every day.

James   When I'm gone, are you going to sit in the house till they take it away from you or you starve first? What are you going to do? Sit here day after day? Stare into space? The fat cats keeping all the money in this country are drooling all over what little bit of milk your babies get. Gonna go live under the overpass with your babies? Or you gonna try to marry a man? Knowing there's no reason he won't leave when the times get hard? You think you'll just fade away?

Shannon   It's in God's hands.

James   I know it is. But here on earth, God's a rich man. You've always been good. Obedient. Never had a problem putting your head down and getting the work done. Never seen anybody that could work as fast or hard as you. Never heard you or Porter complain. Practically raised all three of you and I love you, I do. But you got to stand up, lift your head up and do what needs to be done without anybody telling you. Not doing just whatever William says. You hear me?

Shannon *gets up and dumps the bucket out.*

Shannon   How do you think I can go against William? Who do you think pays the mortgage on this place?

James   Well, just the same.

Scene Five

HEAVEN AND THE UNDERWORLD

It is quiet except for the breeze that laps at the night like tides against strange shores. **Cove**, *now that we can see him, is muscular, tanned, Apollonian, dejected as if fallen from a greater height of heaven. He has come and rested against a rock. When he is present, the stars reveal themselves shining as pinpoints. But if he is absent the stars are obscured by night.* **Porter**, *who has come upon him, watches him, only half hidden.*

On his back he carries stag bones bound together like firewood. Where once flowed the more varietal powers of strength and green quick, now his expression is marked with resignation and pain, and at times a fleeting astonishment or, if he catches a glimpse of his changed appearance, disgust. His hands are stained with the now-extinct fire of work. He tries to sharpen an arrow, but the iron-headed instrument clangs against the ground.

He pulls himself up and gathers a lantern from his things, ignoring **Porter**. *He hangs it up.*

Porter   Have you seen an old man and a boy?

He ignores her.

Have you? (*Beat.*) What are you doing that for?

Cove   Have you looked at the highway? At the edge of the woods. Way in the distance.

Porter No.

Cove Go look at it. Way out there, a couple miles out.

She does.

What do you see?

Porter An empty road. A boarded-up store.

Cove Is that all?

Porter Those tents. Do people live there?

Cove They do. I hang lights for them. I used to work for the electricity company, up in the sky, till I was laid off. (*Beat.*) Electricity lit up the night for seventy years and now they can't afford to keep the lights on at night. No work, the highways are empty and the houses abandoned. The world is going back to darkness. All kingdoms and castles and masses have been washed away. My children sleeping in the back seat of the car, leaning against one another. Their mother took them to her family's when my despair moved through my veins and made me violent. Others stir in restless dreams. I hang the lanterns to lead people here. (*Beat.*) Want a drink?

Porter No.

The firebird shakes its wings.

Cove They say that bird there can break the spell.

Porter What spell?

Cove The one that has left everyone here enchanted. Petrified forest. Greed and violence. Once I had a problem with drink. I let the world eat me up. But now, hell, no amount of poison can dull the hell I'm in.

Porter My cousin tried to shoot it.

Cove Well, if you can catch it, it can bring good luck. But it's double-edged, it can also bring bad.

Porter I don't believe that.

Cove   You don't believe in anything. Many have died when they've caught the bird.

Porter   You don't even believe that.

Cove   I'm a hunter myself but not of feathers.

Porter   Is that where you got those bones?

Cove   I search the woods night after night. I used to have values. My father used to lead us into church and I would look up at the stained-glass windows and the light and feel something calm in me. Goodness. I used to believe that there was a right way to act and if you worked hard you would be rewarded. Now I don't care so much. Now I just take what I want. Whatever is beautiful, I kill. For something to live, something has to die. There is one beast I'm looking for above the others, I've been looking for and I hope to find it tonight. (*Beat.*) Come closer. Have you seen the beast that walks these woods?

Porter   What beast?

Cove   The one that carries the past. And is pure. The stag.

Porter   I haven't.

Cove   I aim to get it before anyone else. Come closer.

Porter   I'm alright.

Cove   You're alone?

Porter   Maybe.

Cove   Have a drink.

Porter   No, thank you.

Cove   It's been a long time since I've known comfort. Been near someone. Felt their hand on my arm. Felt the softness of skin.

Porter   I care nothing about that kind of thing.

Cove   Sure you do. Tell me, do you believe in the devil?

Porter   No, I don't. My cousin does.

Cove   The devil isn't anything to be afraid of. When he fell out of heaven, it wasn't anger he felt. A need of vengeance. Or hate. It was astonishment. Self-loathing. (*Beat.*) Feel him. (*Beat.*) My name is Cove. Like a hidden place. I can show you where they are for a price.

Porter   Who?

Cove   Your father and your son.

Porter   I thought you said you didn't know.

Cove   Maybe I saw. A little boy, about four.

Porter   What do you want?

Cove   Maybe you're like me. It'd take nothing, not hardly the wind, to push you over the edge.

Porter   I have to find my son.

Cove   Then why do you have pills in your pocket? In case things don't turn out right?

Porter   How do you know anything about me?

Cove   You can't help your son. Your blood is tainted with the violence of your family.

Porter   That's not true.

Cove   You let things fall apart. Maybe you want a little sip.

Porter   Hazlitt said she'd come. She's told me she's coming.

Cove   You were drunk the night you conceived your son, I bet. I bet you had a drink or two when things got hard. You're alone, you might as well stay with me here in the dark woods with the ghosts and the spirits.

He grips her tightly.

They told me about your mother. You drained what little bit of nutrients her body had. Her belly swelled while her limbs grew stick thin. Her teeth rotted and death showed in the cracks of her teeth. She died when you were young, didn't she? Have a drink. They don't understand you.

Porter   She died when I was three.

Cove   I know what they used to say. That you were never very good. You didn't do well in school. You never cared the way the others looked at you. You clean the mud from men's boots. You're a whore. Dirty.

Porter   No, I'm not. Don't call me that. You don't even know me.

Cove   Where's your fortitude? Here it is. This is what they think of you. Give in to it.

He shakes the bottle and holds it to her.

It's hard to tell what the truth is. Whether they're making it up or whether you've chosen despair over your son. Drink.

She pushes him away.

She knocks the bottle out of his hands.

Porter   You don't know me.

They wrestle. He gets a hold of her shoe and she takes it off. He tears a piece of her dress. She pulls out her knife, standing with one bare foot. He backs away with a smile.

Cove   You do care and that's your downfall. It's self-loathing and that's what will tear you apart. Not any drink. Not any person. The deprivation of love destroys the world. Just a push. Just a breeze. Your soul has become the weight of a leaf. You can't even hold your head high enough to see that there's no hope for him in this life. He'll end up like you.

She tries to get her boot back. He blocks her way, so she takes off the other and throws it at him.

Porter   You don't know anything.

Cove *disappears into the darkness.*

Cove   Watch in the woods. There's dangerous beasts here.

Porter *finds herself alone, unsure if it was real or a fearful imagining.*

Hazlitt *enters and calls to* **Porter**.

Hazlitt   Porter?

Porter   What?

Hazlitt   Are you alright?

Porter   Yes. You scared the shit out of me.

Hazlitt   I haven't forgotten.

Porter *shakes off the moment.*

Hazlitt   You're shaking like a leaf.

Porter   I'm fine.

Hazlitt   Porter?

Porter   What?

Hazlitt   I think I'm blind in one eye.

Porter   You can't be blind in one eye. You'd know it if you was.

Hazlitt   I used to see things clearly. I used to have an old memory. A memory that was a house I could walk. I could see uncle's house. The bright wood opening to the cathedral of sky. Mammaw. Her cast-iron pan. The tobacco. I could see the valley and the bright sun in spring. Spring in the north is gray but spring in the south is so bright that you can hardly stand it. The wind scattering winged birch seed. But now the world's gone mute. Everything is gone. I'm scared of the dark. I'm waiting for the light. Now I can feel bad spirits around me. I can't see them because of my eye. If it weren't for the one eye, I could see the spirits. I felt them a few times ever since the night when he tried to suffocate you. Do you remember that?

Porter   No.

Hazlitt   Someone had stolen your shoes. Well, I could feel them after that.

Porter   What?

Hazlitt   The spirits. Last night I woke in a jolt, I felt
something terrible approaching. And I could feel them dark as
night. (*Beat.*) I used to crawl over the crib and sit with you in
the dark. I remember you even then. I don't have anybody but
you, Porter.

Porter   You live a better life than us.

Hazlitt   Do you know what I envy when I see the rich? I envy
the luxury of affection they have with their children. I would
have liked to have been a child.

Beat.

Porter   Did you feel bad at all for leaving?

Hazlitt   Yes.

Porter   You never came back.

Hazlitt   I know.

Porter   He liked you. Even if you didn't know it.

Hazlitt   You also left. Porter?

Porter   What?

Hazlitt   Do you think I am good?

Porter   I thought I heard him sigh.

Hazlitt   I think of you when I walk down the streets of
Brooklyn. Maybe I'm the last of the great migrators. Here
the men shove buckets of fish to each other. They are stooped
close to the concrete. Their bones bowed under the city.

Porter   Do you think I made our father sick?

Hazlitt   I don't know. I think you should have left each
other alone. (*Beat.*) Do you think there is such a thing as
goodness, Porter? When I work is the only time I am sure of
myself. I work until I am exhausted and the exhaustion burns
away everything I want to forget. I want to be good. It is not

too late, or these things are not too old-fashioned in this world, to think of what is goodness and spirit, or beauty and truth. These things are eternal. These things are like the air and are apportioned to everyone the same or people fall into despair.

Porter   There is no work.

Hazlitt   But all over the world there is already the murmurs of people rising up. Can't you hear it? I don't think there is anything but work that can save us.

Porter   You picked your freedom over me.

She stands up and looks to the west.

Hazlitt   I never could bear it all. But I promise you I am coming now.

Porter   It might be too late.

Hazlitt   Don't feel lonesome, Porter. I can see the snow when it falls on the clumsy alder and the myrtle bushes. I have never left you. I'm always with you. Always.

Porter *struggles for words.*

Porter   I don't know which way to go.

Hazlitt   Head east. Follow the bird. (*Beat.*) We're like twin planets and where the sun is, there is our father.

Hazlitt *digs in* **Porter**'s *pocket and hands her the knife.*

She disappears. **Porter** *continues her journey and disappears into the woods.*

A new figure moves in the silvered dark. He breathes lightly but with effort and steps forward. He strings a clothes-line from one tree to the other and hangs old photographs along the line with clothes-pins. When he is done, he rests a moment, puts his hand softly over his heart as if it pains him and speaks.

William   There is May Denton, your great aunt. And there her siblings Faith and James and Honor. And there is Rosie Kidd and her siblings June and Little Christie and Hope and

Acki Maxi and Porter, who your mother was named after, all
these were kin of Rosie Kidd. My wife's mother and Jim's
mother. Rosie had twenty-two brothers and sisters. I tell you
this for when I am not here any longer. My days upon this
earth are numbered. Some worked in the factories, but Rosie
and the others worked the farm. And Rosie's folks, Joshua and
Maybelle. And their siblings who lived closer to Oak Ridge.
They had one of the first Model-T's in this area. Then there is
my family. I don't know hardly anything of them. They didn't
stay in one place. I know Crosswhite, my great grandmother,
was half Creek and from Alabama. And her seven sons. I
don't own a piece a paper with their names but I know this
is her half-brother Cotton Stone who was carried off by the
wind. Kids at school used to make fun of me for being Indian.
We never had no land that I know of. And there my mama
Louise Hagaman and my sister Hope. My mother worked in
a seat-belt factory, but it was gone by the time Hope was a
teenager so she worked in a grocery store. I can't really talk
too much about them. It is a shame you don't know them.
And that is Jo, who is your grandmother. And Porter and Hen
as little ones. When we lived in the old house. And there is me
when I was a boy and was eternal. You should know where
you came from.

He picks up a truck door from the ground.

When I was a boy, we used to drive up to the mountains on
Sundays and have picnics, me, my sister and family. A truck
like this, but older. When my limbs were not fettered by old
age. You had never known a prettier place. The hickory trees,
the trees of heaven, and the maples. And the open fields with
heaps of wildflowers and wreath'd honeysuckle. The air so
bright. Almost like there was nothing to weaken that fixed
sunlight. When my sister died, I used to come up here and sit
like I was waiting for her. Once I saw her. Her beauty was so
bright that it blinded me for a minute and I nearly swooned.
There was a deer near her and it was spring and there were
gold seeds and these gold seeds floated through the air like
specks of dust in heaven. She looked prettier than she was

even in life. My memory is weak as the wind but the days of my youth are clear. I don't want to die, but when I do, I want to go back to Cades Cove. The mountains, now that you know them as young as you are, you will never forget them.

He heaves a breath and sits. He takes off his shirt and there is a bandage over his heart.

They put a machine in me to keep my heart going so I could work. Shannon and Jim depend on me, and her girls, and there's you to make sure is alright. I've got to keep going. My poor girls are scattered to the wind. The last time I saw Hen she looked so skinny and wore out. That little baby couldn't even finish the cup of coffee I bought her and I had to let her go, out into the world to live like a dog. (*Beat.*) I have to keep going. It can't be this dark forever, morning has to come soon.

William *disappears back into the darkness as soft-footed as he came.* **Porter** *reappears.*

She sees **William***'s shirt on the ground. She picks it up and puts it on.*

Scene Six

THE INFERNAL DANCE

Coryden, *alone in the woods, drags a rein of flowers and vines. When she comes into the clearing she sees* **Cove**, *sharpening his arrow with a piece of* **Porter***'s dress in his hands.* **Coryden** *freezes, but it's too late. They stare at one another,* **Coryden** *with a staff and* **Cove** *with his arrow. The sound of birds, rustling of leaves. Lanterns move in the wind.*

Scene Seven

THE IMMORTAL KASCHEI OF THE PETRIFIED WOODS

Porter *comes through the woods to a clearing. The bird flies high and lands on a branch. It grows immense and glows, fiery, then resumes its shape.*

She notes the bird and then, laying in the distance, a small empty wooden cage that looks like it has been abandoned ages ago. She puts the cage under her arm and climbs a tree. When she nearly reaches the top she drops the cage and it lands with a thud. The bird flies into an old wood shack. That's when **Porter** *notices the shack. Moonflowers. Ancient. Pieces of the truck lean against it.* **Porter** *approaches it. She tries to see inside by looking through the cracks where the light shows so brightly as if it might be holding the very sun of September.*

She moves a piece of metal from the truck. When she does, **William** *appears.*

He breathes. **Porter** *jumps. They stare at one another. Pain clutches him, then passes.*

William   I must be dying if that's you. If I am seeing you, I'm surprised. Porter.

For a moment, he seems unable to believe she is before him.

Porter   I've been looking for you.

William   I know.

Porter   My son must be here.

William   Did Shannon tell you?

Porter   No, how would she? (*Realising.*) She knew.

William   It wasn't her. I told her to listen to me.

Porter *looks in between the cracks of the shed, full of longing.*

Porter   I want to see him.

William   He's not there. I've already moved him. Go look.

She goes in and pulls out handfuls and handfuls of bright fire feathers.

Porter   Just feathers.

William   You'll make yourself delirious with false imaginings.

Porter *shivers.*

William   Winter. Airish. Do you feel the wind?

Porter   No.

William   Well, you're like the wind to me. I don't know you. I don't feel you.

She sits down on a stump a little ways from him. She waits, like a dog might wait to be let in for ages.

She takes off a ring and hands it to him. He doesn't take it.

Porter   It was Mama's, remember? Twin rings. Hazlitt has one too.

William   I think you ought to leave.

Porter   I have come home now.

William   Even when you were a small girl you always took people for everything you could get. When the plant went on strike. They were shooting people who crossed the picket line. Three months. Even when they were threatening to cut the electricity off you got a new pair of shoes.

Porter   I was just a kid. I didn't understand. What if I promised to let him come over? You'll see him all the time.

William   I don't have anything left to give. (*Beat.*) I used to walk around with all his toys still laying around the house. I used to work on my truck. I wanted Leo to have it one day. My '72 Ford. So powerful it will jump if you tap the gas. Eventually I stopped working on the truck. It lies in rusted bits. There. I began to forget, more like die is what it was. Then the calls began. The night you called me crying, you said, 'Daddy I'm ready to come home.' I said alright. I was so happy when you said you were going to come home last March. I painted your room. Painted his room. When I thought you all were coming home my feet couldn't touch the ground. And then you let me wait all day.

Porter   You could have given me a chance.

William   I took one look at his little face and I knew he needed me.

Porter   You could have gave me a chance.

William   How much is Denel giving you a month?

Porter   Four hundred and fifty dollars.

William   And how much is a place to rent? Even a trailer?

Porter   I don't know.

William   I'm sure you looked.

Porter   Four hundred dollars.

William   That's what I thought.

Porter   I'll make it work. Hazlitt is coming.

William   Hazlitt? Hazlitt is coming? No, she won't. You believe in magical things.

William   If you'll move back home, I'll let you see him.

Porter   I can't do that.

A long silence.

Look, you can see the gold seeds floating through the air. Where do they come from? Maybe you could let me have him. Maybe we could be happy. I'll live nearby.

They have a moment.

William   Didn't I treat you good?

Porter   I guess.

William   We used to go to car shows together.

Porter   I suppose.

William   You were my chicken. Used to buy you candy.

Porter   I know.

William   You could come home and not worry about rent. I have his room still painted. You could go to school for nursing. You too good for that?

Porter   No.

William   You're sick. Drinking and such. It's disgusting.

Porter   I only drank when you kept calling and calling.
I quit it now.

William   Somebody could call the law on you and being
homeless they could take Leo away.

Porter   They can't do that.

William   They can. If you moved home, you'd have a nice
room and things. Maybe learn to not screw things up. Not be
so worthless. Be worth something.

Porter   Maybe.

William   So you'll come.

Porter   I suppose.

William   That'd be good of you. The thing a good mother
would do. Come here.

She does. He starts to hug her but the hug turns too violent, too hard.

You listen to me. You stupid son of a bitching girl.

He changes. Seems to regain his former power. He locks his jaw.

Now you will know how I felt. My heart wrenched out of me.
You will never see your son again. I'll take you to court if
I have to.

He grits his teeth and hits her hard. She falls. He grabs her by the neck.

Last night I saw my sister. She said, 'Billy, it's time. Come on.'
But I told her no. I said I wasn't going. You hear me, you
sonuvabitchin girl? You disgust me. I'm not going.

He lets her go. **Porter** *stays on the ground, defeated but refusing to leave.*

*He is wrenched with pain suddenly. She starts to go to him but he picks up
a rock. The light grows light, pale, almost like daylight though it is still
dark. Gold seeds move through the air. He looks up as if he sees someone
standing behind* **Porter** *although* **Porter** *cannot see her. And then*
William *tosses down the rock. The light fades.*

William *leaves.* **Porter** *struggles to pull herself up.*

Hazlitt *enters.*

Porter   Tell me about the night you left Tennessee.

Hazlitt   Heartache followed. You do have a knife. I would have thought you'd remembered. The problem is that you forget that I wanted you to come with me.

Porter   We both forget.

Hazlitt   We could have got jobs anywhere back then. Seen a new place. I would have gone anywhere.

Porter   Hard to go someplace when you get knocked up.

Hazlitt   I know.

Porter   Doesn't matter. It wouldn't have ended up very different.

Hazlitt   I want to wake up in wild flowers. I am so weary, Porter. I've been coming to see you, but it's a long way. I haven't slept in ages. Sometimes I feel like my life has already happened. That I can tell the story of it. I don't think with our lives that I'll live to be too old.

Porter   Mammaw was sixty-four.

Hazlitt   She could afford to go the doctor. I am small for this age. We both are the size of people who were alive in the Civil War. I read about it.

Porter   I suppose.

Hazlitt   We could have watched the small soldiers pass. And I wouldn't have felt small. I think that I will live to be forty-two. Which seems good. When I die they will say that I was of the poor, that I had a great spirit, and that I was a worker. I lived upon the earth in the last days of labor.

Porter   I'm waiting for you to come home.

Hazlitt   I know.

Porter   I'm not what you think. What he made it out like.
You know I'm no drunk. I drank a little, but when I was
pregnant with Leo I quit. Now you don't believe me.

Hazlitt   I know.

Porter   You don't believe me. No one does.

Hazlitt   I do.

Porter   We both abandoned him. Daddy.

Hazlitt   I know.

Porter   You want me here to take care of him. So you don't
have to.

Hazlitt   That's not true.

Porter   You worry about being good but you don't come
home to take care of your father. You won't even come home
when I need you. You think you're better than us.

Hazlitt   Porter –

Porter   Leave me alone. I don't think you actually care about
anybody. You couldn't even call him on his birthday last year.

Hazlitt   I was no better than a dog to him. I can't stand up
straight, my bones are deformed from cowering.

Porter   You thought you could make it out there. You didn't
belong.

Hazlitt   I don't belong anywhere.

Porter   Look at us, Hazlitt. I can't get a job at a fast-food
restaurant that I used to work when I was fifteen. When we
die, they won't say shit, all people'll say is good riddance.

Hazlitt   I think about our mother sometimes. How she
probably wasn't much different than us. If you gain the world
but lose your soul what good is it? I lived hard years in the
city before I went to work on the farm. I did things I wouldn't
be proud of. I can still feel the weight of his body against me.

My spirit is not pure. But when night falls and you haven't got anywhere to go . . . I used to imagine the little sparrow that used to nest on the porch, want to know what it is to feel safe. At night I imagine angels sleeping around the edge of my bed, if I have a bed, flung haphazard in a lazy guard, sleeping and guarding in turns with wild abandon. I think if I ever knew what it was like, to feel protected and warm, I'd probably die of happiness. When you first lost the house, I told myself it wasn't as bad as it seemed. Who knows what will come for us in winter. But something will. Mothers will call their children home. Children will sleep. We will make sure nothing happens to them. I didn't want to come. I am not good, Porter. I picked my own life over yours. But I aim to make it right.

Porter   He's just a sick old man who loved you.

Hazlitt   Porter –

Porter   I don't know where my son is.

Scene Eight

INTERCESSION OF THE SHEPHERD

Shannon *sits alone on the porch. The table by porchlight is now the only thing that receives light and is lit. Although lonesome, it seems bathed in warmth and familial attention. If her babes were near her, we would imagine her holding the youngest, cherub-faced, stroking the child's wheat-colored hair, the same as her own, gazing toward the mountain, wearing a chain of lavender around her wrist. But her children are not around and she sits still in the chair, her senses unquiet. She plants her bare feet on the porch and feels the wood underneath, something that we would see register pleasure in her, if pleasure was something she felt deserved expression and not kept girded and thatched and bound closely to the soul. She holds her gun close to her.*

She starts to settle when she hears the rustling of leaves.

Shannon   Who's that?

Coryden *appears.*

Coryden   It's me.

Shannon   Coryden? What are you doing there? You look like you seen a ghost.

Coryden   I think that Porter is in trouble and I wanted someone to go help me.

Shannon   Have you seen her?

Coryden   I have.

Shannon   Where is she?

Coryden   I lost her. She went deep into the woods. I followed her a while, further than I said I would, but then I got scared.

Shannon   She walks the woods often. That doesn't mean anything.

Coryden   I saw the devil.

Shannon   It's been a long time since I seen you, Coryden.

Coryden   I know.

Shannon   Are you hungry? Have you ate? Everything is cold. I made it hours ago.

Coryden   No. I don't have in mind to eat. If you won't go, let me wake old Jimmy up.

Shannon   Sure, you go right ahead.

Coryden *sits down on the steps.*

Coryden   Maybe I won't.

Shannon   You look tired.

Coryden   I am. You people've kept me up all night. Damnedest people I ever seen in my life. Raising hell and a carrying on.

Shannon   Normally I would have made the girls go to bed by now but with Porter coming they've been kinda riled. (*Beat.*)

I remember when I met my cousin. I hugged her just as tight as I could. Told her I loved her. I'm worried for her.

Coryden   Well, you could help me.

Shannon   Well, it'd do you good to get something in you.

She brings out a plate of cornbread.

Have a little cornbread at least.

She cuts a slice and puts it on a plate. They stare at it.

Maybe I should cut it in half and we'll split it since there weren't much cornbread.

She splits it and puts the measly cornbread on two plates. They stare at it painfully for a moment. They eat.

But there's heaps of fried squash and greens and tomatoes from the garden. There's beans. I'm keeping them warm on the stove in case they want them later. Daddy didn't even eat. We're waiting for Porter. There's a few biscuits too.

Coryden   No thank ye. This is plenty.

Shannon   Some of the things in the garden didn't do well.

Coryden   Just tell me.

Shannon   Not always enough sun.

Coryden   You know where he is, don't you?

Shannon   I've promised.

Coryden   You're alone except Jimmy, but I have the woods and the stag. The stag doesn't like to get too close, but he follows me if I go too far away. He has the heart of a beast, just muscle. His coat is coarse brown, and a sad look in his eye. Incorruptible. Something everlasting about him. That's why I have to watch him.

Shannon   Daddy lost his job.

Coryden   Jimmy?

Shannon   Fired him. One of the boys came over today to tell me that. He cost the company too much money. He's a danger.

Coryden   They were a bunch of sonuvabitches anyhow.

Shannon   Things happen. I figured I would let him have one more supper as a working man. What could it hurt? I set my sight on the horizon. You get through today maybe and maybe tomorrow, but then what? Wisdom is the food of angels, but I've never seemed to be able to partake any of it, not enough to matter anyhow. I saw Porter when she was wild. And if she was falling down drunk, you can't leave a little child with her alone like that.

Coryden   I don't think she'd be like that.

Shannon   I have to do as William says. We're already slack on the bills this month. Last month they cut the electricity off till William paid it. I don't have money for the girls' things for school. I look for a job, even though it means having to leave the little ones with Daddy. But no one hires a woman with five children and no high-school degree. I have to forget the moral compass of my heart though it is wound tight and sends a tolling bell. I feel bad for Porter.

Coryden   I look at her and I can tell there's somebody who's had the spirit beat out of her just about.

Shannon *looks off. Thinking hard.*

Shannon   No, I can't go into those woods with you.

She holds her silence and looks at the children's shoes.

Coryden   Well, I suppose I will be getting on then. I'll go myself. First I'll make sure the stag is safe – I saw a hunter earlier – then I'll go.

Shannon   But if you wait a minute, I'll tell where the boy sleeps.

A long silence.

He is being kept in the old barn near the road, the one with ivy and morning glories growing up the side. The one not too far from creek. She wouldn't have checked there because it belongs to the Denton family.

Coryden   Thank you. I won't tell anyone you told me.

Shannon   You were close to Hen, weren't you? (*Beat.*) You're not like everybody here. Your capacity to love. Must a' been hard. I saw it. I know that's why you stay away. But you know you don't have to stay away. I know what it is to love, but all my love goes to my father and children. So I don't know exactly how you feel. But what I do know, what I can tell you, Coryden – shepherd, is that what they still call you? A shepherd?

Coryden   The fat men in Knoxville do, when they see me with all my siblings. They don't see me often though.

Shannon   Well, shepherd, sitting by your flock of siblings, there's nothing is wrong with loving.

Coryden   Do you think that's why Hazlitt left?

Shannon   She had a lot of reasons for leaving, without that. She was of a different kith.

Coryden   I still find books she hid and papers she left behind. She left me here with all these things that don't have no place. I wish I were a beast with a brute heart. That it could crush in me all the things I feel.

Shannon   By enduring there is a dignity in that. Whether you're a shepherd or laborer of the earth, you are fulfilling a place in the universe like all the other people who have worked or loved. Whether I die poor, whether I marry or I don't, I don't think it matters. My spirit is pure because my heart is pure. Maybe it is wrong that I have yoked my soul to this house and let my cousin suffer. It sits on my soul. But I love them. I helped raise them when they were babies and I was just a child myself and not anything can tear that bond. She will forgive me. But what's important is that you love – don't wait for it to come back to you. Love more until you are full of love. And all the love you have in you, all the love you give not expecting a return, nothing can be wrong with that. Not everyone really knows what it is to love unselfishly like that. The love you have for Hen, the love you have for the earth and your family, it's a virtue, Coryden, that the world forgets. Try to love even more until your heart is overfilled like a cup and drink of the cup. Love brings more love.

Shannon *watches as* **Coryden** *leaves. More than once she starts to follow until it is too late.*

She tries to settle into the quiet. She looks off the porch nervously, as if spooked, wide-eyed, searching for a sight or movement, and tries to distract herself with tasks.

She sees the line of children's shoes and straightens them, then, mid-shoe, freezes on some realization. She collapses into a moment of grief or guilt, as much as the torn battlement of a guarded castle will reveal the dwellings of its secret and interior chambers. After a few moments she pulls herself up and heads to the garden.

James *comes out to the porch.*

James   Shannon? Shannon?

He walks around the porch and looks toward the garden.

The children must be asleep. I must a' fell asleep. Well.

He gets up with effort and goes into the house to look for her. Returns. **Hazlitt** *enters from the woods and listens to him, with a handful of flowers. He doesn't see her.*

James   Now I don't know where you went off to. Must be in the garden. Sure is a pretty night. With the mountains. I wonder if your children will remember this place when it's gone. I'm part of the old life, I reckon. Already gone. That's what I suppose. Yesterday's trash. The leaves on the trees are beginning to turn. And so, 'The roots shall be dried up beneath, and his branches shall wither above.'

*As **Hazlitt** starts to climb the stairs a pair of doves, or maybe magpies, their wings sounding, for in the dark they are unseen, are startled and take flight by their shadows into the air.* **James** *sees* **Hazlitt** *and stops. He strains his eyes.*

Hazlitt   'And his memory shall perish from the earth.'

James   I believe that's Hazlitt, there. Am I to believe my eyes? The dark makes it hard to see.

Hazlitt   Where is Porter, Uncle?

James   I don't know. In the woods, I believe.

Hazlitt   Has she found Leo? And our father?

James   No, she hasn't. Been looking though.

Hazlitt   Where's Shannon? Is she here?

James   In the house.

Hazlitt   She is?

James   I thought so. Maybe she went down to the garden.

Hazlitt *doesn't move. She tries to see into the house.*

James   You want a little coffee? Shannon cooked all day. Maybe she was hoping for company. You can look and see if she's in the house.

Hazlitt *tries to go through the doorway.* **James** *blocks her way, once, twice.*

James   Can't get too far away from it. This place. It'll call you back. The mountains always be calling you back. It's been a long time, Hen. A few years.

Hazlitt   I know.

James   Your father asks about you.

Hazlitt   I know.

James   Well, I know you been working hard.

Hazlitt   Maybe I have. Maybe I ought to have worked harder.

James   Maybe. Lot of education, gone to waste. How'd you like it up there with those Yankees?

Hazlitt   It's alright.

James   Yeah, that's what I thought. You know I read. I'm as smart as they are. I like reading about the Irish. And US history. I could have given you a job here. If you wanted to work in a field. Porter said you had some people good to you up there in the city.

Hazlitt   They helped me out.

James   Well, I tell you one thing. Nobody is as good as family. They don't care about you when it comes down to it. Did they? Anyone of them hold on to you up there?

Hazlitt   I suppose not.

James   They should have watched out for you. No one out there cares if you live and die. No sense of fortitude, strength of will.

Hazlitt   They helped me some.

James   You'll find yourself alone again out in the world. They only think of themselves. If they cared they would have grabbed hold of you and not let you come back to this place. (*Beat.*) You mark my words. I thought you were going to be somebody. But maybe it's better for you to come back.

Hazlitt   Maybe.

James   That's what I thought.

Hazlitt   I'm going now to look for Porter. If she's out in the woods.

James   Come here.

Hazlitt *goes to him.*

James   My little baby.

The hug lasts a little too long.

Shannon *appears.*

Shannon   Leave her alone, Daddy. Go on into the house.

James   I was talking to her.

Shannon   Well, you're done.

James   Good to see you.

He exits.

Shannon   I didn't know you'd be coming. Now everyone is here.

Hazlitt   Cousin.

Shannon   Ain't seen you in a long time.

Hazlitt   I know.

Shannon   Won't you sit a spell. Let the world soak into you a bit.

Hazlitt   I want to see my sister. I brought you some flowers.

Shannon   Thanks, yeah.

They are shy with one another since they haven't seen each other in a long time.

Hazlitt   Your kids are bigger, I bet.

Shannon   Yeah. Trouble is what they are.

Hazlitt   Pretty things, all of them.

Shannon   And buck wild. I guess you had a long trip.

Hazlitt   I did.

Shannon   You can share a bed. I'll put the kids on the floor, when the morning light comes. I hope Porter's alright. Coryden been here.

Hazlitt   Coryden?

Shannon   Yes. She's trying to help you all. Maybe you could say a few words to her. She misses you.

Hazlitt   I will.

Shannon   See that they don't kill one another. Porter and her daddy.

Hazlitt   I know where she'll be. I know where she used to run when we were little.

Shannon   Y'all still children to me. I could handle Porter leaving. She's so mean. But something about you just always tore me up, seeing you all alone. Your shoulders being so small or something. Like a kid. No gall in you. You were the one I always worried for.

Hazlitt   I did alright.

She starts to leave.

Shannon   If I did anything wrong by not helping you more when we were little –

Hazlitt   You were just a teenager. You took care of me since you were eight and I was glad for it. I kept wanting to come back.

Shannon   Well, maybe now you can stay. If the wind ain't restless.

*She embraces **Hazlitt** and kisses her on the head.*

Shannon   Be careful.

Hazlitt *exits.*

Scene Nine

APPEARANCE OF THE MAGICAL RETINUE

Coryden *carries a lasso of vines and flowers. Stops, exhausted.*

Coryden   Stop, you stupid stag. Come back here. You're so pig-headed you've got me following you. Someone will see you. The devil. And then where will you be? I don't even

know where you're taking me. And I don't have time for this.
I'm going to get this thing around you and pull you back
somewhere safe. You're a mess. Your antler is chipped. Sick
with too much daydreaming.

Somewhere in the woods, **William** *walks. He has to sit down for part
of the journey. It feels uphill even if it's not. He grabs hold of a tree. The
woods seem new again, they light up briefly. New leaves bud on empty
trees. This is not the light of morning but the light of heaven. He looks as
though seeing someone, maybe seeing their bare footsteps as they run through
the woods. He follows a few steps, now more sick than before. The already
antiqued light fades. He trembles and wipes the fevered sweat from his
troubled brow.*

Cove, *in another part of the woods, drowsy from his hunting, props
himself up to rest a moment and falls into the thick, inert sleep of the
despaired.*

Hazlitt *walks among the woods and sees the photographs that*
William *has hung. She looks in the shed and finds* **Porter**'s *shoes,
which* **Porter** *has taken off at some point. She takes off her own shoes
and puts her sister's shoes on her feet.*

After a moment **Hazlitt** *rustles through the dead leaves and finds a
buried book, opens it.* **Coryden** *comes to the edge of the woods, the
lasso still in her hands.*

Coryden   Hazlitt.

Hazlitt   It's me. Is that really you?

Coryden   It is. Don't put it up. Read. A little.

She comes closer. She lies down near **Hazlitt** *and puts her head on the
earth, looking out to the woods, dreaming, listening transfixed.*

Hazlitt (*reading*)   'The Iris is named because of its resemblance
to the rainbow in heaven. It bears leaves like little daggers but
bigger, broader and fatter: the flowers on the stalk are bent in
one over against another and have varied colours for they are
white, pale, black, purple or azure. It is because of the variety
of colours that it is compared to the heavenly rainbow.'

If **Coryden** *hears music – maybe she does – maybe it would register on her expression, maybe not. When the words have drifted up and disappeared into the woods, she reaches up and kisses* **Hazlitt** *lightly, a kiss on the cheek that has lived for ages and finally found a home in the ancient tapestry.* **Coryden** *hears movement in the woods.*

Coryden   You've stirred him. He came closer to hear.

Hazlitt   The deer. He followed me a little. He looked at me with his big eyes. Like he mistook me for someone.

Coryden   I know. You have to go find your sister. She's had a hard time.

Hazlitt   I went to visit her in the desert once. She still had the house but it was empty almost. We put out decorations for fall that she had bought at the dollar general store even though you couldn't even tell it was fall since there weren't any trees. It wasn't even a town. It felt like a life patched together with whatever she could get. How do you live like that? There was no one to help her. I should have stayed there with her. But I turned a blind eye. I think maybe she started drinking then. Maybe just one drink in the afternoon. Maybe they were already having trouble. I don't think she's a drunk though. I know she was just having a hard time. I know her better than our father. She'd sit on the base all afternoon on her patio smoking cigarettes and watching her baby. She'd sit in the sun till the sun got too strong then she'd sit in the shade. Nobody to talk to. She said she was happy, proud to have a house. I should have told her she had done well anyway, told her it was good. I should have stayed. She must have known I didn't think much of it in my fancy city clothes. I bet I made her feel awful.

Coryden   Do you want me to come with you?

Hazlitt   I'd like to go alone.

Coryden   Then I'll tell you where William is hiding Leo.

Hazlitt   I can feel the spirits.

She covers one eye, looking for spirits, then the other.

Coryden   Don't be afraid.

She stands behind her and covers **Hazlitt***'s eyes with her hands one at a time.*

Coryden   What do you see?

Hazlitt   A maple leaf.

Coryden   Now what do you see?

Hazlitt   Honeysuckle.

Coryden   Now what?

Hazlitt   A sparrow.

Coryden   See. Nothing to be scared of.

She whispers **Shannon***'s secret to* **Hazlitt***.*

In the woods **Cove** *awakens.*

Scene Ten

INTERCESSION OF THE GOLDEN PRINCESSES

In the melon patch, the dark-green sugary melons sleep among the elephantine leaves and curling vines. The tendrils of the plants have furled and dried, revealing that the flesh of the fruits is ripe. Beyond, are the first eves of morning heralded with faint light? It is impossible to tell for sure. The birds, the robins and sparrows, are still quiet in their arbors. Leaves twinkle in the dew. It seems surely that morning must come. It is, no doubt, that hour of comfort, the sweetest dream-hour of mortals, the hour when angels, if any, come down from the singing in heaven, the hour of sweetened children's breath. The hour of four o'clock, when no matter how long and desperate the night, if one were to awaken or stir in this dream hour, warmth and hope would seem to embrace one, like lost children, and if alone, if forsaken, become less so in that cradle of confused, tender-footed time between waking and sleep, in the arms of suffered and benevolent darkness. It is at this hour that **Porter** *enters and tries to gather herself. Perhaps not too far off we hear a creek.*

She sees half a cast-iron bell on the ground. In it are little-boy pajamas. After she searches the area, hopeful, knowing he won't be there. Nothing. She holds the feather and waits for the bird. She closes her eyes and waits, then opens them. No bird.

She tries to clean herself up and sits in the middle of the patch. She pulls a melon loose from the vine.

As she cuts open the fruit she notices the knife, the stag-bone handle, the blade. She tosses the melon aside. She looks at the knife a long time. And disappears offstage with the knife and pills.

Coryden *appears with a hoe and works the melon patch, when* **Cove** *appears at the periphery of the woods. They watch one another.*

Cove   You endanger your pet coming here.

Coryden   Not my pet.

Cove   Who do you save it for? Why even bother with people who have destroyed themselves? Are you scared of me?

Coryden   No.

Cove *comes close.*

Coryden   I have no fear of you. There is no love in fear.

Porter *returns, wet, wiping the dirt off her arms with* **William***'s shirt. She's washed herself off a little. She throws the pills away and closes the knife. She looks at the pictures she took from* **William***'s clothes-line.*

She shakily puts the clothes on, but puts her father's work shirt back on almost as an afterthought.

She looks up to the trees. The bird appears. They watch it. **Porter** *takes one of* **Cove***'s unlit lanterns. The firebird glows.*

Carefully, she goes to the bird and puts it inside the lantern. Inside the lantern, the firebird becomes a bright red flame. Out of the shadows **Hazlitt** *appears.*

Porter   Hazlitt?

Porter *and* **Hazlitt** *stare at one another a long time.*

Hazlitt   I've been looking for you. Then I knew where you'd be.

Porter   Is it really you? You've come?

Hazlitt   Yes. I told you I was coming.

Porter   It's too late. You will leave again. And I will end up living with him to be mean as a snake to me. So you might as well not bothered.

Hazlitt   Come on. You won't talk to me? I followed your muddy tracks. I knew you'd go to the place where you always go when you're upset. Like a child, gone looking for arrowheads. We used to come here when we were kids. It's still beautiful. You always run off wanting to be found. I know how you are.

Porter   I'm a mess.

Hazlitt   Well, I've seen you with less mud on your clothes.

Porter   I guess that's true. What if I can't?

Hazlitt   If you can't do it, how do you think I can? I always thought you were stronger than me. I looked up to you, when you were pregnant and working two jobs. I always thought when things got hard, well, Porter could do it. That's how I got by.

Porter   I've had a hard time without you.

Hazlitt   I know. But we were never really apart. Like two stars. Get up.

Porter   It must a' been a long trip.

Hazlitt   I don't mind. (*Beat.*) Are you ready?

Porter   Where are we going?

Hazlitt   To find Leo. I saw Coryden. She told me.

Porter   I'm afraid of him.

Hazlitt   It's alright. The lantern is bright enough to show the path. He can't hurt the both of us. We'll go together.

Hazlitt *takes* **Porter**'s *hand. The lamp guides them through the woods with its fiery light and provides a warmth which encompasses and pushes through the somnolent valley, lighting shadows of mountain lions and beasts along the path.*

Now the stars have gone, except the one bright star of morning.

The bright star of morning is luminescent and spreads its morning beacon, moves as the mover of the earth moves. Somewhere else in the woods **Cove** *draws back his arrow.*

Scene Eleven

LULLABY AND BREAKING OF THE SPELL

William *paces in front of barn doors, delirious with fever. Sometimes, exhausted, he sits.* **Porter** *and* **Hazlitt** *watch him from a distance.* **Porter** *holds the lantern with the bird.*

Porter   The lantern's gone out.

Hazlitt   It's a bird in there.

Porter   I caught him. It's wounded. He's supposed to bring luck.

Hazlitt   I suppose we don't need the light now anyway. Look.

Porter   He must have Leo inside the barn.

Hazlitt   Porter. Our father looks so aged.

Porter *takes the bird out of the cage and holds it.*

Porter   Come on.

William's *breath is troubled, he sets down a shotgun with some effort and when he looks up sees before him both of his daughters together for the first time in years.*

Hazlitt   Father.

William   Hen?

Hazlitt   It's me and Porter. We're both here.

William   I must be dying.

Hazlitt   Maybe you ought to sit down.

William   No. I don't want to.

Hazlitt   I'm sure glad to see you.

William   It's been a long time. A real long time, my girl.

Hazlitt   I know.

William   Well, have you been alright?

Hazlitt   I have.

William   You look thin. The only news I got of you was through Shannon or this one. Now you come back. (*Beat.*) You look just like your mother, Hen.

Hazlitt   I came to see how you were doing.

William   I suppose there's not much to say. Could have done that a long time ago.

Hazlitt   I'd like to stay and talk to you. Sit with you a while.

William   You used to be two little girls sitting on my knee. Would have done anything for you. I know why you're both here now. Not come for me.

He clutches his shoulder with pain. His hands shake. The pain subsides a little.

Hazlitt   Porter. Is he alright?

Porter   Maybe you ought to lay down, Daddy.

William   You're not taking him.

Hazlitt   I hate to see him so sick.

William   My hands won't stop shaking. My heart feels like it's in someone's fist.

Porter *tries to help him. He grabs her by the shoulders.* **Hazlitt** *pulls him off her as he cuffs* **Porter**. *Aiming for* **Porter**, *he accidentally hits* **Hazlitt** *hard. She recoils.*

William Don't touch me. You can't just come back here after being gone – how many years? Five, six years, Hazlitt? You never came back to see your father.

Hazlitt I'm sorry, I wanted to come back. I thought of you all every day.

William How does it feel to be an outsider? A stranger to your own family?

Porter We came to make it right with you, but you're so mean.

The firebird shakes its wings and gleams for a minute with light, then becomes dim again. **Porter** *picks the bird up.*

William There's gold seeds floating through the air. I can see them.

Porter We've come to get Leo and leave. That's all we want.

Hazlitt He belongs to her, Daddy.

Porter *picks up the bird.*

William I told you to leave him.

Porter *and* **Hazlitt** *look at one another confused.*

William I told you to leave him alone. You've got Leo there in your arms. With the gold seeds and the light. Give him to me.

Porter This is just a bird.

He reaches for the bird again. Then clutches his heart in pain.

William I can feel the wind in the cove. I'll kill you. I'll beat your ass till your nose bleeds.

Porter I don't have him.

William   You're a disgusting sonuvabitch. Leave your father to die alone. (*Beat.*) I see him there, he's breathing softly, there's a wreath of light around his head. If you're going to leave me, leave me, Leo. I won't let you trick me. You know that I am close to him.

Porter   He thinks the bird is Leo. He's confused. I'm going to go get him. (*To* **Hazlitt**.) You stay here and watch him.

William   No. Don't you move.

Porter *walks to the door.* **William** *points the gun at her.*

William   I said you're not taking him.

She steps toward the door. He drops the gun. It goes off. The shot hits the ceiling. **Hazlitt** *picks up the gun.* **William** *collapses.*

William   It's so bright here. I can see the wild flowers and the open field where the deer roam.

Frightened, they watch him struggle for a minute.

Porter   Let's lay him down over there. Help me move him.

She picks up an old quilt lying near by and puts it down. She and **Hazlitt** *pick up his arms and legs and move him to it.* **Porter** *takes off his work shirt and puts it under his head.*

Porter   Hazlitt, get that rag and put a little of that water over there on it.

Hazlitt *does so, and wipes* **William**'s *forehead with it. They tend to him.*

Porter   Here's Mama's ring. Maybe you'd like to hold onto it. And Hazlitt has the other.

She turns to **Hazlitt**, *who gives her a ring, and she places them both in* **William**'s *hand. He holds them carefully a moment, then places them gently near his pillow.* **Porter** *takes off* **William**'s *shoes.*

William (*to* **Hazlitt**)   Maybe you could stay a little while.

Porter   We could stay a little while. Sit with you.

William   Not you. (*Long beat.*) Just Hen.

Hazlitt   I'm not staying unless Porter stays.

William   Then you can both go. You're nothing. You disgust me for being weak. I remember even the way you and Hazlitt used to walk down the street with your clomping boots. You couldn't even walk right. Like a couple of bitches. Come back to my life to cause me pain and suffering.

He tries to get up out of bed and reaches for **Porter**. **Hazlitt** *pulls out the knife but before she can open it,* **William** *wrestles it from her and holds the knife to* **Porter**'s *throat.*

William   Put him down, goddamn it.

Hazlitt   Porter. If he thinks the bird is Leo, then give it to him. Do it so we can go.

Porter   You're right. Daddy, just let me go.

William *loosens his grip and lets* **Porter** *loose.*

Porter   I'm going to do what you're telling me. Look. There, I've put him on the bed.

William   I knew it was the right thing to do. When I took him. I looked and saw his little face and saw he needed me. I knew it was the right thing to do.

Porter *lays the sick bird next to* **William**. *She looks at the door where Leo sleeps. Her expression softens and the hardness in her seems to dissipate. She puts her hand on the barn door, feels the texture of the wood and opens it as the light fades.*

Scene Twelve

DAYBREAK

In the woods light flashes, illuminating **Cove** *who follows the stag. He draws back his arrow and releases it. Sparks. It flashes briefly in the shadow of its aerial path and darkness swallows the world. A crack of light. The stag falls.*

Coryden *in the high weeds finds its body by the glow of its red amber heart. She runs her hands along its body as the heart fades.*

Later. The first light of morning hits the porch. **Hazlitt** *and* **Porter** *are on the porch.*

Shannon *comes out of the house with a gallon of ice tea.*

Shannon   How is he?

Porter   Sleeping like a baby.

James *is already at the table. Maybe we see Leo at the table, maybe not.*

Shannon   Well, hoss here is ready to eat if nobody else is. Move your feet out of my way, biggun.

James   Don't talk to me like that.

Shannon   And you're to leave Hazlitt alone. You got that?

James   Yes sir.

Shannon   Well, everybody sit.

They do.

Shannon   I'm sorry I didn't tell you.

Porter   It's okay.

Shannon   Well, I'm sorry. I'm ashamed of it.

Coryden *comes up through the yard, broken.*

Shannon   What's wrong with you?

Coryden   I can't talk about it.

Hazlitt   What's all over your hand?

Porter   The stag.

Coryden   He let himself be seen.

Porter   Sorry about it. Let me wash off your hands.

Shannon   You might as well set down to eat. All of you. You too.

Coryden   I don't feel much like it.

Shannon   Well, sit at least.

Coryden   You found your boy.

Porter   I did.

They sit.

Shannon   I been waiting all night to eat.

James   Where's the girls?

Shannon   Sleeping. I told them we were eating. Too stubborn to live.

James *reaches for a biscuit.* **Shannon** *knocks it out of his hand and slams it back down on the plate.*

Shannon   I wonch you to quit now. Hold your horses.

She looks around at the table. Maybe she bows her head, maybe not. When she is satisfied:

Give us, Lord, our daily bread. And protect us in your valley. (*Beat.*) Now, all 'od's children say 'Amen'.

All   Amen.

They eat.

Later. **Porter** *and* **Hazlitt** *sit on the porch railing. Day has arrived in full blush. The sky is a cathedral of blue and white clouds. The sun is out.* **Hazlitt** *turns the radio on.*

Porter *paints her fingernails.*

Hazlitt   What do you think you'll do for work?

Porter   I'll find something. I'm going to look in the morning. Are you going to stay?

Hazlitt   Maybe. The days will cool off soon. (*Beat.*) Porter?

Porter   What?

Hazlitt   We could go down to Knoxville and listen to the bluegrass at Sullivan's sometime and drink us some strong coffee. I missed that.

Porter   The new old times.

Hazlitt   I suppose. (*Beat.*) Porter.

Porter   What?

Hazlitt   What do you think will become of us?

Porter   I don't know.

Hazlitt   Maybe we'll be alright.

Porter   Maybe.

The sunlight fades softly on them. Somewhere in the woods **William** *lies with the sickly bird and breathes his labored breath.*

Mona Mansour

The Hour of Feeling

*The playwright gratefully acknowledges Mandy Hackett
and Liz Frankel at the Public Theater; Professor Nina Schwartz
for invaluable insights into literary criticism; and fellow playwright
and amazing dramaturg Ismail Khaldi*

The Hour of Feeling received its first UK staged reading at the HighTide Festival, Halesworth, Suffolk, on 6 May 2012 and featured the following cast and creative team.

Adham	Robert Gilbert
Beder	Ishia Bennison
Abir	Sofia Stuart
George	Geoffrey Breton
Theo	Jack Cosgrove
Diana	Olivia Vinall

Director   Richard Fitch

Characters

in order of appearance

Adham, *Palestinian, twenty-five. A scholar. Handsome, intense, equal parts cocky and unsure.*

Beder, *Adham's mother, fifties. As intense as her son. World-weary but fierce. Funny, too. Not a great cook.*

Abir, *Palestinian, nineteen. Smart, beautiful, unself-conscious.*

George, *English scholar, late twenties to early thirties, but could be older. Very polished, more confident than Adham. A bit argumentative, loves the sound of his own voice. The ladies like him.*

Theo, *English scholar, mid-twenties. Affable, energetic, sweet, willing to look foolish at times.*

Diana, *English, early twenties. Ex-scholar, current bohemian. Very friendly, very curious about the world. Sexy in a 'joie de vivre' kind of way.*

The play takes place in the summer of 1967 in two places: London and Beit Hanina, a village considered a 'suburb' of East Jerusalem. In 1948, Beit Hanina was captured by Jordanian forces, so it became part of the Hashemite Kingdom of Jordan. But residents there considered themselves Palestinian first and foremost. This is still the case when the play begins.

About Language

I've indicated surtitles for Arabic translations. There are other ways of conveying these, and I would welcome exploring them. Dialect-wise, it seems to fit the rules of the play that in scenes with just Arab characters, no dialect is present. But in scenes with the British, Adham has a Palestinian accent, as does Abir. The Arabic is transliterated; a capital A indicates the consonant *'ayn*, and a capital H indicates the consonant *Haa*.

Note: On page 119 a scene begins that is entirely in Arabic. While I would strongly suggest this scene play as such, should no surtitles or alternate form of translation be available, there is a slightly modified version of the scene, all in English. See Addendum on page 156 at end of script.

Part One

Prologue

Lights up, very close in on:

Adham *stands, reads out loud from Wordsworth's poem 'To My Sister', first in Arabic:*

Adham
Hunaaka baraka feelhawaa'
Tabdou idraakan lil'ibtihaaj, youhab
Lil'ashjaar aljardaa' wa ljibaal alaariya
Wa lilAushb al 'akhDar fee lHuqoul.

[*There is a blessing in the air,*
Which seems a sense of joy to yield
To the bare trees, and mountains bare,
And grass in the green field.]

Then in English:

My sister! 'Tis a wish of mine
Put on your woodland dress;
And bring no book: for this one day
We'll give to idleness.

Beder Idleness? Hm.

Adham *shushes her.*

Adham
Love, now a universal birth,
From heart to heart is stealing,
From earth to man, from man to earth:
It is the hour of feeling.

Lights widen a little to reveal:

Late afternoon. A small, stifling apartment, in which **Adham**'s *mother,* **Beder**, *fifties, cooks – energetically but not necessarily skillfully.*

Beder   Keep going.

Adham   I can't. It smells terrible in here.

Beder   You don't have to eat it.

Adham   Someone does. All these years and she's never learned to cook.

Beder   So what? No one starved.

Adham   Can I open the window? Please.

Beder   No. I just killed a mosquito. I don't want to have to run around chasing them off all night.

Adham   It's stifling in here. It's only going to get worse when the guests arrive. (*Sarcastic and playful, more the former.*) Whatever guests there are, actually. Who's coming?

Beder   Half the village. They better show up.

Adham   Is that what you said when you invited them? I'm opening a window. I can't breathe in here.

Beder   You're antsy? Have a smoke.

Adham   I will if I feel like it. Not because you told me to.

Beder   So spoiled.

Adham *laughs.*

Beder   Like a child. It's hard to believe you're a college graduate, the way you act.

Adham   Believe it.

Beder   Intellectually, yes. Emotionally?

Adham   What are you doing?

Beder   Putting down a bowl. Is that so shocking?

Adham   For what?

Beder   Nothing you need to worry about!

Adham   Food?

Beder   Maybe.

Adham   I see. So what's with the coins you threw in? Are they edible?

Beder   Leave it alone.

Adham   My God, she has no class! All these festivities to 'celebrate my accomplishments'?

Beder (*rhetorically*)   Do you need money for your trip?

Adham   No! It's funded by a scholarship, all of it!

Beder   Leave it alone.

Adham   So we're begging people for money now?

Beder   We're not going to London with you in that suit.

Adham   'We'? We? Ha.

Beder (*correcting herself*)   You. You.

Adham   She thinks she's coming along? Good God.

Beder   Does the scholarship pay for new shoes and a suit?

Adham   I'm leaving.

Beder   The bowl is for gifts! This is common practice!

Adham   Then why force it upon people?

Beder   These cheap villagers? You have to make it explicit!

Adham   Why don't you put that on the bowl: 'Dear cheap villagers, please pay up or leave!'

Beder   They put on such airs when we got here. Acting superior, because *we* were the refugees!

Adham   Not this again.

Beder   And you don't know this, but people aren't naturally generous. Left to their own devices, they're petty. Selfish. They don't think about things like how much it will cost to get you a new suit, or to bribe someone to get your passport.

Adham   Well, *I* don't want to think about such things.

Beder   You're above all such worldly considerations? I've created a monster.

Adham   Yes, you have.

Beder   Where are you going?

Adham   Out for a walk.

Beder   Where?

Adham   I need to give you a report?

Adham   I'm asking.

Beder   The hill, above the village. Where I used to walk all the time.

Beder   Hm.

Adham   You don't approve?

Beder   It's dangerous.

Adham   What, I'll twist my ankle?

Beder   There are things going on.

Adham   I am reminding you I lived in Cairo. An actual city.

Beder   Bad things happen to Palestinian men walking around these days. Here, not Cairo. You forget how close we are to the border.

Adham (*under his breath*)   No, I don't.

Beder   You think you can just amble along like one of your poets? They think you're involved in some bit of business against the Israelis, and that's it.

Adham   Thank you, Mother. I'll make sure I don't shout political slogans and accidentally amble into No Man's Land.

Beder   You think it's funny? Be careful!

As he goes:

You can't leave! It's your party!

Adham No, it's not.

Adham *exits. As he opens the door, lights widen to reveal* **Adham**'s *world: 1967 West Bank. He pulls across the stage a giant panel, on which is a series of pictures that represent:*

THE CITY — A VILLAGE OUTSIDE JERUSALEM

April 1967.

We hear the sounds that surround **Adham***:*

First, music. Fairuz, the great Lebanese singer: 'Old Jerusalem'.

More sounds: argument and speeches in Arabic, English and Hebrew.

Carrying a book, **Adham** *makes his way up a hill. As he does so, men run in with posters and 'paste' them all over the city: cartoons of 1960s Arab/Israeli figures – Dayan, Eshkol, Nasser – framed by Arabic or Hebrew.*

A beautiful young woman of nineteen, **Abir** *runs in, and flips a panel, revealing a photo of sixties British singer Lulu and the words: 'Lulu Shout'. Into the sound mix we hear a few lines of 'To Sir with Love'.* **Abir** *bops to the music for a split second, then looks around like she might get into trouble – and leaves.*

Fairuz music fades up once more as other sounds fade out.

Adham *walks over to a small panel and turns it, revealing:*

SOMEWHERE IN THE MIDDLE EAST

Then another panel:

IN WHAT USED TO BE CALLED PALESTINE

And one more panel:

AND NOW IS JORDAN.
KIND OF . . . IT'S COMPLICATED

Finally, he finds the spot he loves, top of the hill. Settles in, making notes in his book. Laser focus. Beat.

Abir *enters, seems startled to see him. He's not flustered. Nothing flusters him.*

Adham   Meeting someone?

Abir   Oh. Hello. No. I'm just taking a walk.

Adham   It's a long way up from the village.

Abir   Clears my head. So.

She reaches into a small cloth bag, pulls out a pack of cigarettes, takes one out and lights up.

Adham   Wow!

Abir   Want one?

Adham   Are you allowed to do that?

Abir   No. But I don't ask anyone for permission.

Adham   All right then.

She holds up a cig for him. He reaches to take it.

Your hand is shaking.

Abir   No.

Adham   Okay.

Abir   It's cold up here.

Adham   Sure.

Abir   It is!

Adham   Yes.

Abir   And windy.

They light up, smoke in silence for a beat.

Adham   If you're going to transgress, at least enjoy yourself. I don't know why it's *aayb* [*shameful*] anyway. The prophet never saw a cigarette. If he had, who knows? Maybe he'd have liked Gauloises.

Abir   You shouldn't be talking that way about the Prophet.

Adham   Says the girl who's sneaking a smoke. (*Studies her.*)
You're . . . ? I'm sorry, I know we've met before. But I've been
away for school.

Abir   I'm Abir.

Adham   Abir. (*Playing with her name.*) Abir . . . So why are you
not at my party?

Abir   Well.

Adham   Everyone in the village was invited. I can't believe
you're not attending.

Abir   Why are you not there?

Adham   I don't like smiling and pretending to be gracious.

Abir   But it's your party!

Adham   Let me ask you something.

Abir   Okay.

Adham   You like my shoes? My clothes? You think they're
acceptable?

He 'models' for her for two seconds.

Abir   The shoes are worn out. And you could use a new
pair of pants.

Adham (*amused*)   I see. And they say the village girls have no
taste!

Abir   Who says that?

He laughs. Which makes her mad.

I know what looks good! I read magazines. I see movies.
I speak French fluently and some English.

Adham   And Arabic, of course, with a little bit of a peasant
accent.

She starts to leave.

I mean that in a good way!

Abir (*incensed*)   We had a farm. But I'm probably more educated than most city girls.

Adham (*overlap*)   All right –

Abir   I learned how to draw and design irrigation tunnels from my father. How many people can say that?

Adham (*overlap*)   Of course.

Abir   I was second in my class, overall.

Adham   I believe you! So let's hear some English then.

Abir   What?

Adham   You said you spoke English.

Abir   I mean, just some phrases. Here and there.

Adham   Such as?

Abir (*caught*)   *Tosir widloh.*

Adham   What?

Abir (*hedging*)   Toh. Sir. Widloh. The song? 'To. Sir.' That one. You know that one.

He lets her squirm.

Adham   I really don't.

Abir   The one, 'To. Sir.' Lulu.

Adham   'To Sir with Love'?

Abir   Yes!

Adham   So that's your English.

Abir   And a few lines from a movie. The Julie Christie one. I see all her movies. Do you go to the movies?

Adham   No.

Abir   Are you really going to Oxford to speak?

Adham   Oxford? No. Who said that?

Abir   Someone. I thought I heard that.

Adham   No. University College. London. A conference on Romantic Literature. I'm one of the keynote speakers.

Abir   Oh.

Adham   So I'll deliver a paper. I was chosen out of, uh . . . three hundred or so entries? Every year they highlight one speaker from abroad, and this year it was me.

Abir   Praise to God.

Adham   I'll keep the praise for myself.

Abir   You don't believe God had a hand in this?

Adham   I don't believe he has a hand, a face, an arm, a tooth; I don't think he exists.

Abir (*challenging, a little*)   At least you pray.

Beat.

Adham   Not for a long time.

Beat.

Abir   So . . . what happens after you go to London?

Adham   Who knows? You become well known in Cairo, you teach in Cairo. You become well known in London, you can go anywhere.

Abir   So that's what you want, to teach?

Adham   Well, I've finished my Master's, so that's done. Then when you complete the PhD, teaching is the next step. But then, anyone can do that, you know? It's another thing to be – sought after. To have other scholars, people you respect, say, 'Yes, I've heard of you. I've read your work.' It's an imprimatur, you see. You keep building your reputation, and eventually you chair a department, and then . . . You think I'm too much?

Abir   I think that, to get anywhere, one must have a lot of confidence.

Adham   What do *you* want?

Abir   Well, I studied civic engineering in secondary school.

Adham   And now?

Abir   Now I'm supposed to wait at home for a husband.

Adham   How's that going?

Abir   I don't like any of them. It feels forced.

Adham   Oh no. It should feel natural.

Beat. They both smoke and look out.

Why did you come up here?

Abir   So you don't believe in any god? Not ours, no one's?

Adham   I believe in Fate. If anything.

Abir   Yes?

Adham   When I was a child, my mother took up with a stupid man.

Abir   I don't . . . understand. Your father . . . died?

Adham   May as well have. When we had to – leave the Galilee, we ended up at a refugee camp in Southern Lebanon.

Abir   I'm sorry.

Adham   I was three, barely remember it. Anyway, my mother says she would've killed herself if she stayed. So she got us out of there somehow. Left my father, and we came here.

Abir   And the stupid man? Where does he come in?

Adham   Oh! Well, he was from the next village. He was nice enough, good at fixing things. But not a good fit with my mother. It wasn't his fault! He had a low IQ. Couldn't understand her books or make proper conversation. So he gave up, and she gave up. She stopped speaking to him, except to say, 'Go get flour.' 'Get me a magazine.' 'Shut up.' He finally got the hint and stopped coming around.

Abir   That's terrible! And you?

Adham   I don't want to talk about this.

Abir   Tell me.

Adham   Just. She put all her energies on me. I read to her in the mornings, translated Latin . . . If I didn't get it right? . . .

He laughs at the memory.

She demanded I be her equal.

Abir   Where is the Fate in that?

Adham   If my mother had found a smarter man, I wouldn't have achieved a thing.

Beat.

You think I'm strange.

Abir   I think you say strange things.

Adham (*mock horror*)   Oh, I say terrible things sometimes.

Abir   Do you still read to her every day?

Adham   No!

Abir   She must be proud of you.

Adham   She should be.

Beat.

Why did you come up here?

Abir   You saw. To smoke.

Adham   Why else?

Abir   I don't know.

Adham   Really?

Abir   I don't know.

Adham   You don't?

He keeps getting closer to her.

Why don't you tell me?

Abir   It's wrong.

Reaches out to her, barely brushes her arm.

Adham   What's wrong? Tell me.

Abir   I saw you walk up the hill. And I thought, if I don't talk to him now, I'll never get to talk to him.

And now he runs his hand up her arm.

Adham   And how does it feel? Talking to me?

Abir   I'm not sure. Not altogether good.

Adham   Oh?

Abir   And not altogether bad.

Adham   And how does it feel now?

He lifts his hand to her face.

Abir   Stop making fun of me.

He takes her hand.

Adham   I'm not making fun of you.

Abir   Do you think I'm beautiful?

Adham   You know you are. Don't you? You look like your actress, like Julie Christie.

Abir   No.

Adham   More beautiful.

Abir   I'm not supposed to think that.

Adham   Too late.

She looks at him. She tries to pass, and he doesn't let her. They stand there, a couple feet apart. He leans in, takes her hand, and kisses her on the lips, very lightly, very slowly.

'To Sir with Love' starts playing:

'If you wanted the sky I would write across the sky
With letters, that would soar a thousand feet high.'

AT HOME

May.

Beder*'s apartment.*

*She turns a panel, revealing: a giant picture of Adham, aged fourteen,
looking very serious, holding a certificate. She then sits down next to*
Abir*, who has come in with a plate of food on her lap.* **Adham**
stands, leaning against the door frame.

Beder   That's him getting the Jowett.

Abir   Oh.

Beder *(overlap)*   The youngest recipient in the history of the
award.

Abir *(barely gets it out)*   So impressive.

Beder   And then the Partington. That got him into
university. That one was from the Catholics, they made him
do some of these –

*She waves her hands carelessly in the air, doing something resembling the
Sign of the Cross –*

– and write a letter to the Pope, but I didn't care. They want
to pay for his education, we'll do anything they want.

Adham   It's this.

He makes the Sign of the Cross, doing it the right way.

Left to right. Father, Son, Holy Spirit. *(Teasing her.)* Get it right,
Mother.

Beder   And this is his graduation picture.

She hands **Abir** *a small Polaroid photograph.*

Beder   Careful.

Abir *looks at the picture, anxiously, balancing her plate.* **Adham** *reaches his hand out to take the picture.*

Adham   I'll take that.

Beder   More food?

Abir   Oh. Yes. It's delicious.

Beder   It's passable.

Abir   I don't agree.

Beder   Keep eating.

Mini-beat.

Did my son tell you what I did for him as a child?

Abir   You made him read to you. And uh, you tested him . . . Right?

Beder   That's what he said?

Abir   Well. I mean –

Beder   That's one-tenth of what I did. After an-Nakba . . .

Adham   Oh no . . .

Beder   You want to tell the story?

Adham   Of 1948? I'll pass. She knows, anyway. The Israelis took her family farm. Her father died.

Beder   They killed him?

Abir   No, not from that. It was all the smoking. His lungs. He smoked a couple packs a day.

Beder (*her mind is made up*)   They killed him. What about the rest of your family?

Abir   I live with my sister and her husband. And my mother lives with my brother. In Detroit, Michigan. America.

Beder   What does he do there?

Abir   He makes cars.

Beder (*not impressed*)   Oh.

Abir   He likes it . . . Adham told me you were from the Galilee.

Beder   Before they cleaned out every village, yes.

Abir   And then . . . Lebanon?

Beder   It wasn't a pleasure trip.

Abir   I know that.

Beder   We get there, and we sit in, excuse me, a shithole refugee camp. I realize: this isn't temporary. This place is Death. I grabbed my youngest son, and came back here. With nothing but my education, that's it. Did he tell you I had started a degree in philosophy? Before I was married.

Loud explosions are heard in the distance. Everyone jumps. **Beder** *gets up.*

Beder   God help us.

Another explosion, and now light bursts through the window.

The war is on? It's happening?

Adham   It can't be.

Jumpy, everyone goes outside.

A few beats while the explosions continue.

Adham *and* **Abir** *come back in.*

Adham   I knew it was just fireworks.

Abir   So loud.

He takes the opportunity to get close to her.

Adham   She likes you.

Abir   I don't know about that. She thinks I'm common.

Adham   Doesn't matter. I like you.

He takes her plate away.

And I like *this.*

He kisses her hands.

And this . . .

He kisses her neck.

Abir   We can't.

Adham   She's not religious.

He starts to caress her arms when **Beder** *comes back in.*

Adham   Disappointed, Mother? Did you expect to see
Egyptian jets, here to liberate us all?

Abir   That's not funny.

Beder (*fuming*)   Independence Day fireworks. How can the
Israelis call it Independence Day and not choke on the words?
They celebrate forcibly removing people from their homes?
Killing men, women, children? This is cause for a party?

Adham   Let's not get political.

Beder   Who's getting political? Anyway, we leave Lebanon.
We come here, we know no one. I take a job. Menial labor, a
clerk. Our own people talk to me like I'm nothing. As dumb
as a dog running in the streets: 'Take this number and write
it three times in three books.' Same number, over and over.
I said, What is this? I explain to them: this is inefficient! They
don't care. They're not interested. No wonder the Arab world
hasn't advanced in the last two hundred years!

Adham   Thank God we cleared that up.

Abir (*changing the subject*)   You did so much for him. I know
you did everything to help him be successful.

Beder   When the Quakers opened the new school, I begged
them to let him in. We couldn't afford more than him being a

day student. He was so frightened the first time I took him there.

Abir (*touched*)   Oh?

Beder   You remember?

Adham   No.

Abir   Why do you think he was afraid?

Adham   Who cares.

Beder   Who knows? He'd been at the little village school before that. This one was farther away, toward Ramallah. We had to take a bus every day. There's the entrance, where the gate is. Then you have to go down these stone steps, and you're on a path between a grove of fig trees, the school building in the distance. Well. I get him there and he starts crying. And I am thinking, who is this child? What is wrong with him? So fearful! Did I make him this way?

Adham (*under his breath*)   Yes.

Beder   Then he tells me: he thinks bandits are going to come from behind the trees and slit his throat. You remember?

Adham   No. And I don't remember you, actually. What was your name again?

Beder   And I'm thinking, what to do? I can't send him away like this, his face covered in tears. So I make it a game. This wasn't my nature, this kind of whimsical approach.

Adham   Really.

Beder   I say, Do you see this sign, my son? This entrance to the school? This is a magical entrance. Once you go through these gates, you are safe. Just be careful as you walk these first few steps. He was always running, everywhere. They used very old stones when they built the school. They say these were from the front steps of the great hall that housed Alexander the Great.

Adham   I didn't believe that. Even then.

Beder   Of course you did.

Abir   Did he stop crying?

Beder   No, he didn't.

Adham   Because he didn't recognize this strange new mother, full of kindness!

Beder   That's not the story.

Beat. **Adham** *looks at his mother.*

Beder   We walk through the gate, and I take your hand, and the wind came up. I say, 'Do you feel yourself drifting, as you take this walk?' Because none of us was ever allowed to drift, really. 'Let yourself drift, my son, as the ancient grove makes way for you. The trees will bow to you. See? Each one nods! Each one says, this is a scholar!' Each tree had a name, do you remember this?

Adham   Khallas, mama.

Beder   And you look at me, and you look at the trees, and you say: 'Tell me then. Tell me each tree's name.' This is when I realize, this boy has exceptional intelligence. Such imagination.

Adham   Or he was crazy. Did you consider that?

Beder   And I think, quickly: what is the name of each tree? And I say: 'Al-Mutanabbi, the great poet. Al-Yajizi. Al-Barudi. Aristotle. Shakespeare.' You see? And then you took a breath, and you walked, and you let go of my hand, and it was like I was barely there.

Long beat. **Adham** *waits it out, displaying a rare show of sensitivity.*

Adham   So. I don't want to have to ask your blessing. We're not traditional that way.

Beder   So don't ask.

Adham   I've already talked to her brother-in-law, and we spoke to the sheikh.

Beder   Oh.

Adham   But I'm giving you the chance.

Beder *looks right at* **Abir**.

Beder   You're a beautiful girl.

Abir   Thank you.

Beder   But my son is too young to make his way with a woman.

Adham   What?

Beder   In ten years or so, when he's established, that's when he starts looking for a wife. And then, he'll be at a higher level, if you understand.

Abir   I should . . . go.

Beder   Finish your food.

Adham   I can't believe you!

Beder   We've discussed this. I said the same thing about your Egyptian girlfriends.

Adham   You're unbelievably insulting, on every level.

Abir   I'm leaving.

Beder   I'm insulting? I waited with you for your passport for hours, begging them to issue it to you. They're suspicious of every Palestinian these days, and I'm standing there, pulling out my birth certificate from the British Mandate! Telling them lies, that your father died! Performing the sad widow act! Bribing them!

Abir   I don't want to cause a problem . . .

She starts to leave. **Adham** *grabs her arm.*

Adham   Wait.

Abir   She doesn't want me.

Beder   I didn't say that. I like you.

Abir (*to* **Adham**)   Why would you bring me here, if you knew this would happen?

Adham   I wanted her to see you.

Abir   Well, she saw me, okay?

Beder   You have your mind made up? Then why go through the motions? You're making a mistake if you go with her! I know what mistakes are! So even though you really don't want to hear my opinion, I'm giving it. This is my house!

Adham   You're right. I did just go through the motions. I like her. I liked her the moment I saw her. You've decided everything! This is the one thing that's mine.

Blackout. The sounds of a jet taking off.

Adham *and* **Abir** *are suddenly in travel clothes, holding suitcases, sunglasses on.*

From her apartment, **Beder** *talks to* **Adham***, and he responds, almost in two places at once.*

Beder   There's one thing I never told you, part of this story. I wanted to walk you all the way down the steps, through the trees. I wanted to take you inside the building, and sit next to you, and sit there all day to make sure we were getting our money's worth! I wanted nothing more than to take you all the way in. It was the last thing in the world I wanted, to leave you to go down those steps alone. But I had to. I stood there and watched you go.

Adham   Well, such heroism. It's worthy of an epic poem, really.

Beder   You know what I did after I left you? I came home and I threw away every picture I had of your brother.

Adham (*genuinely shocked*)   What?

Beder   I had very few to begin with. Baby pictures.

Adham   You just tossed them in the trash?

Beder   Tore them to bits, each, and then, yes.

Beat.

Adham   Why on earth would you do that?

Beder   The way I felt with you on the steps. This – feeling this –

She puts her hand on her chest: a pang she doesn't have words for.

This was – this was the same way I felt every time I looked at those pictures. Anyway, I couldn't stand to look at them anymore. What does that emotion serve? It's going to help me get your brother out of Lebanon, rescue him? I knew that if I got rid of him, his pictures, I could do anything. I knew that to get you where you needed to go, all such feelings would have to be gotten rid of.

Adham   You left them. He and my father. That was your choice.

Beder   There was no choice to be had! What a ridiculous thought. Choice. What a myth. Choice is a luxury.

Adham   You left your son there.

Beder   To raise you in a better place! Don't forget that.

Adham   See you later.

STRAND PALACE HOTEL, LONDON

June, late afternoon. Panels have turned to reveal 1967 LONDON, *with parts of the old city still showing.*

Adham *and* **Abir** *enter their hotel room – not huge, but well-appointed. A desk with a lamp. Two chairs and a table, on which has been placed a tea service, and a bottle of champagne. A bed.*

They close the door behind them and take in the room.

Abir   This is, uh –

Adham   Nice.

He carries the suitcase into the room. Leaves it by the window. He peers through the sheer curtains.

Abir   What's out there?

Adham   Theaters. Lots of things.

Abir   Can anyone see in?

Adham   I don't think so. I don't think anyone cares.

Abir *goes into the bathroom.* **Adham** *opens the window. Sounds of the street come in.* **Abir** *comes back.*

Abir   So many towels.

Adham   Yeah?

She giggles a little bit.

Adham (*smiling*)   What's going on?

Abir   Nothing. We just haven't been. Alone.

Adham   Sure we have. That first day. The day of my party.

Beat.

Abir   What was the man talking about, something 'downstairs'?

Adham   Oh, bomb shelters. During the war. Down there.

Abir   He talks so fast.

Adham   Why do you ask? You want to go look at them again?

Abir   No.

She opens a cabinet.

(*Excited.*)   A television set.

Adham   All the nice hotels have them now.

Abir *turns it on. It's Tom Jones on the BBC, singing 'Show Me'. We see it projected on one of the panels behind them.*

Tom Jones (*voice-over*)
Show me a man that's got a good woman.
I'll show you a man that goes to work hummin'.
He knows he's got some sweet love comin'
At the end of his working day.

Because it's Tom Jones, it's kind of amazing and sexual, obviously.
Abir *shuts off the TV. Closes the cabinet. Awkward beat.*

Adham   You like that?

Abir   I don't understand it.

Adham (*flirting*)   I think you do.

She scans the room, sees something on the tea service.

Abir   Tea?

Adham   Not now.

She picks something up off the tea service.

It's an English cookie. Try it.

She takes a bite.

Good?

It's heinous. **Abir** *nods politely.* **Adham** *walks over to her, holds it up to his mouth, eats the rest.*

Adham   That's terrible.

Abir, *exhausted, fluttery, sits on the bed. Bounces back up. Grabs the champagne off the tea service.*

Abir   Let's have some of this.

Adham   You can't have alcohol!

Abir   A little. With my husband.

Adham   A little, huh? You found that out. Read it somewhere?

Abir   No. I know it.

She impulsively starts to open the bottle.

Adham   You don't know what you're doing.

Abir   No one did, the first time they did it.

The cork goes flying. Hits a painting on the wall.

Oh no.

Adham *walks over to look.*

Abir   Do you think anyone could hear it?

Adham *checks the painting.*

Adham   It's fine.

Abir *pours some into a glass, drinks.*

Abir   Oh.

Adham   Good?

Abir   It tastes like juice. Very strong juice.

She pours some for him, holds it out.

You have to have some.

Adham   Look at you.

Abir   Go.

He takes it, drinks it quickly.

Adham   It's good.

She stands and looks at him. He goes over to her, puts his arms on her, runs his hands up her back. This is new for both of them. His grip gets tighter.

Abir   Ouch.

Adham (*letting go*)   Shit.

Abir   No. It's okay.

She takes his hands, places them on her waist. The hands stay there, still firm, but not going anywhere. He stalls. Breaks off.

Did I do something wrong?

Adham   No, no. You. You're beautiful.

He goes to the window. Looks out. Takes a big breath.

Maybe I'm no one to come here and tell them what their poetry is.

Abir   What? No. You're everyone.

She walks up behind **Adham**, *places a hand on his back. He turns. She kisses him quickly, almost surprising herself.*

She takes his face in her hands, looks at him. He kisses her back. Wraps his arms all around her body.

Abir   Everyone.

Now she kisses his face, his chest, his hands. He kisses her hands back, lets go, puts his hands on her breasts. She inhales. Doesn't know where to put her hands.

I want another glass.

Adham *wordlessly goes over to the champagne, pours more. Holds it up to her . . .*

Lights fade on the room, as the two move onto the bed.

WIVES, TOO

Next morning. In bed, **Adham**, *alone, asleep. He rustles, slightly.* **Abir**, *wearing a robe, her hair up, make-up 'done', stands watching him, smiling. She leans over him, studies him. Dares herself to touch his face.*

He reaches for her, touches her breasts, smiling. He half sleeptalks:

Adham   Yes. All right.

Abir (*amused*)   Yes what?

His eyes open suddenly. He pulls his hands away.

Adham   Where am I?

Abir   The hotel, silly.

He bolts up, panicked.

Adham   Oh god. What time is it?

He finds his watch on the nightstand, checks the time.

This is terrible.

Abir   Are you all right?

He looks at her, taking her in for the first time.

Adham   Oh.

Abir (*re: the robe*)   I didn't want to wear it at your mother's.

She suddenly gets self-conscious, pulls the robe more tightly around her waist.

Should I make you tea?

Adham   I'm late.

Abir   Now?

Adham   I will be. Why didn't you wake me? Where are my books? Notes? I need to know where they are at all times!

Abir   I put your things on that desk.

In just his underwear, he goes to the desk, starts to rifle through two neat piles of books and folders.

Abir   Are you speaking today?

Adham   I'm meeting everyone. Why didn't you wake me?

Abir   I tried. I didn't know you had to be somewhere.

Adham   You have to give me a shove. It's – you have to do that till I wake up.

Abir   I'll remember.

Adham   It's not just about presenting the paper. It's about fellowship, camaraderie, you understand?

Abir   I think so.

He finds the folder he was looking for, sets it on the bed, then grabs the pants he wore on the plane, folded over a chair. Puts them on. He goes to his suitcase, pulls out a button-down shirt and puts it on. The shirt is very, very wrinkly.

Adham   Oh no. Oh no.

Abir   I saw an iron.

Adham*, helpless, says nothing.*

Abir   Let me get it for you.

She opens a closet and pulls out an ironing board and iron. Holds her hands out.

Give it to me. Here. I'll take care of it.

Adham   I can do it.

Abir *steps back as he walks his shirt over to the iron. He clearly has no idea what he's doing.*

Adham   Shit!

Abir   I said, let me . . .

Adham   We don't have time for that.

She takes it from him, and irons the damn shirt.

Abir   It just takes a minute . . . I should've hung this up last night when we got here. I didn't know you were going somewhere important today.

Adham   We. You're coming too.

Abir   We?

Adham   Yes. Wives. Wives, too.

Abir   Oh. I have to get dressed.

Adham   You're not interested in going?

Abir   Of course I am.

Adham (*snatching the shirt from her*)   Give me that.

Abir   I only finished one side!

Adham   It'll be fine. I'll keep my jacket on. You keep your coat on at these things.

Abir   It's warm outside. You'll be too hot –

Adham   The jacket stays on. It's fine.

He grabs a thin 1960s tie from the suitcase, puts it on, then puts on the coat he wore on the plane, the only jacket he has.

It's fine.

Rushed, he pulls out of his suitcase some kind of hair cream, gops it into his hair, tries to push it down.

Now you get ready. Why are you laughing?

Abir   Your hair.

She rushes into the bathroom, comes out with a comb, sits him down on the bed.

Adham   No one cares.

Abir   I do. No one will listen to a word you say if this isn't fixed.

Abir *tries to comb his hair . . . As she finishes, she puts her hands through it, slowly, trying not to give away how much she likes it. She steps away.*

Abir   There.

Adham   Okay. So go. Get ready.

She goes back into the bathroom.

He lights a cigarette, then goes to the window and looks out at the city.

Adham   All the fellows in the English Department will be there. They're probably expecting someone older.

A few beats as he smokes and waits. Then:

(*Calling to her.*)   Okay?

Abir (*from inside the bathroom*)   One minute.

Adham   We have to go!

Abir (*from inside the bathroom*)   I know!

Moments later she comes out, wearing her 'travel' dress.

Abir   Do I look like the wife of an academic?

Adham   I don't know. What does one look like?

Stung, she tries to zip the back of her dress.

Let me do that.

She turns her back, lets him.

Abir   Are you upset with me?

Adham (*clueless*)   No.

And now she cries.

Abir   I thought maybe –

Adham   Oh no – what?

Abir   Are you happy with me?

Adham   What? Yes!

She cries for a beat. **Adham** *is lost.*

I'm sorry.

He takes her hands, holds them, softens.

(*Re: her hands.*)   This smell . . .

Abir   You like it?

Adham   It smells like the countryside.

Abir   That's not good!

Adham   Yes, it is.

She throws her heels on.

Can you run in those shoes?

Abir   I don't know.

He throws his cigarette into the ashtray, not bothering to put it out.

Adham   Hold on to me.

As they disappear into the panels, now LONDON, *we hear Petula Clark:* 'Don't Sleep in the Subway'.

THE LUNCH

Lights up. Two English scholars, George and Theo, open the panels to reveal a domed building above the words: UNIVERSITY COLLEGE. *They sit down at a table, and hold up teacups to* **Adham**.

George   To the next wave of literary criticism.

Theo   You're embarrassing him.

George   But he is. You are.

Adham   Thank you.

George   Don't you feel it's so?

Adham (*cocky, pretending to be humble*)   I feel I'm finding an interesting angle in my approach.

George   Angle? You're far too humble. Look how humble he is.

Adham   No one's ever called me that before. Humble, I mean.

They laugh.

George   And funny.

Theo   I think we needed it, frankly. A fresh infusion.

George   What – you didn't think we got that from the German scholar last year? (*To* **Adham**.) Dreadfully boring, he was.

Theo   It's refreshing. A different perspective on our dusty old poets. Will you tackle Tennyson as well?

Adham   I don't find his work particularly engaging, actually.

George   His love has limits. Not willing to take on old Alfred Lord?

Adham   Nothing has inspired me to do so yet.

George   But have you read Tennyson, actually?

Theo   George . . .

George   I'm just asking. Everyone loves to malign Tennyson but most haven't actually bothered to read him.

Adham   No, I have. I appreciate the imagery in his, uh – (*Confidently, but hitting the Arabic 'H' hard.*) *TAHT-oh-nay-us.*

George   Which one?

Adham   One of his blank verse . . . ?

They don't seem to know what he's talking about. **Adham** *covers his panic.*

Adham (*faking confidence, slowing the word*)   *TETH-honus* . . . ?

George   *Tithonus?* Of course. Yes.

Theo   Adham, we've been looking forward to meeting you. We want to show you the town.

George   Where have you been so far?

Adham   Just here. And the hotel.

Theo   Oh, that's unacceptable! We must give you a tour.

Adham   Yes, absolutely.

George   Oh! Forgive my manners. I almost forgot. We have something for you.

He reaches onto the seat next to him, and pulls out a paper bag. He pulls out a large towel-like thing with an old painting on it.

To our most esteemed guest of the international language exchange.

He hands the bag to **Adham**, *who holds it up appreciatively.*

Adham   Oh this is, it's perfect.

Theo   It's hideous!

George   He hasn't a clue as to what the hell it is. Have you?

Adham   No.

George   It's a tea towel.

Adham   Oh. Of course.

Theo   'Cause everyone needs a tea towel.

George *points to the figures on the towel.*

George   Ah, but this is a University College tea towel. These are our founders, Jeremy Bentham et al., fighting our blood enemies from King's College.

Adham   Who's winning?

George/Theo   We are, of course.

Adham   What's the fire?

George   The pits of hell. Into which our rivals will fall. Gorgeous, right? So you'll remember us when you take your tea.

Theo   Or wipe your bum! It's awful. Adham, I for one won't be insulted if you leave it in the hotel when you go.

Adham   I will treasure this. Thank you. I wish I had brought something.

George   Relax. You're our guest.

Theo   Now give him the real gift.

George   That old thing?

He pulls out a book. Hands it to **Adham.**

George   Your Wordsworth. Third edition. It was the oldest one we could find.

Adham   Thank you. I don't know how to thank you.

He opens the book. Amazed. Reads:

Adham   'Third printing, Macmillan Publishing . . . '

George   Didn't believe me, eh?

Theo   Smart fellow.

Adham   'Sixteen Colborn Street.'

George   That's close by.

Adham (*breaks out of his reverie*)   Thank you.

He closes the book and sets it down carefully.

George   I've been meaning to ask, how did you find your way to the English Romantics?

Adham   Find my way?

George   I can't imagine you woke up every day hearing Wordsworth.

Adham   My mother decided I should be a scholar. It was this or Cicero.

George   You chose right. Was she a teacher?

Adham   No. Just full of opinions.

George   You should've brought her along.

Adham (*laughs*)   No, I shouldn't have.

George   And she grew up in, uh, Israel? Or . . . urn, of course. Palestine.

Adham Yes.

Theo The landscape there is splendid. Mountains and the sea, yes?

Adham I don't know. I never get out that way.

Theo Really? The famous road down the coast, on the way to Jerusalem. I'm dying to try it one day. The Phoenicians, the Romans . . .

Adham I've heard that. The road is cut off now, so –

George What do you mean?

Adham We can't go back there. It's off-limits. To – us.

Theo Sorry.

Adham No, no. It's. You can't miss it if you don't know what you're missing.

Just then **Abir** *walks up, a tea in hand.*

Adham My wife – she's from the countryside. You can ask her.

George *Vous êtes de la campagne?*

Abir *Oui.*

George She's delightful. Isn't she delightful? I'm saying you are delightful.

Abir Oh, yes. Yes.

George Have you been to London before?

Abir *nods tentatively.*

Adham That was the extent of her English.

Abir *smiles, nervously, standing there, waiting. Beat.*

Adham Okay.

He nods, as if to say, you're done.

She goes.

George   Ah. Darling girl. So she's never been to England?

Adham   No.

George   Brave girl.

Adham   Why brave?

George   To come all this way.

Adham   I thought you meant, to marry me.

They don't know **Adham** *well enough to know he's joking.*

George   Oh. Well.

Awkward beat.

Adham   In which case I'd agree.

They realize he's joking. They all laugh.

Theo   Because you're a penniless academic like the rest of us?

Adham   Because I have no sense of the practical concerns of life. I'm useless in every way.

George *smiles, leans in to* **Adham**, *confidentially, man to man:*

George   In every way?

Adham *takes a beat: Is he really going to go there? He is.*

Adham   Well . . . no. Not in every way.

They laugh. **George** *puts an arm around* **Adham**.

George   Listen to this, Adam: We've a friend who runs a society called the Old Stagers. They take the month of August, go to a giant house in the Cotswolds and do nothing but play cricket all day and amateur theatricals at night. You must come back and join me there.

Adham   I would love that.

Theo   I can't imagine he'll come all this way to see our countryside before he's seen his own.

Adham   You never know.

Abir *approaches. She speaks to* **Adham** *in Arabic.*

Abir   Shoe akul? (*What should I eat?*)

The following is in Arabic. **Adham** *is jarred – immensely embarrassed to be speaking in his native tongue.*

Adham   Shoe? (*What?*)

Abir   Al akl, maa barif shoe hel aklat. (*The food. I can't tell what anything is.*)

Adham   Kulee shoe biakloo azzawjaat i'taneen. (*Eat what the other wives are eating.*)

She makes a face.

Hazzeree, maashi? (*Just take your best guess, okay?*)

Theo   Everything all right?

Adham (*to* **Theo**, *in English*)   Yes. (*To* **Abir**, *in Arabic.*) RuHee iHna bniHkee. (*Go. We're talking.*)

Abir, *hurt, goes.*

Theo   She doesn't like the food?

George   Can't blame her for that!

Adham   Oh. No. No no. She's fine.

Theo   But she did mention food? Bad food?

Adham   Yes.

Theo (*to* **George**)   See? I'm not as hopeless as you think.

George   Hurray, hurray, you understood one sentence.

Adham   You speak Arabic?

Theo   I try.

George   Very hard, sadly. With little results.

Theo   Not true.

George   Actually, Theo here is a bit of a pan-Arabist.

Theo   An Arabist. Although this pan-Arabist phenomenon is fascinating. Nasser is rather inspiring.

George (*to* **Adham**)   Do you think?

Adham   Do I think?

George   Nasser. I'm curious what the word on the street is about him.

Adham*'s a bit thrown.*

Adham   'On the street'? Well. I guess, he, uh, yes, he's seen as a, savior . . . by most people.

Theo   And you?

Adham   He's very charismatic. Sweats a lot.

George (*enjoying* **Adham***'s assessment*)   Brilliant.

Abir *is back.*

Abir   Inta HatiqAud maAay? (*Are you going to sit with me?*)

Adham   BaAd daqeeqa, itkalamee maA'Hada. (*In a minute. Talk to someone.*)

Abir   MEEN? (*Who?*)

Adham   Ayy Hada. iHkee maAa annas. (*Anyone. Make some conversation.*)

Abir   Aalaa shoe? Wa laa waHda min ha nniswaan biHkoo faransawi. Leesh? Inta ultilee inhum muthaqafaat. (*About what? None of those women speaks French. Why is that? / You said they were educated.*)

Theo   You'd think if they were really educated, those women *would* speak French!

Adham   niHkee baAdin. (*We'll talk later.*)

She stands there for a beat.

Go.

She goes.

Theo   She seems a good sport.

Adham   Ah. Oh yes.

George *offers* **Adham** *a cigarette. He takes it. All three men light up, looking back toward where* **Abir** *went.*

George   You've been married a long time?

Theo   That's rather a personal question, isn't it?

Adham   Not at all. We're just. Married.

George   Just?

Adham   Three weeks ago.

George   By God.

They look at **Adham***.*

Theo   Oh. It's very new, then.

Adham   Yes. We barely know each other. So.

For some reason he starts to laugh.

Here we are.

George   Sometimes that's best.

Adham *looks at them. He feels bad about this talk. But joins in anyway.*

Adham   Why is that?

George   Well, sometimes you need to just jump in. Don't look at how high the cliff is, or that you might hit the rocks on the way down.

Theo   So cynical.

George   How so? I love women.

Theo   Adham, he has three girlfriends. Three. And he rotates them from week to week. I can't fathom why they put up with it.

George   I mislead none of them! They're happier than if they were my only ones. They're all beautiful, Adam. Just gorgeous . . . Really, my man, we could take you to some parties . . .

Theo   Tell him about your theory.

George   So you'll make fun of me?

Theo   Of course. Tell him anyway.

George   Well, as I said, I love women. Always have. I love every bit of them. Their minds. Bodies. Their clothing. I mean, when a girl asks me what she should wear to go out, I put some thought into it! My father was the same way.

Theo   The theory – ?

George   My theory is, well, my father and I both were raised by women, you see? Just women. Both our fathers were off at wars. So we spent an inordinate amount of time with the fair sex. We've got a sixth sense about how they operate, what goes on in their heads. (*To* **Theo**, *re:* **Adham**.) He thinks I'm touched.

Adham   No no. It makes sense to me. I was, uh, raised by a woman, also.

George   So you see? You're the same way.

Adham   I'm . . . not so sure about that.

Abir *returns, and this time sits down next to* **Adham**.

Abir   Ana jeet kul hal masaafa. Laa yumkin tatjahalnee. (*I came all this way. You can't ignore me.*)

George (*to* **Abir**)   Would you care for a cigarette?

He holds up a cigarette to her.

Abir   Thank you.

He lights it. She inhales, exhales. Smiles at **Adham**.

Adham   She's not supposed to, so this is a special treat for her.

George   I'm sorry. It hadn't even occurred to me. Is she not allowed . . . ?

Adham   She can do whatever she wants, as far as I'm concerned.

George   Ah. But it's not in line with the religion?

Adham   It's not about the religion. People talk.

Theo   I can't imagine how difficult it must be right now, down there. In your homeland, I mean. (*Re:* **Abir**.) I feel terrible leaving her out. (*In Arabic, to* **Abir**.) bHiss inno da raheeb . . . lam nushrikuki fil hadith. (*I feel terrible . . . leaving you out of the conversation.*)

Abir   Ashkuruka Alaa qawlika haathal. (*Thank you for saying that.*)

Theo   al Aarabi bitaAi, taAban, mish kidda? (*My Arabic is terrible, isn't it?*)

Abir   Laa. (*Not at all.*)

George   Can she understand a word he's saying?

Theo   Of course she can. (*To* **Abir** *again, in Arabic.*) mabastaAmilhash kitheer. bi ged mish battal? (*I get to use it so infrequently. It's really not bad?*)

Abir   Laa. tiHkee ka annak min Masr. Hadha she ghareeb. (*No. You sound like you're from Egypt. That's the only strange thing.*)

Theo (*in English, to* **Adham**)   What's that?

Adham   Egypt. She said it sounds like you're from Egypt.

George   So he is a pan-Arabist. One of Nasser's cronies. A spy, very likely. A rather inept spy, but still.

Theo (*to* **George**)   Would you please be quiet? (*To* **Abir**.) Ma kansh Aindee ayy fikra. kunt fakir inno huwa da' el mustawa? (*I had no idea. Imagine that. I suppose that's the standard?*)

Abir *shrugs.*

Theo   She's absolutely unimpressed with me. She's very beautiful if you don't mind me saying.

Abir (*she understands this*)   Thank you.

She smiles.

Adham   You understood that . . . (*In Arabic.*) Mahay?

He puts his arm around **Abir**.

Adham   You see? So we can speak in English.

Abir   Aal aqal zumalaa'ak Habbounee. Amma anniswaan, kullhum Aajaayiz wa ghaseesaat. (*At least your colleagues like me. The women were all old and mean.*)

Theo   I agree! The women over there *are* old and mean.

He and **Abir** *laugh.*

Theo   Rest assured they're not our wives. I mean, we don't have them.

Abir *nods politely, not getting it.*

Theo   I wish my Arabic were better! (*To* **Adham**.) They are the repressed trophies of our doddery old faculty.

Awkward beat.

Beer, anyone?

Adham   Oh. Yes, thank you.

Theo   Certainly. Would your wife . . . ?

Adham   No, no.

Theo *leaves.*

George   Are you ready for your talk tomorrow?

Adham   Oh, yes. Yes.

George   Some of our colleagues have got pretty worked up about the poem on which you're speaking.

Adham   Oh.

George   They take issue with Wordsworth's way of seeing. He sees something, then he doesn't.

Theo *returns with three beers.*

Theo   Oh no. Is this your hedgerows discussion again?

Adham   Let me hear it.

George   Early on in 'Lines Composed a Few Miles Above Tintern Abbey, on Revisiting the Banks of the Wye During a Tour, July 13, 1798' – you'll forgive me if I don't abbreviate – Wordsworth mentions the hedgerows he sees. But then in the same line, backs off from the observation. He who is the master observer of nature backs away from what he sees.

Adham (*not sure where it's going*)   Um-hmm . . .

Theo   That's what I say! 'Um-hmmm.' It doesn't go anywhere, this line of thinking. Trust me, Adham.

Abir *reaches for the beer glass, but* **Adham** *stops her.*

George   It's been said – not by me – that these hedgerows are a sign of enclosure, and, and, rural impoverishment.

Theo   By one neo-Marxist historian! Not even a Romantic specialist. (*To* **Adham**.) Should I get her a beer? (*To* **Abir**, *in Arabic*.) *Bedik tarabeeza?*

Abir *laughs and shakes her head.*

Theo   Oh no. What did I say? What've I done?

George   What *did* he say?

Abir (*in Arabic*)   Quit 'tarabeeza'.

Adham (*in English*)   You asked her if she wanted a table.

Theo   Oh dear. Just when I think I've made progress.

Adham   She's fine.

George (*resuming his argument*)   Do you feel this is way off the mark?

Adham   I don't understand.

George   That Wordsworth backs off from an indictment of the landed class?

Theo   So now it's an 'indictment'? That reading isn't supported.

George   Some critics are taking that path, my friend.

Theo (*to* **Adham**)   Tiny pocket of scholars out of Cambridge. They're just interested in being trendy. Most of their colleagues have said as much.

George   It's a reasonable discussion. Wordsworth sees this sign of social stratification, of the subjugation of the peasant, and then dismisses it. It bears some investigation.

Abir *sneaks in another sip of* **Adham***'s beer.*

Abir (*to* **Theo**)   Aagabitnee hay mahma kaanat. Hataa law kaanat tarabeeza. (*I like whatever this is. I don't care if it's a table.*)

She laughs, as does **Theo**.

Theo   Should I get her something?

But **Adham** *is caught up in the discussion.*

Adham   I read it as simply, Wordsworth says, 'Once again I see these hedgerows, hardly hedgerows, little lines of sportive wood run wild.' He sees the structures, the outlines of them, but then he reflects on what he's seen, almost instantaneously, and amends it. 'Hardly hedgerows.' Not because he's disturbed by the implication. But for the simple reason that the hedgerows have become overgrown with grass. That's what he sees.

George   That's the traditional reading of the poem, of course.

Theo   And the one that most readers of English adhere to.

Adham   He's giving himself license to let things fade in tableaux as they fade in the mind.

Theo   Ah. I like that!

George   Hm. What about the vagrant then?

Adham   From 'The Ruined Cottage'?

George   No, from the same poem we're discussing. 'Tintern Abbey.' What about him?

Adham   Forgive me, but what about him? I don't understand the question.

George   My dear man, you need to be ready for this kind of question.

Theo   You're making him feel unwelcome.

George   Not at all. We're having a discussion. Exchange of ideas. You don't feel I'm making you unwelcome, do you?

Adham *shakes his head.*

George   So, yes, in this same poem. Wordsworth suggests this life, this vagrant is there, but he clearly finds it distasteful, moves on.

Adham   I don't think he finds the vagrant distasteful.

George   There are readings that contradict that. That imply that the vagrant is tucked away, something marring the poetic vision.

Adham   What more did Wordsworth need to say about the vagrant?

Abir   Laa tsarrekh. (*Don't yell.*)

Adham   Ana mneeH. (*I'm fine.*)

Theo (*to* **George**)   Right. Did you want an epic poem about the vagrant? If you want a bloody epic poem about the bloody vagrant perhaps you should write it yourself. Sorry, Madam.

Abir *smiles. She hasn't understood, but decides to respond anyway, in English.*

Abir   It's all right. Where's my table?

Theo   Good lord, Adham, I had no idea your wife was a comedienne. She's perfectly charming.

George   I'm saying that no discussion of Wordsworth should be considered complete without an acknowledgment of this unseemly underbelly. Our friend Adam is in a perfect position to understand.

Adham   I am?

Theo   Ha.

Adham   I don't know how.

George   As Palestinian, a, a, refugee.

Adham   Sorry, I don't understand.

George   Your world. Where you live. I mean, what's going on now. The sublime mixed with the horrific. The Egyptian army building up in the Sinai . . .

Theo   Some of that is overblown.

George   Not at all. And the Israeli generals panicking, taking the reins from the Prime Minister. We have been hearing about how dire it is, all over the Middle East.

Adham   I've never known things not to be dire.

Beat.

Theo   There was an, uh, interesting article in *The Times*. Saying that basically Nasser is bluffing, with no intention of going to war. But Moshe Dayan, who says he won't go to war, is actually readying the rifle, so to speak.

Abir (*alerted*)   Dayan kdh-dhaab. (*Dayan is a liar.*)

Adham *tries to quiet her.*

Adham   All right, all right.

George   What'd she say?

Theo   She believes Dayan's a liar.

George   Well he may be, Madam, but he's saddled with the task of protecting his country. Israel is surrounded by those who wish them extinct. They must fight back if provoked. Clearly you grant them that?

Abir   aysh beeyqoul? BeeydaafiA Aal israa'eelyeen? (*What's he saying? He's defending the Israelis?*)

Adham (*to* **Abir**)   *Laal.* (*To the men.*) I'm sorry.

George   No need to apologize. I like the passion.

Abir   Eash yaHkee? (*What did he say?*)

Adham   Wala yhimmik. (*Don't worry about it.*)

Abir (*in Arabic*)   Dayan bass byaAmal al Aamal al wisikh. Fee nafs el waqt Eshkol biyhibb yiqAad wara w'ubeeAamil Halou inno ma'beeyarof shi. Hada kullu mukhattat Aashaan ybanou abriyya' mustafazzeen. (*Dayan is just doing the dirty work while Eshkol gets to sit back and pretend he knows nothing about it. It's all part of their plan to look innocently provoked.*)

Theo   What's all that?

Adham   I guess this is an area she has strong feelings about.

Abir   Annas lazim yaArafou. Mumkin yastamAou li dayan, bas tisAa w tisAeen feel meyya min elli beyqoulou kithib bi kithib. (*People should know. You can listen to Dayan, but ninety-nine percent of what comes out of his mouth is lies.*)

Adham   Ma jeenash houn naHkee Aan haadhaa? (*We didn't come here to talk about this, all right?*)

Abir (*to* **George**)   Bas ibtiAraf eash, iza bidak itdalee jahel, khaleek jahel. Eash badar aAmal? (*But you know, if you want to stay ignorant, stay ignorant. What can I do?*)

Adham   uskutee! (*Shut up!*)

Theo   What's she saying?

Abir   Laa teHkee maAee heek. Leesh ibteHkee maAee heek? (*Don't talk to me like that. Why would you talk to me like that?*)

Adham   I think Wordsworth sees the vagrant as much as he cares to. As much as he sees anything else in the poem. And that I for one don't feel any particular affinity for the vagrant dweller in that poem, or any other.

Adham *takes the beer away from* **Abir** *again, and downs the rest.*

REHEARSAL

Adham *enters, turns a panel, revealing:* ADHAM'S REHEARSAL. *A beat of panic upon seeing this title, then he takes his place behind a podium, leans into a microphone, and starts his lecture.*

Adham   Wordsworth's poem –

He backs away. There's a tremendous echo, almost surreal.

– begins with the mention of time passing: 'Five years have passed.' Is this the way it's supposed to sound?

The others are heard but not seen.

George   Sounds good to us.

Adham   It's very loud.

George   That's this hall. You have to fill it up or you get swallowed.

Adham *looks supremely uncomfortable.*

Theo   You okay up there?

George   It's just a rehearsal.

Adham   It's uh – yes. (*He laughs.*) It's so big in here. What's the word – (*In Arabic.*) WasiA. (*Cavernous.*) I don't know it in English. (*Laughs again, nervously.*) Oh well. WasiA. Leave it at that.

He wipes sweat from his face.

Theo   Take the coat off, you'll feel better.

Adham   Yes, thank you. (*Starts to take his coat off, stops.*) I'll be all right.

We hear the low sounds of Fairuz's song 'Dabke Libnan'. **Adham** *adjusts his coat.*

George   Just a few more words.

Adham *begins again, trying to be louder than the music he (and we) seems to hear. But the music rises as well, until it drowns out his words.*

Adham
    Five summers, with the length
    Of five long winters . . . Once again
    Do I behold these steep and lofty cliffs
    Which on a wild secluded scene impress
    Thoughts of more deep seclusion . . .
    I have owed to them
    In hours of weariness, sensations sweet
    Felt in the blood, and felt along the heart,
    And passing even into my purer mind,
    With tranquil restoration: – feelings too
    Of unremembered pleasure: such, perhaps
    As have no slight or trivial influence
    On that best portion of a good man's life.

Lights out.

Part Two

ADHAM CONFRONTS HIS MEDIOCRITY

Early evening. **Adham***, in some kind of torment, enters the hotel room. Rain has come through the open windows, drenching the curtains.* **Adham** *doesn't seem to notice. He takes off his jacket, throws it on the floor. Starts to unbutton his sweat-stained, wrinkly shirt. Lies on the bed.*

Suddenly, his mother, **Beder***, appears in the window – all garbed-out, wearing a hijab, totally different from how she looked at home.*

Beder   Tell me again why you brought the girl.

Adham (*springing up*)   What the hell?

Beder   Tell me.

He goes to the window. She disappears. He slams it shut. Now we hear her voice, from the opposite side of the stage.

(*Offstage.*) Answer my question.

Now she comes out of the bathroom, dressed normally.

She brought a lot of make-up. What is she hiding?

He looks at her, decides not to question her being there, lies back down.

Adham   She helps me.

Beder   By ironing your shirt? Half ironing it? She didn't even have it on the right setting.

Adham   She's not my maid. She's my wife. She's beautiful. She makes me look good.

Beder   A word to you: you didn't look so good at that event.

Adham   What event?

Beder   The tea. Whatever that was. You looked sideswiped. Like someone who'd never spent a day in a library. You made us look badl

Adham   Well, thank goodness you're not here then, right? What a relief.

Beder   I'd have helped you handle that.

Adham   Handle what?

Beder   The argument he made, the Englishman. You needed a minute to think about it. You'd have found the answer.

Adham   There is no answer. It's a literary discussion.

Beder   One-sided! He made his point and you retreated.

Adham   I'd never heard it before –

Beder (*overlap*)   Doesn't matter –

Adham (*overlap*)   What he was saying –

Beder (*overlap*)   You're educated! An educated man comes up with answers!

Adham   He had an entirely new approach.

Beder   Based on Marxism. So what? Like you've never heard any of that? It's the same babble we hear every day coming out of Cairo. These English want to be Marxists, let them. They have all the time in the world up here to sit and philosophize. Like the bourgeoisie that they are!

Adham   I did answer him. I told him that line of thinking doesn't interest me.

Beder   What 'interests' you doesn't matter. No one cares about that. You didn't dismantle what he said as irrelevant.

Adham   You're right.

Beder   I knew I should've sent you away when you were five. I had the chance. Just packed you up and sent you to the States. Instead, we both stayed. What a waste. All that work! How was I to know those schools weren't halfway decent? What a fool I was, thinking I'd set you up with a proper education.

Adham   I've done well!

Beder   For an Arab in Palestine. Up here, you're practically a Bedouin, as far as they're concerned.

He sinks.

Money, connections. We had nothing. And those teachers put on such airs, as if it was the Sorbonne! It just isn't enough, in the end. You can't hold your own here. God, I should've seen that. I should've seen how limited your education was.

His hands start to shake.

Adham   I'm not giving up on myself.

Beder   This could be the end of you.

Adham   How's that possible? Washed up at twenty-five, Mother?

Beder   Not that unusual in our part of the world.

And she's gone. **Adham** *lies back down on the bed. Long beat of him alone.*

Abir *enters. Switches on the light. Shocked to see one of the windows still open. The scene is in Arabic, with surscript titles on the panels.*

Abir   Leash nayam wa mkhali al-matar yadkhul? Hasis innak mneeH? (*You're lying here letting the rain in? Are you all right?*)

Adham   Mashi ilHaal. (*Sure, sure.*)

She rushes to close the window.

Abir   Inshallah ma kharabish ishi. (*I hope it didn't damage anything.*)

Adham   Hadhi ghurfat funduq. maa byehtamou. (*It's a hotel room. They don't care.*)

She looks at him.

Abir   Laysh roHt heek bisor3ah? Dawaret Aallak taHet. II Aadjooz – il imwazaf? – kaan bidou iyfarjeani suwar Omar E-Sharif lama kaan houn. Fakarny mehtameh. (*Why did you go* *ahead so fast? I looked for you downstairs. The old man − the clerk? − wanted to show me the pictures from when Omar Sharif stayed here. He thought I'd be interested.*)

Adham (*sarcastic*)   Wa kunti. (*And you were.*)

Abir *sees the jacket on the floor, walks to it, picks it up, shakes it out.*

Abir   Shoo fee? (*What is it?*)

Adham   Walla shee. (*Nothing.*)

*She takes the cigarettes out of the pockets and sets them on the desk. Hangs the jacket in the closet, looks at **Adham**, who goes to look out the window.*

Abir   Inta taAbaan. RaH aAmilak shay. (*You're tired. I'll make you a cup of tea.*)

Adham   Ma bidi ishi. (*I don't want anything.*)

He sulks. She studies him.

Abir   Fee ishi ghalat. (*Something's wrong.*)

Adham   Walla ishi. Inti bi vacances. Lazim itrooHi titbasati fee halik. (*Forget it. You're on vacation. You should have a good time!*)

Beat.

Abir   Hader. (*Okay.*)

*She goes into the bathroom. Stunned, **Adham** watches her go. He walks to the desk, grabs a cigarette and lights up. Goes back to the window. **Abir** comes back out, her hair down.*

Abir   Tdayib shoe al' usah? (*So what is it?*)

Adham (*incredulous*)   Aanjad, lazim tisalil (*If you have to ask!*)

Now she walks over to him. Just stands there, waiting.

Kaan shaklee zay il-liHmar. Fshilt. (*I looked like a fool. Ridiculous! I failed.*)

Abir   Fshilt? Bi-eesh? (*Failed? At what?*)

Adham   ItdalaAou feeye, zay, inti shufteehoum. 'Meen halahbal?' 'Leesh iHna jibnaa la noun?' Hada shafaa' Aallee. Aw fakarou inhoum jaboony la houm Aashaan ifarjeehoum adeysh houmin azkieh. Ma bitifra'. (*They looked at me, like, you saw them – 'Who is this idiot?' 'Why did we bring him here?' 'Someone felt sorry for him.' Or they assumed I was brought here to show them how smart they are. Either way.*)

Abir   Walla Hada fakar haek. (*No one thought that.*)

Adham   Kunt bahdaleh. Aaam bafatish Aalia jawaab, Aaam bataleA takhareef, ou walla ishi. (*I was an embarrassment. Scrambling for an answer, coming up with mish-mash, nothing.*)

Abir   Ma bayanish haek. (*It didn't sound like that!*)

Adham   Ma btitkallami il-lugha ya habibti. (*You don't speak the language, my dear.*)

Abir   BaHki shwaye. (*Some.*)

Adham (*in English only*)   Beer. Please. Thank you.

Abir   Shufthoum biyihkou maAak. Aajabt-houm. Ya reet lao inta shuft hada. (*I saw them talk to you. They liked you. I wish you could see that.*)

Adham   Lazim ti'rafee minee. Wa'aafit fisaleh, wa itdalaAit, sakaAo rukabi, ma Himlouni. Maa raH a'adar. Mish a'adar. (*You should be disgusted with me. I stood in that hall, and looked out . . . My legs beneath me, they couldn't hold me. I can't do it. I can't.*)

Abir   Kaanat ibroova. (*It was just practice.*)

Adham   Yadoob tdiliA ilkalaam min tommee. Ma shufteesh? (*I could barely get the words out. You didn't see that?*)

Abir   Laa. (*No.*)

Adham   Khalleeni afasirlek. Joozek. Mish maAqool inek ma shufteel Saa'louni adafiA Aan raayi wa iysh aAtdethoum? Nazariyaat Aumourha khamastaAshar saneh. Afkaar qadeemeh, nazariyaat qadeemeh. Faashil. (*Well, then let me explain something. Your husband was flailing. I can't believe you couldn't* *see that! They ask me to defend my point of view, and what do I give them? Theories that took fifteen years to trickle down to us. Old thoughts, old theories. I'm useless.)*

Abir   Walla mish saH. *(By God, that's not true.)*

Adham   Wallah saaH. IHna mutakhalafeen. AAdeen minHarib Aalla nitfeh min houn ou sha'afih min ha saHrah il kharah, Aamin walwil Aalla akher ikhtiyal. Ou houmin Aaysheen maA al afkaar el-Aatheemah. DaaA el wa'et mina. *(By God, it is! We're backwards! While we've been fighting over this and that scrap of desert, crying over the last assassination, they've been living with the great thoughts. We've wasted so much time.)*

He looks like he might cry, but he holds it together. She goes to him, touches his back.

Abir   Afkarak Aatheemah. *(You have a great mind.)*

Adham *laughs.*

Adham   Aah. *(Is that right.)*

Abir   Aah haek aal. *(He said that.)*

Adham   Meen? *(Who?)*

Abir   Hada Theodore. Bil Aarabi. Haek aal. *(The, uh, Theodore. In Arabic. He said that.)*

Adham   Aemta? *(When?)*

Abir   Lamma kunt bil-brova. *(When you were practicing.)*

Adham   Howeh aalik haek? Kaan bas bidou yitarab Aalla waHdeh helweh mitlek. *(He said that to you? He just wanted to get close to a beautiful woman.)*

Beat.

AaAid biyAaksik. Ma intabahti? Ilirijaal biyolou aya ishi la yitdalaAou biAaneen waHdeh. *(Flirting. You didn't know he was doing that? Men will say anything to look into a woman's eyes.)*

Abir   Ana ma baAraf. Ma bafaker fee haltdaree'a. Bihimush. Ou kaman allino wajhit nazrak raheebeh. *(I don't*

*know. I don't even think of it that way. It doesn't matter. He also said
you have a unique scholarly voice.*)

Adham   Aashaan bakkey maA lahjeh. (*Because it comes with an
accent.*)

Abir   Ana mish Aarfel leesh inseet adeesh inta zaki. El rujal
illy baAarafou − (*I don't know why you've forgotten how smart you
are. The man I met −*)

Adham   El rujal illy ibteArafeel − (*The man you met! −*)

Abir   − kan zaki, ow mitakid min nafsou, ou ma ihtamish,
eesh il naas bifakfoufee.(− *was smart, and sure of himself, and
didn't care about what anyone thought.*)

Adham   Yumkin hada il-roujal mish ana. (*Well, maybe that
wasn't really me.*)

He looks at her.

Yumkin hada ana. (*Maybe* this *is me.*)

Beat.

Abir   Ana bidi al-itnaen. (*Then I want them both.*)

She reaches for his head, touches it.

Ana ba'adar Aalla al-tnaen. (*I can handle both.*)

She takes his hands.

Edaek biyroujou. (*Your hands are shaking.*)

Adham *pulls his hands away. She places her hands on his head, runs
her hands through his hair, trying to fix it.*

Abir (*re: his hair*)   Mish Aarfeh eash biysear bi ha-shaArat.
(*I don't know what happens with this hair.*)

*He relaxes, just a little. She takes his cigarette from him, smokes, studies
him . . .*

Adham   Madmaneh? (*Wondering what you got yourself into?*)

Abir   Laa. (*No.*)

Adham   Kazaabeh. (*You lie.*)

She goes and grabs his Wordsworth book.

Abir   Oulee eash bi-yia'oul. (*Tell me what it says.*)

Adham   Ha tizha'aee. (*You'll be bored.*)

Abir   BtiAraaf inak inta kteer a'leel il-adab. (*You're so insulting, you know that?*)

Adham   Hadi gheer lughah. (*It's in a different language!*)

Abir   Ou kamaan? (*So?*)

She starts reading it, in English. It's barely recognizable:

Thus by day . . .

She stops, but keeps her eyes on the page, as if she's reading and comprehending it.

Adham   Inti mish fahmeh ishi bil-marah. (*You don't understand a damn thing.*)

Abir   Ana fahmeh shwaye minou. Ana kteer zakiyeh kamaan. (*I get some of it. I'm very smart, too.*)

Adham   BaAraf. (*I know.*)

She hands the book to him.

Abir   Yallah. Iqraa'. (*Go. Read.*)

He shrugs. She watches intently. He takes a beat, then reads, speaking in English:

Adham   'Thus by day / Subjected to the discipline of love – '

Abir   Tarjim. (*Translate.*)

Adham *shakes his head at first.* **Abir** *waits. He then translates it into Arabic, haltingly. This feels very unfamiliar to him.*

Adham   Wa hakatha maA el waqt, wa huwa khadiAan li qaAidati lHob.

Abir   Kamaan. (*More.*)

Adham 'His organs and recipient faculties / Are quickened, are more vigorous.'

He looks at her. Translates again, into Arabic.

Ada'uhou wa quduratuhu lHissiyya tatasaraA, tatazayadu nashatan.

Abir Aajibnee hada il-shaAir. Ma Biyzahi'. (*I like this poet. He's not boring.*)

Adham Ma bitarjam inmeeH. (*It doesn't translate well.*)

Abir Em-balah. (*I disagree.*)

Adham Mish mafroud itkhalfee jouzek. (*You're not supposed to disagree with your husband.*)

Abir Halaa' serhan taqleediyeen. (*I thought you weren't traditional.*)

Adham Aah aHyanan. (*Sometimes I am.*)

Abir *gives him a look.*

Abir Kaman. (*More. *)

Adham Ou Aam ibtida'amaree fiyeh! (*Ordering me about!*)

Abir Yallah. (*Go.*)

Adham 'His mind spreads, tenacious of the forms which it receives.'

And translates again:

Adham Aaqluhu yanshareH, yatashabbathu bil 'ashkaali yalqaha.

As he finishes translating this last part, **Abir** *moves closer to him.*

Both of them are on the bed now. She kneels, places her hands on his hipbones. Leans in, kisses him there.

Lights shift: early morning light.

RIGHT AT EXETER STREET

Abir *is gone. It's raining again. We hear a shower. As* **Adham** *says the following, he gets out of bed very slowly. He's naked.*

Adham   No flinch, no fear.

Face. Eyes. Swallow. Normal swallow.

Hands, still. Hand, still.

He puts on his shirt.

Shirt? Pretend it's nice. Pretend it's dry. Breathe. Slow. Slow.

He breathes in and out, fast. Almost cries. Stops himself.

Remember why you're here.

He puts his pants on. His jacket.

A proper gentleman. A student.

He leaves the room and goes 'outside,' into and through the panels:
LONDON.

On his way to do his work:

Right at Exeter Street, left at Wellington Street, Bow Street, Long Acre, Endell Street, High Holborn, Shaftesbury Avenue, Gower Street.

The Darwin Lecture Theatre, University College.

Inside. A simple washroom. A single sink, and a mirror. He takes a towel hanging there, and dries his hands.

Adham   A clean towel. With letters. England's letters.

He hangs the towel. Looks in the mirror.

Vain.

He fixes his hair for a second. He likes what he sees.

Not bad.

He walks away from the mirror, goes through the vast hallways of the building.

New shoes. Clean shoes. Tight. On marble. Solid. History in this floor. Scholars buried here. This history. Scholars underneath, learned men. Here. Shoes click above the great scholars. The poets. The poetry. And me. And me walking past, and through, and history, and honor, and great thoughts, and those that abide by language. Its laws, and its mandates. Me above, moving through.

He arrives at the door that takes him backstage.

Last breath. Hands, still.

He finds a folder, his folder.

Folder.

Pants zipped.

Checks his zipper.

Papers.

Hands still.

Pants zipped.

Goddamn, hands still!

He opens the door, and steps into darkness, into the backstage area.

Darkness.

Breath. Last big breath.

Dust. Old air. A small light on a table. 'How are you, sir? Do you have everything you need, sir? Glass of water for you, sir?' Glass of water for the scholar, for the man, for me. No smile, no thanks, this is expected, this is how it goes.

This is my birthright. I've earned this. I'm in a long line. Shoes, shirt, zipper. Yes.

And now he takes his place at a podium, stepping into a very bright light.

Stand still. Paper. Light. Light.

We hear very faint, muffled clapping. He looks out over the audience:

Glasses. Hair. No one I know. Glasses, hair. Small, easy breath. Easy. You know how to talk. No rolling 'R's. No attack. The British, the English, they don't attack the language.

You know this: in England, the words are like water. One false sound, and a man is exposed. We Arabs? Our words are like hammers, hitting nails.

A thousand breaths, waiting for me. For this man, this scholar, ready to do the Work of God.

Adham *stands at the podium, the lights go as bright as they can, and then –*

Blackout.

Music: Joni Mitchell, 'Night in the City'.

> Light up, light up, light up your lazy blue eyes
> Moon's up, night's up,
> Taking the town by surprise.
> Nighttime, nighttime,
> They left an hour ago.
> City light time,
> Must you get ready so slow?
> There are places to come from and places to go.

THE PARTY

Lights up at a party in an apartment. **Theo** *is there, as is* **George**, *as is a very beautiful English woman,* **Diana**, *twenties, who sits languidly on a couch next to* **Theo**. **Adham** *and* **Abir**, *having just arrived, stand and look at the group, awkward.*

George (*to* **Adham**)   Have you met Diana?

Diana   I'm George's girlfriend. (*Re:* **George**.) How he hates that word. He flinches, don't you, George?

George   Not in the least.

Staying on the couch, **Diana** *reaches her hand out to shake* **Adham**'s.

Adham   Pleasure to meet you.

Diana   Actually, we spoke for a moment right after your talk.

Adham   I'm sorry –

Diana   It's all right. There were loads of people. As well there should've been.

Theo   And this is Adham's wife. Abir.

Diana   Oh! My goodness. Yes. They said you were married.

Adham   Sorry – yes.

Diana (*to* **Abir**)   You sat in front of me. I admired your dress.

Abir   Hello.

Beat.

Adham   She doesn't speak English.

Diana   Sorry. (*Now waving to* **Abir**, *as if to make it clear.*) Hello.

Abir   Hi.

Theo (*to* **Abir**, *in Arabic*)   Ana Hakoun mutarjimak allila. Da Iza kunti Aayza tismaAee el Aabataat illi btitlaA min bu'ina. (*I'll be your translator tonight. If you even want to hear any of the nonsense that comes out of our mouths.*)

Adham (*to* **Theo**, *in Arabic*)   Wala yahimmak. (*It's all right.*)

Theo   'ana bHeb et kalem Aarabee. (*I love speaking Arabic.*)

Abir   Serit ktheer aHsan. Aanjad. (*You've gotten better already!*)

Adham   Ah, sar. aHsan. (*He has.*)

Theo   Shukran. (*Thank you.*)

Beat. They realize they are leaving the others out.

Diana (*re: hearing the language*)   Marvelous. Don't stop.

George   I think we all need more of – whatever we're drinking. Adham, can I get you started?

Adham *nods.* **George** *goes.*

Diana   So, she couldn't understand any of what you said tonight?

Adham   No, not so much.

Diana   Tragic.

Adham   Maybe it was a relief. She has to listen to me a lot.

Diana   Ridiculous! (*To* **Abir**.) Your husband did very well. (*To* **Theo**.) Tell her that. (*To* **Abir**.) Could you see how well he did?

Adham (*to* **Abir**, *in Arabic*)   Bidha teAraf keef shufteeni ilaylee. (*She wants to know how it was to watch me tonight.*)

Abir (*to* **Adham**, *in Arabic*)   Kunt im bayan martaaH ktheer. (*You were the most comfortable I've ever seen you.*)

Diana   What did she say?

Theo   She –

Adham (*cutting him off*)   She enjoyed it.

Diana   And how does she find London?

Abir (*to* **Adham**, *in Arabic*)   Shoe? (*What?*)

Adham   Bidha teAraf keef Habbeetee London. (*She wants to know how you like London.*)

Abir (*to* **Adham**, *re:* **Diana**)   Meen hiya? (*Who is she?*)

Adham/Theo   SaHbitou. (*His girlfriend.*)

Abir   SaHbit meen? (*Whose?*)

Adham   Laa tiqlaqee. (*Don't worry about it.*)

Theo (*overlap*)   George's.

Diana   What did she say?

Abir   Hiya qaalat Inni Hilweh? (*Did she say I was pretty?*)

Adham (*to* **Diana**)   Oh. Uh . . . she likes London very much.

Theo (*to* **Abir**)   Naam. (*Yes, she did.*)

Abir (*to* **Theo**)   Hiya jameela. Mush zaAlaana, houn – (*Points to her mouth, pouty.*) – mithl ktheer min anniswaan al Engleeziat. (She's beautiful. Not angry, here – like so many of your English women.)

Diana   What did she say?

Theo *starts to translate.*

Theo   She says you're beautiful, not like –

Adham (*cutting him off*)   We both like London very much.

Diana   Well. You should both stay. Finish your studies here. I think Adham would do well. Don't you, Teddy?

Theo (*feigning nonchalance*)   Eh.

Diana (*to* **Theo**)   Stop it. (*To* **Adham**.) They're so gruff, these academics. No wonder I had to drop out.

Theo   Diana was halfway through her literature course.

Diana   I met George, and that was it. He seduced me, and I couldn't concentrate anymore. I wasn't cut out for it anyway, though. Focus your whole life on one poet, or one bloody poem? I need variety.

Theo   Really? According to whom? Your fortune teller?

Diana   She's been right about a lot of things.

She smiles at **Adham**. **George** *returns with a fresh bottle of wine and two glasses. He fills everyone's glasses, and pours for* **Adham** *and* **Abir**.

George   To a great speech!

Theo   Hear, hear!

Adham   You're too kind.

Diana   No kindness. We're impressed.

Theo   Don't start being humble now, my dear chap.

George   You were good.

Adham   I mentioned your vagrant.

George   I noticed.

Theo   Funny that. The vagrant made it in. Satisfied, Georgie?

George   Surprised.

Adham   The vagrant had his place. Just a smaller place than you'd have liked.

Diana   I heard all that. But I didn't remember a vagrant in the poem. I'm sorry.

Theo   Aw, Georgie, that's got to be hard to hear.

Diana   I mean, it was really just about Wordsworth, this man. The individual. Oh God. You're afraid I'll massacre your point.

Adham   I'm not worried.

Theo   You haven't read her work, Adham. / Maybe you should.

George   Let's hear it.

Diana   Well, really, it was all sort of ironic, wasn't it? The way you put it. Old William was sort of going on and on about Nature, but in the end, it's not the things he sees at all. Or even the place . . . It's the imprint it leaves. He could be anywhere.

Theo   See? People were listening.

Adham (*to* **Diana**)   Maybe you should go back into academics.

Diana   Right.

Theo (*to* **George**)   Maybe she had the wrong teacher.

Diana   Maybe.

George   I admit. It's a very close reading of the text. Not accounting for the socio-economic underpinnings . . .

Theo   Oh no . . .

George   But it worked. In your hands, the poem was vital. Alive.

Diana (*to* **Adham**)   Did I get it right, though?

Adham   Well, it's the paradox of . . .

He stops himself.

I don't want to go on too much. She . . . (*Meaning* **Abir**.) doesn't understand any of this.

Everyone looks at **Abir**, *who's been listening, smiling, not getting any of it.*

Diana   Isn't she a dear? She must be bored out of her mind.

Abir (*in Arabic, to* **Adham**)   Eash? (*What?*)

Adham (*in Arabic*)   ma fee she, ma bidi akhaleeqEE liwaHdik ktheer. (*Nothing. I don't want to leave you out for too long.*)

Abir   La. Ana martaaHa. Hadhi leeltak. (*No. I'm all right. This is your night.*)

She takes his hand, moves close into him.

Talk.

Adham *smiles. As he speaks, we see his passion for the work unleashed.*

Adham   For Wordsworth, this, uh, this meaning of home, it comes to him only after leaving. His tie to this part of Nature, uh, paradoxically helps him transcend the specific place itself. Line 63:

> The picture of the mind revives again:
> While here I stand, not only with the sense
> Of present pleasure, but with pleasing thoughts
> That in this moment there is life and food
> For future years . . .

Essentially it's – Should I go on?

Diana Yes!

Adham It's – the paradox is: Wordsworth, great poet of nature, comes to know himself as part of the grand scheme of Spirit only when he lets go of his attachment to the very landscape that inspired him to write in the first place.

Diana And then he forgets all about it?

Adham No. It stays here.

Points to his head.

And here.

Points to his heart.

Beat. He catches himself in his own reverie.

Well, enough. Can I have another drink?

He holds up his glass.

George I can do even better.

He goes.

Theo George just might be a bit pissed off.

Adham I'm sorry – ?

Diana He's fine.

Adham I don't mean to cause any problem.

Diana George deserves a little trouble. He's got another girlfriend, you know. I'm not the only one.

Adham I see.

Theo You're the most important.

Diana He said that?

Theo It's clear.

Diana That's too bad. Poor Theo's being forced to lie! What do you think, Adham – should a man be confined to one woman?

Adham   Yes.

Diana   Ha!

Adham   If it's the right woman, of course.

Abir, *exhausted from the day, slowly falls asleep on* **Adham**'s *shoulder. He takes her glass.*

Diana   Sweet. I wish I could fall asleep like that.

Adham   I think she's just tired.

Theo   Been a long day for both of you.

Diana   So one woman if it's the right one. It's conditional to you.

Adham   Well. Yes.

Diana   Are there no gentlemen to be found anywhere?

Theo   Don't lump us in with Georgie.

Diana   Too late. You're lumped.

George *returns with a rolled-up joint.*

George   I didn't think anyone would object if I – (*Sees* **Abir**.) Oh look at that. We've bored her.

Theo   No different than some of your first-years.

George   I've taken a fair amount of beating tonight.

Theo   Aw. Did you bring something to ease the pain?

George   I did. Adham, will you join us? It's good stuff. From Morocco, I believe.

George *lights up, takes a hit. Passes it to* **Theo**. *He passes it to* **Diana**, *who takes a long drag, then passes it to* **Adham**.

Diana   It's all right – for you to – ?

Adham   Oh. Uh, yes.

He takes a hit, holds it as the others have, exhales.

George   We've established all that. Adham is not a man of faith.

Adham   Not really, anyway.

Diana   I went out with a man from Morocco.

Theo   Oh ho!

Diana   Claimed he was some kind of royalty.

George   I'm sure he was.

Diana   Spoke six languages.

Theo   I bet he did.

Diana   He was lovely. My flatmates adored him. I found out later he was selling hash to everyone.

Theo   And none to you?

Diana   It's not really my thing.

Realizes she's holding the joint. Laughs.

God, present circumstances excluded. Adham, you must think we're all so decadent.

Adham   No.

Diana   You know, the children of the faded empire / and all that.

Theo   'Faded empire'? / Good God.

George   Let me have that.

He takes her hand, wrestles the joint from her. Leans in and kisses her.

Theo   Ah, love.

Diana   Fine, shut me up.

George   Never.

Diana (*to* **Adham**)   When do you go back?

Adham   To the hotel?

Diana   No! You're so funny. Home. To your, to your country. Oh God, I've messed it up. It's not really a country, is it?

Theo   Not for twenty years.

Adham   Day after tomorrow.

Diana   You should stay longer.

Adham   For more parties?

Diana   To see London. Didn't you just get here? Why are we sending him off so quickly?

Theo   That's how the university works these things out. They rush you in, pat you on the back, and rush you out.

Diana   Well, it's silly. There's so much to see.

Theo   I agree.

George   Seriously, Adham. You can't want to go back home now?

Adham   After meeting all of you?

George   After hearing the news.

Adham   What news?

George   The war is on. You didn't hear? *Evening Standard* said the Israelis destroyed the entire Egyptian air force this morning.

Diana   No.

Theo   But that's not confirmed. / Radio Cairo is saying Egypt took down Israeli jets.

Adham   What?

George   Where did you see that?

Theo   I heard it on the Home Service. They say there was dancing on the streets of Damascus.

Diana   So who's lying?

George   And it commences. The muddle of wartime rubbish begins promptly on schedule.

Theo   I didn't realize we were getting our news from the *Standard*.

George   I don't. / Normally.

Diana   It's half past midnight.

Adham   Do you have the paper here? / Can I see it?

George   Downstairs.

Theo   Adham, you shouldn't put any credence in the *Standard*. It's biased.

George   Not always.

Diana   Isn't tomorrow's *Guardian* out?

George   And they're not biased at all.

Theo   Yes! Let's nip down to Euston Station for the first edition. Adham?

Adham *gets up and joins them.*

Theo (*to* **Diana**)   Be right back.

They leave. Beat. **Abir** *sleeps,* **Diana** *watches. Lights up a cigarette, stretches . . .*

Diana   Hm.

Abir, *feeling* **Adham** *gone from next to her, wakes up, slowly. Sees* **Diana**.

Diana   Oh. Sorry. They'll be right back.

Abir   Wein zowji? (*Where did my husband go?*)

Diana   Oh. Em.

Abir   Où est mon mari?

Abir *speaks some Arabic here.*

Diana   Oh, dear. No parlez vous pas. I mean, beyond that.
So sorry. I'm sorry.

Abir *gets up, looks around.* **Diana** *gets it.*

Diana   Oh! Sorry. Yes. He left. Just for a moment. They left.
Just to get the newspaper. They'll come right back.

She smiles, trying to reassure.

I promise, it'll be all right.

Abir   Andek cigarah? (*Do you have a cigarette?*)

She gestures: a smoke.

Diana   Cigarette? Oh, yes. Of course.

She gets a cigarette, lights one for **Abir**. *They smoke for a moment.*

Abir   ShaArek helou. (*I like your hair.*)

Diana *doesn't seem to understand.* **Abir** *reaches over, touches her hair
lightly.*

Diana   Oh! I like your hair. I mean, it's beautiful.

Abir *seems to get this. They smoke, and smile at each other
appreciatively.*

Diana   Yes? God. I'm afraid they left you with the most
illiterate of the bunch . . . Studied Ancient Greek, of course.
Ancient Greek? 'Thalassa! Thalassa!' Which is of course
wildly helpful out in the real world.

Beat.

You. Like. It Here?

Abir (*shy*)   'Tosir wid loh'?

Diana   What's that – *To Sir with Love?* You like that film?

Abir *nods.*

Diana   It is rather good, isn't it?

Abir *smiles. Emboldened, throws out:*

Abir Julie Christie.

Diana You like her? I love her. God, did you see her in *Darling*?

Abir *nods.*

Diana Wasn't she fabulous?

Abir Three times.

Diana Really?

She does a bit from the film – Julie Christie, of course, furious:

'A pound's not enough! A pound's not enough!'

And another moment:

'We're not married! At least not to each other!'

Abir So good.

The men return, each holding newspapers.

Theo It doesn't look good for the Arabs.

Adham *scans the newspaper. It's hard to tell how it's affecting him.*

Adham It doesn't, does it?

George Well, then. They overplayed their hands, didn't they? They had to have known Israel would take their threats seriously.

Theo *shakes his head to shush* **George**. **Abir** *has been intently studying* **Adham**.

Abir Eash hadha? (*What's this?*)

Adham Akhbaar. (*News.*)

Abir Eash tiHkee? (*What does it say?*)

Adham Kulla raheeba. aHkee lak baAdeen. (*It's all bad. I'll tell you later.*)

Abir iHkee li hela. (*Tell me now.*)

Adham Mou qadir. (*I can't.*)

Abir   Eash hadha Aan Masr? (*What's that about Egypt?*)

Adham   silaH aljaw. Yabdou innou raaH. (*The air force. Apparently it's gone.*)

Abir   Fe youm? Ana chakkeet kullu kan khidaaA. (*In a day? I thought the whole thing was a bluff.*)

Adham   yabdou al khidaaA inkashfAT. (*The bluff got called, apparently.*)

Abir   Ya, ilahi. (*Oh, God.*)

Adham   Laa tiqlaqee. (*Don't worry.*)

Abir   Leesh maqlaqsh? Laazim nirouH. inShouf eash saar. (*Why shouldn't I? We should go. Find out what's happening.*)

Adham   Kullu raH lil khara. Eesh akthar badina naAraf. (*It's all gone to shit! What else do we need to know?*)

Abir, *upset, grabs the paper from* **Adham**, *scours it.*

Theo   I'm so sorry. I thought you knew.

Adham   Not today. We've been preoccupied. (*Recovers.*) The news is always bad. We learn not to jump at every rumor.

Diana   That's understandable. One hears so many things.

Adham   The Israelis have been digging trenches for months, getting ready. But no one thought anything would really happen.

Theo   We can put the wireless on if you want. I'm sure they're still covering it.

Adham   No, no, not now.

George   Egypt's jets were parked in the open air. No hangars or sandbags, even. Shocking.

Adham (*trying to keep panic down*)   Yes, it is.

Theo   I didn't think Israel would move first without getting the green light from Johnson.

George   That wasn't going to happen. America can't be seen as giving a green light –

Theo   Not explicitly.

Diana (*cutting them off*)   God. It's all so confusing. How can one keep track of any of it?

Adham   No one does.

Diana   That settles it. You have to stay. Couldn't we work something out, with Adham's visa?

George   I suppose so.

Theo   Would you even want to?

Diana   Of course they would. Why wouldn't they?

Adham   Uh –

Abir   Sorat eash hadhi? (*What is this a picture of?*)

Theo   With the war happening, we could try to get the department heads to push through a fellowship.

Abir   Fen maHjuzeen? (*Where are these hostages?*)

Adham   I wouldn't quite call it a war.

Abir   Masr? (*Egypt?*)

Theo   The reporters are. Most assuredly.

Adham   How long would a fellowship last?

Theo   Depends. Six or seven months?

George   One term.

Abir   Wein fee Masr hadha? (*Where in Egypt?*)

Diana   At least wait for things to calm down before you go back.

Abir *stands up.*

Abir   Yallah. (*Let's go.*)

Adham   Well. There's a lot to think about. (*Repeats this to* **Abir**, *in Arabic.*) Fee ketheer lazmou tafkeer.

Abir (*in Arabic*)   Fakkar wa iHna mashiyeen. (*You can do that as we walk.*)

She stands up, looks at **Adham***: time's up.*

Abir   (*Let's go.*) Yallah.

SEVEN DIALS

Outside. Midnight. It's dark. Panels reveal a London intersection where a large monument stands. **Adham** *is a combination of cocky, drunk and stoned, mixed with a rising panic he tries desperately to push down.*

Abir   I don't recognize this.

Adham   We were here yesterday. You don't remember it, civic engineer?

Abir   It's dark.

Adham   Just look.

She looks around: lights, sounds of automobiles . . .

Abir   We've seen a lot of places.

He steps close to her, puts his hands on her shoulders.

Adham   Boo!

Abir (*jumps*)   Stop it! That's not funny.

Adham   Sorry.

He turns her slowly round 360 degrees.

Adham   This will help: One, two, three, four . . .

Abir   Seven streets –

Adham   – connect here.

Abir   Seven Dials.

Adham   You remember. (*Pointing places out.*) Thieves and prostitutes were over there, pubs were here.

Abir   Right. He told us that.

Adham   So we have options.

Again, he turns her slowly, showing her each intersection as he does so:

We can take Monmouth Street, Mercer, Earlham . . . Monmouth, the other way, Mercer, the other way, Earlham, and – shit. What's the other one? Can you remember?

Abir *shakes her head.* **Adham** *pulls her closer, touches her hair, face.*

Adham   You looked so beautiful today. I saw the way people were looking at you. Did you see the way people were looking at you?

Beat.

No. You've been taught not to notice things like that.

Abir   I noticed.

He laughs.

Adham   Ha! Shorts Gardens. That's the other street. I knew I'd think of it. Damn I'm good.

He sits down on the steps in front of the monument, lights a cigarette.

Come here.

Abir   Why?

Adham   It's a nice night. Sit for a minute.

Abir   I don't want to.

Adham   Why not?

Abir   I don't feel safe.

Adham   What?

Abir   Theo said this was a bad area.

Adham   During Dickens's time. Not now.

Abir (*shrugs*)   Well.

Beat. She still doesn't sit down. Something occurs to **Adham**, *and he laughs, shaking his head.*

Abir   What's so funny?

Adham   Nothing.

Abir   Tell me.

Adham   It's wrong. I shouldn't think it.

Abir   Well now you have to tell me.

Adham   Just – Your family was living in the country, the middle of nowhere, and they got pulled out of their house, guns on them, and watched it burn down. But you feel scared here.

Abir   Don't make light / of what happened.

Adham   I'm not!

Abir   Don't you dare / make light of it.

Adham   I'm not!

Abir   You think it's a game. You think everything is a game.

Adham   I don't, *habibti*! Not you and me.

He springs up, gets close to her, kisses her hard.

Abir   How much alcohol did you drink?

Adham (*overlap*)   Oh no.

Abir (*overlap*)   How much?

Adham   I'm in trouble now. The wife is upset!

Abir   You're so mean / tonight.

Adham   I'm not mean, my dear –

Abir   'My dear'? As if I'm your child?

Adham   Of course not! I'm being silly. I'm happy. I spoke in front of people. I succeeded. Did you not see that? They listened to me, a foreigner, tell them about their Poet Laureate. What he meant, what he didn't mean, why he used a comma, a semicolon, a dash.

Abir   I know!

Adham   No you don't. Not really. (*Challenging her.*) You barely understood it.

Abir   I don't speak English! You want an Englishwoman, is that what you want?

Adham *is stunned she even asked, speechless.*

Abir   Do you?

Adham   No! – No . . . I want you. You can't tell? (*Softens, takes her in.*) Habibti.

Beat.

They offered me a fellowship.

Abir   What?

Adham   Well, they didn't offer. But they think it can be arranged. It can be pushed through, maybe, they said. There's a lot to work out, but – (*Almost pleading.*) Come sit down. Why are you in such a rush?

Abir   I want to hear the news.

Adham   I told you all of it.

Abir   On the radio.

Adham   Paper, radio, it's all bad. You want specifics? Egypt lost its air force.

Abir   I want to know what's happening now.

Adham   And uh, I'm not sure about Jordan, but I think they fired a few rounds and are making, what do they say in military terms, a hasty retreat? The Arabs lost. We lost. The whole thing's a bust. / But the British are happy. The Americans are happy. No world war. So far.

Abir   Oh God. What's going to happen now? I can't believe it. There was so much talk / about the Egyptians being superior.

Adham   Yes, yes, talk. Talk talk talk, bullshit bullshit bullshit. It's all bullshit, my dear.

Abir   You talk like an old man.

Adham   That's what I'll be if we go back!

Beat.

Please. Listen to me. We have, we have here, I have, this window of opportunity. You see? We should leave, just leave, our so-called lives and stay where we're wanted.

Abir   We know no one here!

Adham   Sometimes that's preferable.

Abir   You're crazy!

Adham   Please, come sit. Just for a minute.

She relents, goes and sits next to him. He puts his arms around her.

See? All the world connects here.

He takes her in, caresses her hands . . .

Abir   If the Israeli army goes into Jerusalem –

Adham   They won't. They can't. It's their 'holy place'. Everyone's 'holy place'. 'It's so 'holy', they don't want to destroy it.

Abir   But if they do?

Adham   Then the old bat can fend for herself.

Abir   You talk about your mother this way? At a time like this?

Adham *shrugs, laughs. Beat, as she just watches him.*

Abir   Some of the things you say . . . You joke now, but
one day –

Adham   What? God will punish me?

Beat.

Abir   Everything she's done, she's done for you! To advance
your career.

Adham   Everything she's done, she's done for herself! Be
careful what you believe, my love.

Abir   You would leave her there to die?

Adham   She's always had a flair for the dramatic.

Abir   I know you don't mean that.

Beat. They look at each other.

Abir   At least, let's go get her, bring her here / to live with us!

Adham   A man, his wife, and his mother!

Abir   Everyone lives like that.

Adham   Not here! Not here! These are civilized people! Do
you not understand that? She doesn't even like you – why
plead her case?

Abir (*stung, tries to keep her cool*)   I'm thinking only of her
safety. You wouldn't be here if not for her. We have to go
home and wait for the situation to stabilize.

Adham   Stabilize! Stabilize? Where? Where? Where are you
talking about? When have we ever known stability, you stupid
peasant girl?

Abir *is shocked. It's as if he's slapped her.*

Abir   You . . .

Adham   Shit.

Abir   You mean that.

Adham   Goddamnit.

Abir   When you look at me. That's what you –

Adham   I didn't mean it. I'm drunk, don't listen to me!

Abir   That's what you think I am? I'm a village girl you rescued, some girl with the smell of shit on her boots –

Adham   Okay, okay . . .

Abir   – and dirt on her hands, who you get to show the world, is that how you think of me?

Adham   No.

He tries to comfort her.

Abir   Don't touch me! Don't you ever touch me again!

She bursts into tears. Goes. Stunned, he stands, watching her. Long, long beat. He doesn't know what to do with himself. Suddenly looks very lost. He sits. Hands start to shake. Spent, spent, he runs them through his hair.

On the panels around him, we see:

A SILENT FILM, DATED JUNE 6, 1967.

No sound, a handheld camera, almost a home movie, of bombs going off, civilians running through the streets, soldiers. This is Jerusalem. The war. **Adham** *just sits there in these images for a couple minutes.* **Beder** *appears again.*

Adham (*jumps*)   Oh God, can you go away?

Beder   Please. I know things are bad, but let's not start invoking God. You look like a beggar.

Adham   I walked all over the city today.

Beder   Boo hoo. In '48, I ran out of the village, you on my back, and we walked for three days.

Adham   And now you're a refugee again.

Beder (*finds this funny*)   I never stopped being one. You never stop being one. I've been packed for twenty years.

She comes toward him, then sits on the steps at the foot of the monument.

Adham   Are you all right?

Beder   I'm tired. Just tired. Even I get tired sometimes.

Adham *studies her face, seems to notice as if for the first time:*

Adham   You look old.

Beat.

Beder
  'Many rich
  Sunk down as in a dream among the poor.'

Adham   'The Ruined Cottage'.

Beder   He wrote that poem, you know, to show who he would have been if he'd been born under different circumstances.

  'And of the poor did many cease to be.
  And their place knew them not.'

Considers, says it again.

  'And their place knew them not.'

Adham   Shall we discuss poetry now, Mother? Is that what you want? To talk to your son, the scholar, about Wordsworth?

Beder   Actually, no. I just want to rest for a while.

Adham   Are you all right?

Beder *just sits there.*

Adham   Are you?

She doesn't look at him. Doesn't answer.

Adham   Will you miss me if I don't come back? Will you?

She shakes her head no. But she lies as she says:

Beder   I've forgotten you already.

THE RUINED COTTAGE

The hotel room. It's very, very late. Lights are off. The television is on, volume down – we see the images of the ground war in Jerusalem reflected on **Abir**'s *face.* **Adham** *enters.*

Adham   I was almost hoping I would fail. I was! If I failed, you see, then. Then it's not complicated. I go home, fade into obscurity. No choice. See? Where we come from, we get one chance. You know that, right? That's it. We, uh, we're not, uh, designed for success, we. Arabs. From Palestine. It's – we're good at packing up, and leaving places, and waiting.

Abir   You let me walk alone.

Adham   What was I supposed to do, run after you, like in one of your movies?

Abir   I can figure these things out on my own if I have to. I studied engineering. I should've stayed an engineer. I should've stayed home with all that was going on. I shouldn't have left my family with a war coming. I was foolish to come.

Adham (*gently*)   If we stayed every time a war seemed near none of us would ever leave the house.

Abir   Maybe.

Adham   I know I behaved badly.

He turns a light on. Sees on the floor a packed suitcase.

What's this?

Abir   I'm leaving.

Adham   No, no, no, you're not. It's been a big day, okay? I talk sometimes, I don't know what I'm saying.

Abir   I think you do.

Adham   Why are you doing this?

Abir   What's 'this'?

Adham   Packing your bag. Ruining everything for me?

Abir   I'm leaving you. Don't you understand?

Adham   And going where?

Abir   Home! My home. I tried calling my sister – I couldn't get through. All the lines are down. I don't know where they are.

Adham   Chaos. Wherever they are.

Abir   I have to go back. I want to be with her.

Adham   Why? So we can all be refugees together?

Abir   You don't know that.

Adham   So I don't. Maybe everything will turn out fine.

Abir   I want to be with my family! There's something *wrong* with people who don't.

Adham   You can't even get near the country –

Abir   I'll go to the airport, and I'll wait. I can't be with you for another minute.

Adham   You're being ridiculous –

Abir   I am? You're leaving your mother to die, Adham.

Adham   She's not dying –

Abir   What is that? Who does this? I don't understand a man who has no ties! Who are you?

Adham   She taught me to be that way! She did! Because there was nothing in her life that wasn't taken away at some point or another. So she taught me to love that way – easy come, easy go.

Abir   That's love.

Adham   That's –

Abir   So if I leave you now, just leave, and we, we separate, and get a divorce –

Adham   She's so modern now! Listen to her!

Abir   – you would have no feelings about it. Would you? Would your heart break?

Adham   I don't talk that way. Use phrases like that.

Abir   I'm asking you. Would you have a broken heart? Because I would.

He can't answer. She tries not to cry.

Okay. Well. At least I know now. It's only been a month. I have to go back. I was such an idiot to come here.

Adham   Just slow down, okay?

Abir   Too late.

Adham   You can't get home now anyway.

Abir   I don't care. I'll sleep at the Consulate until I get a ticket –

Adham   'Sleep at the Consulate'? You're crazy! It's going to get better.

Abir   What is?

Adham   Everything.

She looks at him incredulously.

Abir   What, what is 'everything'?

Adham   . . . My career.

Abir (*stinging him*)   Your 'career'? You gave one lecture. That's it.

Adham (*stung*)   So she can be cruel, too.

Abir   I never was before.

Adham   So I've done good work then. Brought out the best in you.

Abir *starts packing again, crying as she does so.*

Adham   Please, stop. It's okay.

Abir   No it's not.

He watches helplessly as she cries.

Adham   I have no idea what to do.

Abir   I do.

She gets up to leave. He grabs her arm.

Adham   I didn't say you could walk away!

Abir (*wresting free*)   You don't get to pick and choose your traditions!

She goes to the bathroom, comes back with a little make-up bag, puts it in her suitcase, zips it up.

Adham   Don't tell me I don't love my mother. I *love* her. She made me everything I am. But I don't need to be with her, you see. It's here − (*Points to his head.*) It's all in here, you see? She made an imprint. I *have* her. She knows this. And I know this.

Abir   If you don't come with me now, you may never get to go back. Do you know that, Adham?

Beat. From somewhere inside him, the answer:

Adham   . . . Yes. Yes.

Abir   Okay.

She packs up the last of her things, grabs her suitcase. He gets in front of her.

Adham   Don't do this. Please.

She stands there facing him.

You'll regret it.

Beat.

I don't want you to go.

Beat.

Come on. Look what you'd be giving up.

Beat.

Abir   This feels like nowhere to me.

Adham (*half joking?*)   Well then, it suits me.

She shakes her head, grabs her suitcase. He watches her go. Door shuts. He suddenly is completely alone.

Okay. Okay . . .

Slowly, without much emotion, **Adham** *opens a panel that stretches the length of the room: blankness. Nothing.*

He goes over to the window, looks out. Goes to his desk, straightens his papers. Does it again. Picks up his book. Goes to the bed. Sits on it. Opens the book. Begins to read. As he does, we see:

Abir *on one side of the stage, suitcase in hand,* **Beder** *on the other, holding cloth sacks, and* **Adham** *in the middle, with nothing.*

Adham   The Ruined Cottage.

The house-clock struck eight:
I turned and saw her distant a few steps.
Her face was pale and thin, her figure too
Was changed . . .
She told me she had lost her elder child.
Today
I have been travelling far, and many days
About the fields I wander, knowing this
Only, that what I seek I cannot find.
And so I waste my time: for I am changed.
For I am changed.

As film freezes, so do **Adham**, **Abir** *and* **Beder**.

Addendum

Should surtitles be impossible, and no other way of doing live translation present itself, below is a version of the hotel room scene, entirely in English. This would replace the scene beginning on page 119.

And she's gone. **Adham** *lies back down on the bed. Long beat of him alone.*

Abir *enters. Switches on the light. Shocked to see one of the windows still open.*

Abir   You're lying here letting the rain in? Are you all right?

Adham   Sure, sure.

She rushes to close the window.

Abir   I hope it didn't damage anything.

Adham   It's a hotel room. They don't care.

She looks at him.

Abir   Why did you go ahead so fast? I looked for you downstairs. The old man – the clerk? – wanted to show me the pictures from when Omar Sharif stayed here. He thought I'd be interested.

Adham (*sarcastic*)   And you were.

Abir *sees the jacket on the floor, walks to it, picks it up, shakes it out.*

Abir   What is it?

Adham   Nothing.

She takes the cigarettes out of the pockets and sets them on the desk. Hangs the jacket in the closet, looks at **Adham***, who goes to look out the window.*

Abir   You're tired. I'll make you a cup of tea.

Adham   I don't want anything.

He sulks. She studies him.

Abir   Something's wrong.

Adham   Forget it. You're on vacation. You should have a good time!

Beat.

Abir   Okay.

She goes into the bathroom. Stunned, **Adham** *watches her go. He walks to the desk, grabs a cigarette and lights up. Goes back to the window.* **Abir** *comes back out, her hair down.*

Abir   So what is it?

Adham (*incredulous*)   If you have to ask!

Now she walks over to him. Just stands there, waiting.

I looked like a fool. Ridiculous! I failed.

Abir   Failed? At what?

Adham   They looked at me, like, you saw them – 'Who is this idiot?' 'Why did we bring him here?' 'Someone felt sorry for him.' Or they assumed I was brought here to show them how smart they are. Either way.

Abir   No one thought that.

Adham   I was an embarrassment. Scrambling for an answer, coming up with mish-mash, nothing.

Abir   It didn't sound like that!

Adham   You don't speak the language, my dear.

Abir   Some.

Adham   'Beer. Please. Thank you.'

Abir   I saw them talk to you. They liked you. I wish you could see that.

Adham   You should be disgusted with me. I stood in that hall, and looked out . . . My legs beneath me, they couldn't hold me. I can't do it. I can't.

Abir   It was just practice.

Adham   I could barely get the words out. You didn't see that?

Abir   No.

Adham   No?

She shakes her head.

Well, then let me explain something. Your husband was flailing. I can't believe you couldn't see that! They ask me to defend my point of view, and what do I give them? Theories that took fifteen years to trickle down to us. Old thoughts, old theories. I'm useless.

Abir   By God, that's not true.

Adham   By God, it is! We're backwards! While we've been fighting over this and that scrap of desert, crying over the last assassination, they've been living with the great thoughts. We've wasted so much time.

He looks like he might cry, but he holds it together. She goes to him, touches his back.

Abir   You have a great mind.

Adham (*laughs*)   Is that right.

Abir   He said that.

Adham   Who?

Abir   The, uh, Theodore. In Arabic. He said that.

Adham   When?

Abir   When you were practicing.

Adham   He said that to you? He just wanted to get close to a beautiful woman.

Beat.

Adham   Flirting. You didn't know he was doing that? Men will say anything to look into a woman's eyes.

Abir   I don't know. I don't even think of it that way. It doesn't matter. He also said you have a unique scholarly voice.

Adham   Because it comes with an accent.

Abir   I don't know why you've forgotten how smart you are. The man I met −

Adham   The man you met −

Abir   − was smart, and sure of himself, and didn't care about what anyone thought.

Adham   Well, maybe that wasn't really me.

He looks at her.

Maybe *this* is me.

Beat.

Abir   Then I want them both.

She reaches for his head, touches it.

I can handle both.

She takes his hands.

Your hands are shaking.

He pulls his hands away. She places her hands on his head, runs her hands through his hair, trying to fix it.

Abir (*re: his hair*)   I don't know what happens with this hair.

He relaxes, just a little. She takes his cigarette from him, smokes, studies him . . .

Adham   Wondering what you got yourself into?

Abir   No.

Adham   You lie.

She goes and grabs his Wordsworth book.

Abir   Tell me what it says.

Adham   You'll be bored.

Abir   You're so insulting, you know that?

She starts reading it.

Abir   'Thus by day . . . '

Adham   You want to hear something from 'The Prelude'?

Abir   I don't care. I just want to hear it, coming from your mouth.

Adham   Which poem?

Abir   I don't care.

He shrugs. She watches intently. He takes a beat, then reads.

Adham
   'Thus by day
   Subjected to the discipline of love – '

Abir   I like it. More.

Adham
   'His organs and recipient faculties
   Are quickened, are more vigorous.'

Abir   I like this poet. He's not boring.

Adham   We don't use such criteria to measure a poet's work.

Abir   I disagree.

Adham   You're not supposed to disagree with your husband.

Abir   I thought you weren't traditional.

Adham   Sometimes I am.

Abir *gives him a look.*

Abir   More.

Adham   Ordering me about!

Abir   Go. Just read. Read to me.

Adham
'His mind spreads, tenacious of the forms which it receives.'

As he finishes reading this last part, **Abir** *moves closer to him.*

Both of them are on the bed now. She kneels, places her hands on his hipbones. Leans in, kisses him there.

Lights shift: early morning light.

Laura Marks

Bethany

'Do you know the definition of charisma?
Believing in your own bullshit!'

Lukas Foss

For Eleanor and Clarissa, always

Bethany *was developed at the Lark Play Development Center in
New York. Warmest thanks to Marsha Norman, Christopher Durang
and Tanya Barfield at Juilliard; to Liz Frankel, Mandy Hackett
and Oskar Eustis at the Public Theater; the Women's Project and the
Leah Ryan Fund; G.T. Upchurch, Davis McCallum and Evan Cabnet;
Jessica Amato at Gersh; and to Ken Marks, indispensable both to me
and the play*

Bethany received its first UK staged reading at the HighTide Festival, Halesworth, Suffolk, on 12 May 2012, and featured the following cast and creative team.

Charlie	Louis Hilyer
Crystal	Elizabeth Healey
Gary	Phillip James
Shannon	Abi Titmuss
Toni	Lynne Miller
Patricia	Lynne Miller

Director   Steven Atkinson

Characters
in order of appearance

Charlie
Crystal
Gary
Shannon
Toni
Patricia

Time: early 2009.

Place: the exurbs of a small city in America.

Prologue

A middle-aged man in a bathrobe stands facing out, practicing a speech in his bathroom mirror. His style is presentational, yet intimate and folksy – think Rick Warren at Saddleback. He uses a Q-tip to clean out his ears.

Charlie   There's a reason you're here today. You might not believe that, but I do.

You see, there's a higher power that guides our destiny. I don't care if you call it God or Yahweh or Uncle Fred, doesn't matter.

And I'll tell you one thing about this higher power: He wants you to be rich. Rich beyond your wildest dreams.

He doesn't want you to lie awake all night, wondering how you're gonna make that mortgage payment when your kid's college tuition is due, and your credit cards are already maxed to the limit.

You know, last year, in the town where I live, over thirty-five thousand people lost their homes to foreclosure. Thirty-five thousand!

There are some neighborhoods where you can go for a walk and you won't hardly see *anyone*.

And do you know what's the saddest part about all that? Those people could have saved their homes . . . if they'd known the secrets that I'm about to share with you today. These secrets are as old as the hills, and as powerful as a thunderstorm.

They're the reason that I live in a beautiful five-bedroom home with a hot tub, and a flat-screen TV, and everything else a man could ever want.

If you've been living a life based on hard work, and anxiety, or even fear, your life is about to change forever. So if you haven't already, open up your notebooks; and while you're at it, open up your minds.

He thinks for a moment.

(*To himself.*) That's when I should do that thing with the kazoos.

Scene One

Night. The empty, eat-in kitchen of a small house in the suburbs. Built-in cabinets but no furniture. The counters are bare except for a pile of mail. After some lengthy fumbling with the sliding glass door, a woman enters from outside. She has a small wheeled suitcase, purse and garment bag. She's conservatively dressed, in a suit jacket, skirt and heels, and attractive.

She puts down her things. She's cautious, listening. Turns on the small light over the stove. Quickly looks through the pile of mail. She opens the refrigerator and realizes it's not running. As she kneels down to check the plug, she suddenly stops.

Crystal   Hello?

No answer. She plugs in the fridge. There's an audible hum as it starts to run. She opens the refrigerator again, and this time the light comes on. It takes a few seconds for her to notice the man who has silently entered the room.

Crystal   Oh my God –

Gary (*overlapping*)   It's okay –

Crystal   Oh, I'm so sorry –

Gary (*overlapping*)   Shh. It's okay, I'm going –

Crystal   You know? I think – I, I, I must have just wandered into the wrong house by mistake, I'm so terribly sorry, I'll just be on my –

A long moment while they stare at each other.

Crystal (*grabbing something from her purse*)   I have pepper spray.

Gary   I won't hurt you.

Crystal   I'll just get my things here –

Gary   You don't have to go. I'm leaving right now.

Crystal   What are you saying?

Gary   It's okay. You don't have to call the police.

Crystal   I'm sorry, what's the deal? Do you live here?

Gary   No. Do you?

Crystal   . . . Yes. I mean –

Not exactly, but my friend. It belongs to my friend.

Gary   What's his name?

Crystal   Joe. Parker.

Pause. He laughs.

Crystal   What?

Gary   You got that from looking at the mail.

Crystal   It's true. Joe is my boyfriend.

Gary   Joe is eighty.

Pause.

Crystal   What are you doing here?

Gary   I just need a place to lay my head. I won't bother you. You won't need your 'pepper spray'.

Pause.

Crystal   It's really just breath spray.

She sprays some in her mouth.

Fresh breath is important in my line of work.

Gary   What do you do?

Crystal   Sales. You?

He laughs. From the looks of him, he hasn't held a job in quite a while. She laughs too, nervously.

Gary   What?

She shuts the refrigerator door.

Crystal   It's good that the electric still works. He's only been gone a few days, right?

Gary   More like a week.

Crystal   That makes sense. Who wants to wait around for the marshals?

Gary   Do you know how much he owed?

Crystal   No.

Gary   Two hundred and fifty-four thousand.

Crystal   Unbelievable. Did he have a line of credit?

Gary   How can people be so dumb?

Crystal   He might have been sick.

Gary   He might have been stupid.

Crystal   Well, why don't you go buy a house someday and show us all how it works.

Pause. She backs away slightly.

Gary   Do I smell bad?

Crystal   No – not really, I can't really tell –

Gary   I haven't been showering.

Crystal   Is the water shut off already?

Gary   No. Sometimes I just forget.

A pause while she looks at him, weighing her options.

Crystal   Where are you sleeping?

Gary   Upstairs. So I guess you could have the downstairs if you want. The living-room carpet is pretty soft.

Crystal   How long do you think – I mean –

Gary   Water should stay on until the end of the month. Electric, who knows. Eventually the bank'll put it up for auction, but at this point it might not be worth the trouble.

She's silent, considering.

Crystal   What's your name?

Gary   Gary.

Crystal   Hi Gary. I'm Crystal.

She initiates a handshake. Pause. She reaches into her purse, gets out a packet of nuts and opens it.

Are you hungry? Come here:

She hands him the packet. He pours some into his hand and wolfs them down.

Gary   Thanks.

He offers the packet back to her.

Crystal   Go ahead, have the rest. I already had Quizno's.

Pause.

Oh Christ. I can't do this. Fuck, fuck fuck fuck fuck.

She starts frantically gathering her things. A contradictory impulse stops her. She leans on the counter, trying to think.

Gary   You don't have to go. I'm pretty harmless. But if you have another option, by all means . . . There's always the park, but people can come and fuck with you in the park. I mean, literally. If I were you, I'd go with the devil you know, so to speak.

Pause.

Think it over. I'm going upstairs.

Crystal   Are you going to sleep?

Gary   No, probably just a little meditation. Maybe jerk off if I need to. But I don't think I do.

Pause.

If I do, I'll shut the door.

Crystal   Okay.

Gary   Good night.

He leaves. After a moment she slides her purse off her shoulder and sets it down. She digs in the purse and gets out a photograph: it's wallet-sized, like a school picture. She looks at it as the lights dim.

Scene Two

The next day. **Crystal** *stands on the sales floor of a Saturn dealership. Light background music.* **Charlie** *stands next to her, holding a couple of glossy spec sheets.*

Crystal   . . . The five-door XE has a hundred and thirty-eight horsepower engine, five-speed manual transmission, cruise control; it's virtually the same as the XR except that it doesn't have the sixteen-inch alloy wheels or the advanced audio system, or the sport bucket seats with driver-side lumbar, which I'm thinking you might actually need since you say you do a lot of driving. If you want to save fifteen hundred dollars, hey, in this economic climate, I completely understand. But I see that iPod in your pocket so I know you're a man who likes his music, and I gotta say, having all those audio controls right on the steering wheel is an amazing feeling: it's like, you're heading down the highway and you've got the whole world right there . . .

Charlie   How did you learn so much about cars? Did your boyfriend teach you?

Crystal   I don't have a boyfriend.

Charlie   I was here about a month ago, but I didn't see you then. Are you new?

Her smile abruptly vanishes.

Crystal   Did you work with a salesperson the last time you were here?

Charlie   A girl named Tammy.

Crystal   Oh no. I should . . .

I should probably get Tammy for you then.

Charlie   You trying to get rid of me?

Crystal   Oh, God no! It's just that we're really not allowed to take each other's customers. It's really complicated, but basically, you see, we work on straight commission –

Charlie   How about we just pretend I never told you?

She looks around.

I don't want to work with her anyway. I'd rather work with you.

Pause.

Come on. 'The customer is always right.'

Crystal   I know, but –

Charlie   Shhh, I love this song:

A new song surges forward on the dealership soundtrack: 'Sea of Love', or something equally lush and romantic. They listen to it together for a while.

I swear I've seen you somewhere before.

Crystal   I used to work at the Ford dealership.

Charlie   No, that's not it.

Crystal   Well, I just have one of those faces; people always think they went to high school with me.

Charlie   You were in diapers when I was in high school.

Pause.

Anyway, I filled out the form.

He hands her a thin Lucite clipboard.

And here's my card.

She looks at it.

Crystal   . . . 'Transformative Motivational Speaker' – wait a minute. I know you. I went to that free talk you gave at the Holiday Inn.

Charlie   See, there you go.

Crystal   I still have my notebook. And I remember when I got home, I made a list of all my bills and put it out to the universe, just like you said.

Charlie   And look at you now. You're doing great.

Crystal   Well . . .

You know, that same week, I did have a couple of parking tickets and when I went to pay them, they couldn't find one in the computer, so it was free.

Charlie   We call that 'synchronicity'. The more you use the tools, the more it starts to happen.

Crystal   I don't know. I probably wasn't doing it right.

Charlie   That lecture was just the tip of the iceberg. You should have signed up for my boot camp. That's where we really get into challenging your assumptions.

Crystal   You know, I just didn't have the money –

Charlie   People always say that. It's an investment. But it ends up paying for itself, a hundred times over.

Pause.

Well, speaking of investments . . . Aren't you gonna offer me a test drive?

Crystal   Would you like to go for a test drive?

She has the keys. He offers her his arm with mock formality. She takes it, and they start off.

Scene Three

Evening of the same day. **Crystal** *comes into the kitchen again through the sliding glass door. This time it's apparent that she's using a thin, plastic ID card to jimmy the lock. She does it more easily now. She has her luggage as before, along with a couple of stuffed, no-label shopping bags and a greasy bag of takeout.*

Crystal   Gary?

Are you still here?

Gary *pops up from behind the counter. He's holding a two-by-four.*

Crystal   Oh Jesus –

Gary   Sorry.

Crystal   What the hell is that for?

Gary   Just . . . protection.

Crystal   Protection from what?

He thinks for a moment. He gently lays the two-by-four on the counter.

I brought hamburgers. Are you hungry?

She starts unpacking the bag.

Gary   I was just going to fix some C-rations.

Crystal   What are those?

He shows her a small cardboard box.

Gary   From the Army-Navy store. They keep forever.

Crystal   Well, great, keep it for another night. I'm buying.

Gary   Do you always wear a suit?

Crystal   It's . . . you know. I have to.

But I can't afford to get anything dry-cleaned. Pretty soon I'm gonna smell like a . . .

Embarrassed silence.

Gary   I took a shower.

Crystal   That's great!

They start eating picnic-style on the floor.

So tell me about your day. Did you go anywhere?

Gary *shakes his head.*

Crystal   It was really nice out.

Gary   I didn't have anywhere to go.

Crystal   Well, I hear you, but you could go hang out at the library, or . . . I don't know . . .

Gary   I mean I didn't *need* to go anywhere.

Crystal   So you don't go anywhere unless you need to?

Gary   Pretty much.

Crystal   Do you have . . . like, a phobia, or something?

No answer.

I'm sorry, I'm usually not this rude . . .

Pause.

Gary   I don't like crowds. Crowding is unnatural; it causes stress and aggression. They've proved it with animals.

Crystal   Okay.

Pause.

Anyway, I had a good day at work. I think, maybe, I've finally met someone who wants to buy a goddamned car.

Gary   Hooray for fossil fuels.

Crystal   Hooray for seven-percent commission.

Gary   Is it new, or used?

Crystal   Do I look like the used-car type?

This guy is strictly top-of-the-line. He's looking at a Sky RedLine, fully loaded.

Gary   I only know cars from the seventies and eighties. Nowadays they make them out of plastic.

Crystal   It's polymer.

Gary   That's because the government is saving the metal. They're hoarding it.

Crystal   What for?

Gary   Think about it. Metal is going to be one of the key substances in the new barter economy. As long as your fire is hot enough, you can make metal do whatever you want. Plastic just melts and turns into poison.

Crystal   Okay.

Gary   You should take your seven-percent commission and invest in a scrap-metal yard.

She laughs.

Crystal   You know . . . investing is not really my top priority right now.

She starts unpacking the shopping bags, stocking the kitchen with various things: paper towels, china plates and cutlery from Goodwill.

Gary   Don't tell me you're gonna go rent some apartment. That's just throwing money away.

Crystal   So how does it work: you just stay someplace until the water gets turned off, and then you go and try to find some other house?

Gary   There's always another house; the hard part is finding one with lights and water. Take a look outside. You see any lights in those houses? It's a ghost town.

She looks out the glass door for a long while, realizing how alone they are.

Crystal   That street light's not on.

Pause.

Well, at least it's quiet.

You can see the stars.

Did you ever do any camping?

I mean . . . voluntarily?

I went once. I couldn't believe the sky. Like it was just dusted with white.

Gary   Plenty more where that came from. The days of trying to get 'back to nature' – that's all over. Nature's coming back to us.

Crystal   What do you mean?

Gary   These cheap-ass houses – they're just scrap now. We're sitting in a drywall junkyard.

Pretty soon you're gonna see squirrels nesting in these cabinets. Vines crawling over the floor.

Crystal   That's insane.

Gary   You'll see people start to change too. Fighting to survive. It doesn't bring out the best in a person.

Pause.

Crystal   Listen: I need to ask a couple of favors of you.

Gary   This oughta be good.

Crystal   Will you be home during the day tomorrow?

He nods.

Okay, good. I'm having some stuff delivered. Just a table and chair set, from Goodwill. I just need someone here to open the door. And the other thing is even easier.

The day after tomorrow, I have this appointment. This person needs to come over and see where I live. So I was wondering if you could maybe just . . . not be here.

Gary   That's a problem.

Crystal   Just for a couple of hours. You could go for a walk, or run some errands . . . It's not like you'd run into crowds or anything.

Gary   What time?

Crystal   Afternoon.

Gary   No way.

Crystal   Come on. You must go out all the time to get your C-rations or whatever.

Gary   Only when I *need* to.

Crystal Please, Gary, I can't – I can't even begin to tell you how important this is.

Gary Do you seriously expect me to go out and wander around the neighborhood for *two hours*?

Crystal So go to the library.

Gary You and that fucking library!

No. No way. I see your M.O.

You buy me a hamburger like I'm your buddy, and now you want to kick me out and change the locks on me. I was here first, lady.

Crystal I'm really hurt that you would think that, Gary.

I've never been anything but nice to you. And you've been so kind to me, letting me stay here.

I don't know if I could do this if I didn't have you here to help me.

I appreciate it so much.

Pause.

Gary What if I just stay upstairs?

Crystal They need to see the whole house.

Gary Who does?

Crystal It's complicated.

Gary Why can't you just say, 'This is my friend, Gary?' I'll take a shower.

Crystal Because they'll assume that I'm involved with you.

Gary And that would be deeply embarrassing to you; I get it. Because I'm such a disgusting specimen –

Crystal No, I swear, you could be Brad Pitt – I mean, you're perfectly attractive, as far as I can tell, but I absolutely cannot look like I'm involved with anyone or living with anyone. At all.

Gary   Okay.

So, I got it.

I'll be the plumber.

Crystal   What?

Gary   Like they say in the porno films: 'I'm just here to fix the sink.'

Crystal   Do you . . . do you have any tools, or anything?

Gary   One or two. I can improvise.

Crystal   I don't know.

Gary   It's a good cover. And you know, if you're having the place worked on, it helps it look like you really live here. Because a table and chair set isn't gonna cut it.

Crystal   I bought other things too, like toilet paper and some sheets to put on the bed, I mean, *your* bed. I'll say that I just moved in.

Gary   That's true enough.

Crystal   Gary: don't take this the wrong way, but I need to know that you're not gonna screw this up. If we do this, you have to be completely quiet. Let me do all the talking.

Gary   I know what I'm doing.

I've been living under the radar for a long time.

Crystal   Okay! We're a team, right?

Gary *starts sliding his pants down.*

Crystal   What the hell are you doing?

Gary   Just . . . that's how the plumbers wear their jeans . . . 'Cause when they bend over –

Crystal   Okay, that's too far.

Gary   Just trying to look realistic . . .

Crystal   You should go to bed now.

Gary You're not the boss of me.

Crystal Oh God, I'm sorry, that just slipped out. I guess it's a mom thing.

Gary A mom thing?

Crystal *looks stricken. She gathers up her things and starts heading toward the living room.*

Gary Hey.

It's all fine.

I'm not gonna screw anything up.

I don't want you to worry.

She tries to smile.

Crystal Good night.

Gary Good night.

She exits.

Scene Four

Charlie *stands alone at his bathroom mirror, in his undershirt this time. He practices a speech while he tweezes his ear hair.*

Charlie What do you want?

He points to an imaginary person, as if calling on someone, and holds for their response, which he repeats.

Okay. 'More money.' Anyone have a more specific answer?

The same thing with more 'people'.

'More sales.' 'More commissions.'

Ah. 'I want to be rich.' Okay, let's hold for a minute.

This is my favorite answer: 'I Want To Be Rich.'

Come here a minute:

(*To himself.*) I have to make sure I have a nickel.

Here's a nickel.

Now you're richer than when you came in.

Seriously, though: why do you want to be rich? Why?

Calling on people, as before.

'So you don't have to worry anymore.'

More answers, come on.

'So you won't lose your house.'

'Medical expenses.'

'So your wife will respect you.'

'So you can buy things.'

Okay, stop. Let me ask you this: what things?

Uh uh, don't tell me: close your eyes.

Now visualize the first thing that comes to mind.

How big is it? What color is it?

Is the light hitting it in a special way?

Now stretch out your hand – can you see your hand? – and run your fingers over it. How does it feel?

Now come right up next to it, and see if you can press your face against it.

What does it smell like?

What does *she* smell like? Ha, just kidding.

Now: I want you to say something to yourself.

Don't say, 'I want this.'

Say: 'This is mine.'

Scene Five

*Sounds of rain and thunder. Lights rise on **Shannon,** a woman in her thirties, who stands on the sales floor of the dealership reviewing a checklist on a clipboard. **Crystal** rushes in. She's soaked.*

Crystal   Sorry I'm late, I took the –

Shannon   Did you punch in?

Crystal   No, I'll go do it right now.

Shannon   Do it later. You have a customer.

Crystal   No way.

Shannon   He's in the men's room. Are you . . . ?

Flushing sounds from offstage.

Crystal   What?

Shannon   Is something up?

Crystal   I'm fine. Do I look all right?

Shannon   We need to talk when you have a second.

Crystal   Sure.

Shannon *moves away as* **Charlie** *walks in with a newspaper.*

Charlie   . . . There's my girl.

Crystal   Wow, you're a real early bird.

Charlie   Do I need to buy you an umbrella?

Crystal   It's weird, I can never manage to keep one.

He takes off his raincoat and puts it around her shoulders.

Charlie   Here you go.

Crystal   Thank you.

Charlie   I was getting cold just looking at you.

Pause.

Crystal   So . . . what can I help you with today?

Charlie   I was thinking I'd like to see how that car handles in the rain.

Crystal   You're a smart shopper. I like that.

Charlie   Well, it's a big investment.

Crystal   Absolutely. A car is like your second skin. Well, I'll get you the keys and you can go spend the whole day out there if you want.

Charlie   You free to ride shotgun?

Crystal   Oh gee, I'd love to, but I, uh, I have this meeting with my supervisor.

Charlie   I don't mind waiting. You all have free coffee in the lounge.

Crystal   . . . Okay then. Great. I'll come find you.

He exits.

Shannon   What's his deal?

Crystal   He's pre-qualified.

Shannon   A twelve-year-old can get pre-qualified.

Crystal   What did you want to talk about?

Shannon   We're closing.

Crystal   Closing early?

Shannon   No, closing forever. The service center's hanging on for a little while, but the sales floor is toast.

Crystal   Oh my God.

Shannon   So if you're working on any deals you need to close 'em by the end of the week.

Crystal   Why didn't you tell me before?

Shannon   Crystal: get a grip, okay? We've been operating in the red for two straight quarters; half the associates are gone;

what did you think was gonna happen?

Crystal   But that's not what you do in a change cycle; you have to – you have to hang in there, you know? Because times like these are all about thinning the herd, and that's good for us, but we have to ride it out, we have to; it's all just – it's just part of the cycle.

Shannon   You sound like my 401k guy.

Crystal   Did you talk to headquarters? Because all they have to do is find someone else to buy out the franchise, this is crazy –

Shannon   HQ doesn't give two shits about it. They're busy trying to sell the whole company.

Crystal   What? Who could they sell it to?

Shannon   I don't know. Japanese.

Pause.

Crystal   Shannon: I just want to say . . .

If we get any more walk-ins . . . I know today, with the rain – but tomorrow morning, I'm here, or Thursday or Friday . . .

Shannon, please: I was salesperson of the month twice in a row when I was at Ford.

If anyone else walks through that door, you give that person to me and I will close them.

You know I will.

I will absolutely close them, and I will give you, personally, twenty-five percent of my commission.

Pause.

Shannon   Did you steal a customer from Tammy?

Crystal   No, I –

Shannon   Because she told me you did.

Crystal   It's not . . . no, it wasn't like that, this guy just –

Shannon   Whatever, I don't wanna hear excuses, but you know what? Tammy's husband is on disability. And she may not be as pretty as you, but she's been here a heck of a lot longer and worked her butt off.

So if we get any walk-ins, which at this point is about as likely as Pluto crash-landing into the parking lot, I think I'm gonna give them to Tammy.

Because you know what?

There's a special place in hell for women who don't help other women.

Shannon *exits. After a moment,* **Crystal** *slips the borrowed coat off her shoulders and looks at it. It's an expensive raincoat. She reads the designer label in the collar, folds the coat over her arm, and exits to go find* **Charlie**.

Scene Six

The next day. The kitchen. The table-and-chair set has arrived. **Gary** *kneels in front of the open sink cabinet, wrench in hand. He starts futzing convincingly with the pipes when he hears* **Crystal** *coming down from upstairs along with* **Toni**, *an alert, fortyish woman in a muted pants set.*

Toni (*making notes in a folder*)   . . . So the living room, we saw.

Crystal   I wanted to get a couch, but they said it takes eight weeks.

Toni   Not a problem. I'd rather see you wait eight weeks than go to one of those rental places. I had a client get bedbugs.

Crystal   Oh my God.

Toni   You mind if I look in your fridge?

Crystal *nods, and she does.*

Toni   All right, I'd like to see more fresh vegetables in here, but I know you just moved in. Cleaning products?

Crystal   Oh sure, I have . . . let's see . . . Joy, and 409 . . .

Toni   Where do you store your cleaning products?

Crystal   I . . .

Toni   Under the sink?

Crystal   No.

Toni   Never under the sink. Not even if you have one of those little door latches.

Crystal   Absolutely –

Toni   Because kids are smart, they figure out how to open those things up in about two minutes.

Crystal   I keep everything up high.

Toni *goes to the sliding glass door and looks closely at the handle. She sits down at the table.*

Toni (*writing*)   Let me just catch up on my notes.

Crystal   Take your time.

She sits and waits.

Toni   Okay.

Here's what I still need to see:

Crystal*'s face falls.*

Toni   Don't get upset on me. You're getting there. You have a pen?

Crystal (*not moving*)   Sure.

Toni *hands her a pen and paper.*

Toni   Number one: window guards. On every second-floor window. Write that down.

You get them at the hardware store, about twenty bucks a pop. Your handyman here probably knows how to put them in.

Number two: another bed.

Crystal   I thought she could just share with me for a while.

Toni   You know, she could, but we discourage it. You just don't want to know the stories I've heard. Mostly having to do with the fathers, but still.

Crystal   So, I'm sorry, I don't get it. She's not supposed to be old enough to know not to drink Drano or climb out a second-floor window, but she's too old to sleep in her mommy's bed?

Toni   I don't write the standards, I'm just trying to tell you, I know what my supervisor is going to say −

Crystal   All right −

Toni   If you were in a motel that would be one thing, but you have plenty of room so I don't see what the problem −

Crystal   Fine, I'll get a bed.

Toni   Let's say you have a gentleman who wants to spend the night −

Crystal   That's not going to happen. Let's move on.

Toni   That's about it. I'll just need a copy of your lease, for the file.

Crystal   . . . Great.

Toni   Or if you just have the original, I can just take it with me and run it off at the office.

Crystal   You know, the landlord still has my copy, so I can just make a copy at work and mail it to you, would that work?

Toni   Are you still at the Saturn dealership?

Crystal   Yep, it's a great team over there.

Toni *looks over at* **Gary**, *who by now has run out of things to do to the pipes. He's just sitting there.*

Toni   I'd like to ask you about something a little more sensitive.

Crystal   Gary, while you're here, could you also take a look at the upstairs bathroom? The faucet is a little drippy.

Gary   Sure.

He exits.

Toni   I should get his number from you. Is he reasonable?

Crystal   You know, the landlord is paying, so I'm not really sure.

Toni   Crystal, I just need to ask you.

Do you have any other issues that we should know about? Any addiction problems?

Crystal   No.

Toni   Drugs? Gambling? QVC?

Crystal   No.

Toni   Mental health issues?

Crystal   I went over all this with the other guy −

Toni   I don't care if you did. I'm asking you now.

Crystal   There's nothing wrong with me.

Toni   But you see, when I go back to my supervisor and say 'She's a nice-looking, clean woman who finished school and has a job,' he's going to say, 'So what exactly is her problem?'

Crystal   My only problem is I lost my house. And when I applied for the shelter, you people said, 'Sorry, the shelter's full, but why don't we take that little girl off your hands?'

Toni   You wouldn't want to be in that shelter anyway.

And you can't have a child sleep in a car. It's just not right.

Crystal   Can you at least tell me when I can see her? I stopped by on Sunday just like you said, but the neighbor said they'd all gone to church, so I sat there for three hours −

Toni   I'll talk to them –

Crystal   And when I showed up at school they wouldn't let me see her either –

Toni   Unscheduled visits are against our policy. It can get unsettling for the children.

Crystal *gets an envelope from her purse.*

Crystal   Can you at least give her this letter? And make sure those people read it to her?

Toni (*taking the letter*)   I'll see what I can do.

Crystal   Is she okay, or does she seem like . . .

Toni   She acts out a little at school, but at home they say she's fine.

Crystal   Oh shit, I forgot the stickers.

She gets a sheet of Hello Kitty stickers out of her purse, takes the letter back and starts feverishly decorating the envelope.

Toni   Just bear in mind that we're going to need to open that letter.

Crystal   Why?

Toni   It's just policy, like everything else. And just one piece of advice: I know you'd never say anything intentionally to hurt her, believe me; but we try to discourage parents from making promises they can't keep.

Crystal *clutches the letter, looking for a moment like she might rip it up, but she gives it back to* **Toni**.

Crystal   I'm just telling her I've found us a house. And I'm coming to get her soon.

Toni   All right. I'll stop by again next week, same time. If everything looks good, then I'll make a recommendation to my supervisor.

Crystal   Great. That's great. Thank you.

Toni *gets up.*

Crystal   I'll walk you out.

Toni   Don't bother, my car is out this way.

She heads for the sliding glass door.

But when you get a chance . . . you need to get a better lock over here.

Anybody can bust this thing open with a credit card.

Toni *exits. We hear her car starting as* **Gary** *comes downstairs.*

Gary   You're in some deep shit.

Crystal   No I'm not – what are you talking about? All I have to do is forge a lease; that's the easiest thing in the world.

Pause.

You were perfect. Thank you.

Gary   I told you you didn't have to worry about me. See, I'm the kind of guy you want in your foxhole.

. . . Um, that's a war reference.

Pause.

You have a kid.

Crystal   I do.

Gary   Interesting.

Crystal   Why?

Gary   I don't know. I guess I didn't think you'd ever done anything worthwhile with your life.

Crystal   Are you serious?

Gary   How old is she?

Crystal   Five. She's in kindergarten.

Gary   Is she moving in?

Crystal   I don't know.

Gary   For a long time I thought having kids was a bad idea, because of overpopulation; but now I think the people who know what's going on should have as many kids as they can, because the revolution won't be over in one person's lifetime.

Crystal   What revolution?

Gary   But you have to choose the right genes. You're a good specimen; I can see why someone wanted to mate with you. You have to be a pretty tough animal to keep your genetic material alive. There's so much that can happen, like you were saying, drinking Drano or –

Crystal   That lady is unbelievable. My kid is five; she knows not to drink the goddamned Drano.

And where the hell am I supposed to find two hundred bucks for window guards? And a bed? (*Pause.*) Where did you find that bed you have?

Gary   You don't want to know.

Crystal   I just have to make this sale. I have to.

She gets out the wallet-sized photograph from before and looks at it. **Gary** *comes and looks over her shoulder.*

Gary   What's her name?

Crystal   Bethany.

He takes the picture for a closer look.

Gary   What are they teaching her in school?

Crystal   . . . Um, the usual stuff. Two plus two.

Gary   That's what you think.

Crystal   What are you talking about?

Gary   They're socializing her.

They're teaching her not to hit other kids, and to keep her skirt down, and raise her hand when she has to go to the bathroom.

Every single thing her body wants to do is getting smashed down by the military-industrial complex, and the worst part is that it happens all day, every day, to everyone, and everyone just lets it happen.

Look at you: you go around all day with that big, fake smile pasted across your face, selling people a bunch of crap they don't need so you can go buy crap *you* don't need. 'I just *have* to make this sale.'

You completely bought the government messages: but what happens now? Are you gonna just curl up and die? Or are you gonna fight back?

Because when you have to struggle for food and shelter, just like we did millions of years ago, boom! You start getting your mind back.

And we have to take advantage of this time and fight the system until we obliterate it.

You and me, we'll never recover a hundred percent; but your daughter's young; she might still have a chance . . .

You see, it won't be a collective society anymore where technology controls the masses. It'll just be individuals and small groups.

And when the centers of technology and finance go down, we need to be ready to survive.

Small, nomadic groups have the best shot at it. I know how to trap food and I know all the edible plants.

Crystal   That's great.

Gary   You said, 'I don't know.' How come?

Crystal   I didn't say that.

Gary   No, before when I said, 'Is your daughter moving in?' you said, 'I don't know.' How come?

Crystal   I – I haven't decided what to do yet.

Gary   I'll tell you what you should do. You pick her up from school.

You say, 'Don't worry, honey, we're never going back there again.'

Then the three of us get in your car and we start driving. We drive until we hit wilderness. Someplace without all this EMF radiation.

We build a shelter. Or find one. And we've got the seeds of a new society.

XX . . . XX . . . XY.

Crystal   That's really sweet, Gary.

Gary   I'm not being sweet.

Crystal   I have to think about it.

Gary   Yeah, see, that's not a good answer because your mind is full of all that system bullshit. But I'm thinking about your daughter; and if you were thinking about what's best for her long-term survival you'd be down on your knees thanking me right now.

Crystal   I'm very grateful, I promise, I just – Could I have that picture back?

Gary   God, women always act like there's something wrong with me. But every time I go into a public bathroom, some guy tries to blow me. Why is that?

Crystal   Gary, right now we need to focus on getting her back.

Gary   Right.

Crystal   I need your help. I really need it. You were so great today. We just have to stay here for one more week.

Gary *stiffens and stares out the window at the street light, which has started to sputter on uncertainly.*

Crystal   What is it? Is someone out there?

Gary   It's happening.

Crystal   What is?

Gary They know.

Crystal Who does?

Gary The government.

Crystal . . . It's just the street light. I think it's broken.

Gary Don't say that! I know what I'm talking about! Do you want to end up dead?

Crystal I'm sorry.

He turns off the light over the stove.

Gary No lights tonight.

Crystal I won't. I promise.

Gary I'll go upstairs and keep a lookout. Think about what I said.

He grabs her hand and holds it between his hands for a minute like it's a precious object, then lets go and runs upstairs. Lights fade.

Scene Seven

Charlie's *alone at his mirror again. He's carefully tying his tie.*

Charlie Are you busy after work? Because . . .

He revises his approach.

Do you like Mexican? Because . . .

You look like you could use a good meal. I'll drive.

No, don't bother. Save your gas . . .

This car's been good to me, but it's time to trade up, you know?

. . . No, I didn't even bring my checkbook today. This is just a social visit.

(*Revising*) No, I forgot my checkbook. But I'll be sure and bring it tomorrow. I just felt like saying hello.

(*Revising again.*) Oh, hell, I forgot it. I'll have to come back tomorrow.

He undoes the knot and starts tying his tie all over again.

Did you get enough to eat?

Another margarita? . . .

In that case, why don't I just take you home?

(*Revising.*) You know, instead of going to get your car, why don't I just drive you straight home?

A lot of bored cops on the road these days, waiting to pull someone over.

. . . I don't know. Let's do a little drunk test. Close your eyes.

Now hold out your arms like this.

Now see if you can touch your nose . . .

That does it. I'm driving you home.

Blackout.

Scene Eight

Outside the house. Night. **Charlie** *walks up to the sliding glass door with* **Crystal***, holding her elbow as if he's helping an old lady across the street.*

Crystal   Okay, I'm good now. Thanks.

Charlie   It's so dark out here.

Crystal   That stupid bulb must have burned out.

Charlie   Nice house.

Crystal   Thanks. I really like it here.

Pause. She holds out her hand for a handshake.

Well . . . thanks again for dinner. It's been a pleasure working with you.

He laughs at this and she joins in, lightly.

Charlie   Would you mind if I just came in and used your restroom?

Crystal   . . . Oh. Sure.

Charlie   I'll be careful not to wake up your daughter.

Crystal   Oh, she's not here . . . she's at a sleepover.

She starts automatically to reach for her ID card, but stops herself. At a loss, she feigns digging through her purse for an imaginary key.

Crystal   Oh shit. I don't have my house key.

Charlie   That's a setback.

Crystal   I must have left it in my car.

Charlie   Do you need me to break in?

Crystal   No, I . . . , You know what? My roommate's probably here, he can let me in.

She starts knocking.

Gary! . . . Gary!

Charlie (*to himself*)   Roommate.

Gary *comes down from upstairs looking worse than ever, disheveled and confused. He's holding the two-by-four.*

Crystal   Gary, it's me! Open the door!

Gary *comes through the kitchen, stares at* **Charlie**, *and after an eternity, opens the door.* **Charlie** *offers* **Gary** *his hand.*

Charlie   Sorry to wake you. Crystal forgot her key.

Crystal   Gary, this is Charlie. He's a client from work.

Gary *doesn't take* **Charlie**'s *hand.*

Charlie   So. Bathroom?

Crystal   Straight ahead on your left.

Charlie *exits.*

Crystal   Gary, I need you to be my helper again, okay?
You're my roommate, and you're a nice guy, not hostile; and –
you know what? Just go back to bed. Go.

Gary   What's he doing here?

Crystal   He gave me a ride. It's complicated. It's really
good that he knows you're here, but now I need you to clear
out, let me handle him.

Gary   Which of his parts do you plan to 'handle'?

Crystal   That's disgusting, please, just go –

Gary   I'll be listening.

Crystal   Gary –

He goes upstairs and **Crystal** *composes herself as* **Charlie** *returns.*
Charlie *takes the scenic route, peering into the living room and looking
around.*

Crystal   I just moved in.

Charlie   That guy a friend of yours?

Crystal   You know . . . he's more of a family friend.

He's new in town. So I agreed to let him stay with us for a
little while.

Charlie   He's a little strange.

Crystal   Oh, he's only like that when you wake him up.

Charlie   I don't know if you really want him around your
daughter, you know what I mean?

Crystal (*softly*)   I know.

Pause.

Charlie   You mind if I sit down for a minute? I have a long
ride home.

Crystal   I'm sorry you went out of your way.

Charlie   No trouble. My back just locks up if I drive too
much.

Crystal   That's why you need that adjustable lumbar seat.

Charlie   I don't know. I might have blown my car budget tonight on all those margaritas.

Pause.

Crystal   Can I get you a glass of water or anything?

Charlie   Sure.

Crystal   I hope you don't have an early day tomorrow.

Charlie   No, just prep work for that keynote address I have on Monday.

Crystal   Who is it for again?

Charlie   United Federation of Soybean Suppliers. It's a tri-state organization.

Crystal   Wow.

Charlie   It's their quarterly meeting, and the theme is 'Keeping Optimistic in Hard Times'.

Crystal   And you're the keynote speaker. That's amazing.

Charlie   It's a nice gig. I'm hoping they'll have me back sometime, because I also do a speech on relating sports trivia to your life.

Crystal   What's your speech about? Is it like the Holiday Inn one?

Charlie   Kind of. It's called 'Getting the Wealth of Your Dreams'.

Crystal   Can you do some of it for me?

Charlie   Sure, if you want to pay my speaker's fee –

Crystal (*laughing*)   Oh, great –

Charlie   I'm serious. I do private sessions.

See, the secret laws that allow you to create prosperity are simple to use.

Anyone can do it; you just have to be ready to receive the transmission.

But one of the laws is the 'Law of Compensation'.

So in other words, I can't just give it away.

You have to commit – emotionally, mentally, spiritually and financially – or the laws won't work.

You should think about doing some sessions with me, though. I could triple your commissions, overnight.

Crystal   I'll think about it.

Charlie   I have powerful intuition about people, and I keep having this feeling like I was meant to meet you . . . like there's something I have to teach you . . . or maybe something you have to teach me.

Crystal   Well, I don't have much of a budget for extras right now.

Charlie   Maybe we should work out a trade. Say, a dozen sessions for a new car?

Crystal   If it was my car, instead of the dealer's, I'd be all over that.

Charlie   All over it, huh?

Pause.

Crystal   More water?

Charlie   Sure. Unless you have something stronger.

Your buddy upstairs looks like he might know where to score some weed.

Crystal   You have a long ride home, so that's probably a bad idea.

Charlie   I actually drive better with a little something on board, you know what I mean?

Crystal   Well, driving your new Sky RedLine is gonna be the best high you've ever had.

Charlie   This is starting to seem like kind of a hard sell, you know? I'm sick of hearing about the goddamned car.

Crystal   Okay.

Charlie   Let me ask you this:

If I had come in today and said, 'Look, I've decided to go with a Honda instead,' would you have still gone out to dinner with me?

Pause.

Crystal   But it's so important right now to buy American.

Charlie   Is that your answer?

Crystal   What's the question?

Charlie   I get it.

Pause.

The thing about the Honda dealership is, they're willing to negotiate.

Crystal   What our customers have found is that the places that say they negotiate are really just jacking up the price to begin with, so that's the great thing about Saturn: total price transparency. We put it all right there on a sheet of paper.

Charlie   So in other words, you're not willing to negotiate.

Crystal   . . . I might be able to throw in some free Saturn merchandise.

Charlie   Like what? A travel mug?

Crystal   But if buying American is something that doesn't matter to you then I don't know what else I can say. If you want to buy something that came from a factory in Oki-saka-whatever, then go right ahead. But when you buy a Saturn you're buying American ingenuity and American jobs; from the person who hands you the keys all the way back to the guys on the line in Spring Hill, Tennessee; it's like a family. And when you buy a Saturn, you can feel yourself becoming a part of that family; we even do a little sort of 'thing' when you buy a car, everyone on the floor stands around and does this . . .

Charlie   What?

Crystal   Well, it's supposed to be a surprise.

Charlie   Tell me.

Crystal   We just sing a little song.

Charlie   How does it go?

Crystal   You need a lot of people to do it, and I'm a bad singer.

Charlie   Do you want me to buy this car?

Crystal   . . . Yes.

Charlie   Then sing me a song. Now.

Hesitantly, she stands in front of him and sings the following, to the tune of 'La Cucaracha'. There's some humiliating choreography involving hand-clapping.

Crystal
  You bought a Saturn, you bought a Saturn,
  Put our service to the test.
  You bought a Saturn, you bought a Saturn,
  Saturn owners are the best!
  Go-o-o-o-o, Saturn!
  Yay!

Pause.

Charlie   Not bad. Can you do that last part again?

Crystal   Charlie, I don't think you're really undecided. I think you know exactly what you want to do. I've told you about the features of this car until I'm blue in the face –

Charlie   Stop right there.

You see, I'm not really interested in the features. I'm interested in the benefits.

Crystal   So you want to know how this car is going to change your life.

Charlie   Exactly.

Crystal   Oh, Charlie.

You've hit on the exact reason why I love selling cars.

Because other than a house, I think a car is the single most life-enhancing purchase a person can make.

Your car is like a second skin. You're in it every day. You live in it, you escape in it, you can even sleep in it . . .

I've done that.

It's one of the most important decisions you'll ever make.

If you have a family, it can change your relationship with your kids.

If you're a single guy, it can be the thing that gets you laid. It's the face you show the world. It's you.

Charlie   Can you be more specific? How exactly is this car going to get me laid?

Crystal   It's a really hot car. Women are going to love it.

Charlie   Like you, for example.

Crystal   Obviously I think it's a great car.

Charlie   So if I buy this car, you'll be all over me like a cheap suit.

Crystal   . . . I'm not really in the market these days for any kind of . . . romantic entanglements . . .

Charlie   Why? Because of that guy upstairs?

Crystal   Oh, God no.

Charlie   So what's the problem?

I took you out for a nice dinner and drove you home, but no, that's not enough for you.

You want me to buy a car first.

Crystal   It's not like that, I was just trying to help you make your decision –

Charlie   Just as a charity thing, out of the goodness of your heart. Because it's not like this sale is going to make your month or anything, oh no . . . I mean that dealership is just *teeming* with customers . . .

Crystal   Of course I want to make the sale, but I like you, Charlie, I'm just not –

Charlie   How much do you like me? Because I like you about thirty-two thousand, five hundred and ninety-four dollars plus tax.

Do you want me to sign?

Crystal   Yes I do.

Charlie   So where do we go?

My place is no good.

(*Indicating the living room.*) In there?

She doesn't move. **Gary** *comes in with his two-by-four.*

Gary (*to* **Charlie**)   Get out.

Charlie   Easy there.

Gary   Get out before I hurt you.

Crystal   Gary, don't be stupid; put that thing down –

Charlie (*to* **Crystal**)   Let's go.

Crystal   Gary, I wasn't – it wasn't what you think –

Gary (*to* **Crystal**)   I heard what you said.

Crystal   What am I supposed to do?

Charlie   I'm out of here. Are you coming?

She looks bewildered.

Last call.

Gary   Get the fuck out of here!

Gary *lifts up the two-by-four, but* **Crystal** *grabs his arm. She holds him for a moment in a sort of restraining embrace, looking into his face, keeping his arms at his sides.*

Crystal   Shhh. It's all going to be okay. I promise.

She lets go of him, grabs her purse, and leaves with **Charlie***. The sliding glass door closes.* **Gary** *flings the two-by-four after them.*

The glass cracks into a suspended bull's eye. He starts opening the cabinets and flinging the contents around the room, creating as much destruction as he can. Blackout.

Scene Nine

The dealership. The next morning. **Shannon***'s on the sales floor.* **Crystal** *enters, looking haggard.*

Shannon   Long night?

Crystal   Kind of, why?

Shannon   I just wondered, since you're wearing the exact same outfit you had on yesterday.

Crystal *looks at her with unveiled hostility.*

Crystal   Has anyone come by to drop off a check?

Shannon   Today? No. But someone's here to see you.

Crystal   Thank God.

Shannon *points out a middle-aged woman who's been standing some distance away, watching them and listening.*

Shannon   She was asking about you.

Crystal *approaches the woman with her hand out.*

Crystal   Hi, I'm Crystal. Is there a specific model you'd like to hear more about?

Patricia   Are you a friend of Charlie's?

Pause.

Crystal   Shannon, could you give us a moment please?

Shannon   . . . O . . . kay.

She exits.

Crystal   What's this about? Did he send you here?

Patricia   No.

Crystal   Are you –

Patricia   I'm his wife.

Crystal *finds a chair and sits down.*

Patricia   I checked his GPS. I know he's been spending all this time here but when I ask him about his day he just tells me he's been at the library or the Y.

He likes to have his secrets. I go easy on him.

He got laid off eighteen months ago, and that's so hard on a man's ego.

Now he wants to go around giving these 'speeches', but honestly, no one will even give him the time of day; companies don't have money for that kind of silliness right now.

We're okay, thank God; my investment advisor is a genius; but I know it hurts when he has to ask me for money just so he can pick up the dry cleaning.

Please don't tell him I came here. I just . . . got nervous, I guess.

He didn't come home until two o'clock last night. He said he had a few drinks with an old friend and then his friend's car got towed . . . but I just had this feeling that his friend was not a man. I think he tells little lies sometimes, just so I won't get jealous.

And I couldn't help hearing that you're wearing the same clothes you had on yesterday, so I think maybe you're the friend he was helping, is that right?

Crystal *doesn't answer.*

Patricia   I had my car towed once, so I know what a pain it is, you have to get someone to drive you all the way across town . . . But he's that kind of guy. He makes friends wherever he goes.

And I think for a man his age to spend time talking with pretty young women, maybe even flirting a little bit . . . if it makes him feel better about himself, there's nothing wrong with it. But now . . .

I know you'll think this is really out of line, but I looked up his GPS addresses from last night and one of them is a motel. So I'm thinking it all makes sense, because maybe you couldn't get home for some reason because of the car situation, and he's a gentleman, he wouldn't go home until he was sure that you at least had a safe place to spend the night.

The only thing that doesn't make sense is why he's been coming here in the first place, because he's certainly not in the market for a new car; I'm the one who needs an upgrade; but my birthday is coming up next month, so it occurred to me that maybe he's planning some kind of surprise – and if that is true, you have to tell me so I can put a stop to it, because we do *not* have that kind of money right now. But that's how he is, even after twenty-two years of marriage.

So I suppose what I'm saying is: if there's anything I should know, you can tell me.

Pause.

Crystal   How much do you want to know?

Patricia   . . . I don't think I want to know anything . . .

Crystal   Well, you came here, so I think you do –

Patricia   No, I don't, thanks for your time, but I'll just – I'll just go now –

She starts to leave.

Crystal   Look, I'm sorry, but I don't have much time. I'll tell you the truth if you want, but this is a one-time offer. Now or never.

Patricia *looks at* **Crystal**. *A long pause.*

Crystal   I love him. With all my heart. And he loves me. We've, uh – We've been planning to run away together.

Patricia   Oh no . . .

Crystal   We've been planning it for months now.

Patricia   . . . Oh no, oh no . . .

Crystal   I'm so sorry.

Patricia *is overcome. She sinks into a chair.*

Crystal   I didn't know he was married, at least – not at first.

We met at one of his speeches.

He said he – he had this feeling like he was – supposed to meet me.

Like there was something we were supposed to teach each other.

You know how he is . . .

We both tried to resist it for so long . . .

And he said – he said he couldn't bring himself to tell you, he was just going to leave a note.

But I have to tell you . . . what's your name?

Patricia   . . . Patricia.

Crystal   Patricia, I have to tell you that until today, I would have thought that nothing in the world could keep us apart. It's just . . . so powerful.

Only now that you're here, and I've seen you, I just don't know.

Pause.

I can see how much you love him.

And it makes me angry that he would turn his back on that.

Patricia   . . . It's not his fault; I think I just . . . love him too much sometimes. I've been working on that.

Crystal   No, you're right, it's not his fault. It's *my* fault. Because men – we know how they are, right? They're like children. And it's up to us to keep them on track, isn't it?

Patricia   I guess so.

Crystal   So what are we going to do?

Pause.

Oh Patricia, you're going to think this is crazy, and it's the hardest thing I've ever done, but I have to do it. I see that now . . .

I need to leave town. Just disappear and never see him again.

If I stay, eventually we'll run into each other and the whole thing will start all over again.

Patricia   Where would you go?

Crystal   Well, you see, that's the problem. I don't know. You see . . . I'm sorry, bear with me – I'm just thinking out loud here . . . We've been planning to leave town *together* . . . So I sold my house at a huge loss, and I've given my notice here at work.

I don't have any savings at all; but he said not to worry, he'd take care of everything.

Patricia   How did he think he was going to do that?

Crystal   I don't know, but the point is: because of him, I have *nothing.*

Pause.

Patricia   Do you need me to buy you a bus ticket or . . .

Crystal   Patricia, how would you manage if you took a bus to someplace where you didn't know anyone, and then got out and stood there with no money?

No, it's not going to work. I'll just have to stay here and try my best to break it off with him. Promise me you won't worry, Patricia, because I hate to think of you sitting at home and worrying every time he's fifteen minutes late, worrying that he's with me. I would hate to think that I'm haunting you like that, maybe for years, maybe even for the rest of your life.

Patricia   How much do you need?

Crystal   Oh Patricia, I can't take money from you.

Patricia   Tell me.

Crystal   Well, let's see . . . first month's rent, food . . . and the job market is so terrible; I'm sure I'll be out of work for a long time . . .

Patricia   Five thousand?

Crystal   That would be gone in a heartbeat. Plus there's childcare; I have a daughter.

Patricia   Just say a number.

Crystal   I don't see how I can do it for less than ten.

Patricia *shakes her head.*

Crystal   You see? It's impossible. Excuse me. I'd better go beg for my job back.

Patricia   Assuming I could get it – and I have no idea if that's true – how soon would you be gone?

Crystal   A few weeks.

Patricia *makes a move to leave.*

Crystal   But if I had the money, let's say . . . tomorrow, I could do it a lot faster.

Patricia   I have to think.

Crystal Don't think too much about it, Patricia, or you'll start to hate me.

I can tell you're a smart woman.

If you really listen to yourself, I know you'll make the right choice.

Patricia *exits.*

Scene Ten

Evening of the same day. **Crystal** *comes home. She sees the bull's eye of broken glass in the sliding glass door. She pushes the door open. The kitchen is trashed. The word 'WHORE' has been written in huge letters on the cabinets, daubed in some dark substance. She comes closer, trying to figure out what the substance is, and then quickly recoils. She's shaking. She finds paper towels and spray cleaner and starts cleaning off the cabinets.* **Gary** *comes in and watches her.*

Crystal Why did you do this?

Gary I don't know.

I thought about a few other words but they had too many letters.

She keeps cleaning. He watches.

Crystal I thought I could trust you.

Gary Yeah . . .

Welcome home.

Tough day at work?

She flings everything she can reach at him – the spray bottle and paper towels – missing him by a mile. For a moment, no one moves. She goes and picks up the things again, and goes on cleaning.

Gary You're lucky. I could have done so much more.

Crystal I've never been anything but kind to you.

Gary (*mimicking* **Charlie** *and* **Crystal**)   'I don't know if he's the kind of guy you want around your daughter.' 'I know!'

Crystal   I was just saying what he wanted to hear.

Gary   He was never gonna buy that car.

Crystal   I didn't know that.

Gary   You're a terrible prostitute. Here's a tip: get the money up front next time.

Crystal   Look: we've all done things we're not proud of. You need to get over it, or get out of this house.

Gary   No. You get out.

Pause.

Crystal   Gary: let's both take a minute and count to ten. I don't want this to ruin our friendship.

Gary   Friendship. You crack me up.

Crystal   It's true. Nothing's changed; I made a mistake, that's all.

Gary   Helen of Troy, Tokyo Rose.

Fucking women. It's always the same thing.

If I had a kid with you, I'd never know if it was mine.

Crystal   Gary, please, I can't think about the future; I just need to focus on right now.

We just have five more days until that lady comes back. You were so great before; can you please just help me a little while longer, and then I'll do anything you want, I promise –

Gary   Why are you always calling me Gary? That's not my name.

Crystal   It's not?

Gary   That's just what it says in my underwear.

Crystal   What's your real name?

Gary   I don't know.

Pause.

Crystal   I think you need to eat something. Can I fix you some dinner?

She opens the refrigerator door, and a big mess of something flops and oozes out onto the floor.

Gary   Surprise.

She slams the door. She doesn't speak for a moment.

Crystal   Why don't we go out and I'll buy you something to eat?

Gary   Negative.

Crystal   Come on. I'll drive you. You won't even have to get out of the car.

Gary   You think I'm so stupid.

You had me going for a while there.

You're sick, you make me sick, you're a sickness.

She needs a piece of the teacher, the greens are too much, but she can't eat, can't eat, she can't help it.

She's gonna turn out just like you . . .

Someone needs to help that little girl . . .

Crystal   She needs your help, Gary, so why don't we go help her. We can go right now.

Gary   No way, no, no way, Mata Hari. Why do you want her so badly? What are you gonna do to her?

Crystal   She needs me.

Gary   Nobody needs anyone, least of all you, fucking white-bread government whore.

Crystal   That's not true.

Gary   We're done. Get out of my house.

She doesn't move.

Gary   Get out.

Crystal   Please, Gary –

*He suddenly runs at her, trying to push her out by force. She resists and pushes him off. He stares at her for a moment, shocked. He lunges at her again, trying to choke her. They grapple and struggle for a while, slipping on the detritus that still litters the floor. She manages to push him backward and he falls, hitting the back of his neck against the edge of the counter. He falls to the ground. She grabs **Gary**'s two-by-four off the counter and watches him. He doesn't move.*

Outside, the street light flicks on. She stares at it for a moment, then keeps watching **Gary**.

He twitches. She goes over to him, lifts the two-by-four, and swings it down as hard as she can, bludgeoning him over and over.

The street light blinks off, then on again. She staggers away and begins to clean up the kitchen.

Crystal   Oh God.

She goes on cleaning. She looks back at **Gary**. *She goes to him and looks at him closely.*

Crystal   Oh God oh God oh God –

She goes back to cleaning. The street light blinks off/on again. She stares at it. She goes on cleaning. Elsewhere lights also rise on **Charlie**, *alone at his mirror.*

Charlie   Let me tell you something:

The hardest part of making your dreams come true is simply believing that you deserve it.

The first time someone offered me these secrets, I was resistant.

I didn't accept what they had to offer, because I couldn't accept my own personal potential.

Now, that was stupid, wasn't it?

When a gift is offered to you, you should accept it.

Crystal *stops, goes back to* **Gary***, hooks her arms under his armpits and drags his dead body, with difficulty, out of the kitchen. Throughout all this the street light keeps blinking on and off, seemingly at random.*

Charlie   And you tell yourself: this is the Universe taking care of me, giving me everything I deserve.

Scene Eleven

Lights change. The Saturn dealership. **Shannon** *is alone, wearing a party hat and holding a drink. She sings the Saturn song to herself, making up her own choreography, which is slightly more lascivious than* **Crystal***'s. While she sings,* **Crystal** *enters.*

Shannon
    You bought a Saturn, you bought a Saturn,
    Put our service to the test,
    You bought a Saturn . . .

She sees **Crystal***.*

Shannon   Hey, Crystal.

Happy Last Day.

Drinks are in the lounge.

Crystal *gives her a dazed stare and keeps going, back toward the offices.*

Shannon   Oh! Check your box.

Some lady dropped off an envelope for you.

Pause.

Crystal   Thanks.

She exits.

Shannon   Anytime.

Scene Twelve

The kitchen. Early evening, just before dusk. **Toni** *and* **Crystal** *sit at the kitchen table.* **Toni** *makes notes in a folder.* **Crystal** *tries to sneak a glance at what she's writing, but* **Toni** *is casually positioned to prevent this. Finally she stops writing and closes the folder.*

Toni   Your file looks good. And this is your lease?

Crystal *nods and slides some papers across the table to her.*

Toni   'Joe Parker'. Huh. I used to know a fellow by that name.

She shrugs and tucks the lease into the file. They look at each other for a moment.

Crystal   So what's next?

Toni   We're done.

Crystal   Done?

Toni   I'll tell my supervisor you've remediated all the problems we discussed. And I'll recommend reinstatement of custody.

Crystal   So I can go get her?

Toni   We'll need to schedule a time. It'll probably take a day or two.

Pause.

Crystal?

Are you all right?

I know it's hard, dealing with all this. It probably seems like it's been going on forever.

Crystal *can't speak.* **Toni** *pats her on the hand.*

Toni   Look at everything you've done. You've turned your whole life around.

Crystal   I'd do anything for her.

Toni   I know you would.

Pause.

Well. I'd better get on the road. Three more stops on my way home. Goddamned budget cuts.

They get up and move to the sliding glass door. **Toni** *sees the splintered bull's eye in the glass.*

Crystal   Oh . . . I forgot to tell you . . . I'm getting this fixed. They're coming tomorrow.

Toni   Bird?

Crystal   Pardon?

Toni   Did a bird fly into it?

Crystal   Yes. It was so sad.

Toni *steps outside.*

Toni   Take care now.

Crystal *manages a polite half-smile but doesn't answer. She stands framed in the doorway, watching* **Toni** *leave. She waves as* **Toni** *drives away. It's darker out now. For a long moment,* **Crystal** *seems frozen, almost catatonic, rooted in the doorway. The street light blinks on. She stares at it. She slides the door closed and locks it. Blackout.*

Branden Jacobs-Jenkins

Neighbors

Neighbors received its first UK staged reading at the HighTide Festival, Halesworth, Suffolk, on 13 May 2012, and featured the following cast and creative team.

Richard	William Byrd Wilkins
Jean	Jessica Pidsley
Melody	Nicole Lecky
Mammy	Clare Perkins
Ryan (**Track**) / **Zip**	Miles Mitchell
Sambo	Jonathan Livingstone
Jim	Marcel Miller
Topsy	Pearl Mackie

Director   Melanie Spencer

Characters
in order of appearance

THE PATTERSONS
Richard, *thirty-nine, father, black*
Jean, *thirty-nine, mother, white*
Melody, *fifteen, daughter, biracial*

THE CROWS
Mammy, *mother, in blackface*
Zip Coon, *uncle, in blackface*
Sambo, *oldest, in blackface*
Jim, *middle, in blackface*
Topsy, *youngest, in blackface*

Setting: a distorted present.

Note: the ethnicity and/or gender of the actors playing the Crows is not specified.

Punctuation

A dash (–) connotes a revised or broken thought if it comes within a line or an interruption if it comes at the end.

An ellipsis (. . .) connotes a slight pause or 'searching' if it comes within a line or a trailing off if it comes at the end.

A slash (/) is where the following line, spoken by whoever speaks next, begins, creating an overlap.

Overture

*A barely, barely, barely, barely, barely, barely, barely, barely, barely,
barely, barely, barely, barely, barely, barely, barely, barely, barely, barely,
barely, barely, barely, barely, barely, barely, barely, barely, barely, barely,
barely, barely, barely, barely, barely, barely, barely, barely, barely, barely,
barely, barely, barely, barely, barely, barely, barely, barely, barely, barely,
barely, barely, barely, barely, barely, barely, barely lit stage. Almost black.*

Almost.

And totally silent. (You can't even hear me.)

*The song 'Dixie' is heard playing somewhere far away, coming closer and
closer and closer and closer, just as five people – a family – suddenly enter
the near emptiness from every direction, toting boxes, carrying furniture,
moving in. They communicate in a hundred thousand ways as they
converge and traverse the space: talking, hooting, hollering, joking,
fighting, scolding, laughing, gossiping – louder and louder, as the music
swells and, whatever they're saying, it's funny. If only we could see them.*

Amidst the ruckus, a deep amber light comes up somewhere, revealing
Richard, *who stands behind a window, watching the family wander
about as though he were watching himself have a bad dream. After a
moment of this, 'Dixie', at its loudest, quickly cuts out and a voice from
the darkness behind* **Richard** *is heard.*

Jean   What do you see? What is it?

Lights change and immediately:

Scene One

An early morning in the Pattersons' kitchen. **Richard** *stands at the
window, tense-looking, distracted, disgusted and confused.* **Jean** *still
bustles about the stove and counter, brightly handling the business of a
big breakfast. There is a kitchen table cluttered with books and papers:*
Richard's *notes.*

Richard (*re: what he sees*)   What?

Jean Richard?

Richard Baby, come here.

Jean What?

Richard Come here and look at this.

Jean *tosses off a sigh, wipes her hands, comes over to the window. She looks. She reacts.*

Jean Okay, now . . . (*Sees, beat.*) Oh.

Richard What is this?

Silhouettes pass by, moving in. Silence, while the Pattersons watch.

Jean New neighbors. This is . . . great?

Richard Great?

The tea kettle screeches or something happens that summons **Jean** *back to the stove.* **Richard** *continues watching.*

Jean They finally sold that house. It was just sitting there. And we're not the only new faces anymore. That's great.

Richard Yeah, just great. (*Audibly mumbling*) A bunch of . . . niggers.

Jean *freezes, maybe drops something.*

Jean What?

Richard (*confused*) What?

They study each other across the kitchen.

Jean What did you say?

Richard What? When?

Jean Just now.

Richard Just now? Did I say something?

They stare at each other across the kitchen.

Jean (*confused*) I thought – (*Beat, moving on.*) Never mind.

Richard   Do you actually think they bought that house?

Jean   I thought it was for sale, but I don't know. Why do you care?

Richard   Because maybe we should have bought it.

Jean   Um, but we have our own house?

Richard   We're renting.

Jean   With option to buy?

Richard   I mean, who are these people?

Jean   Do you want to go over and say hi?

Richard   What – Jean, no! No. We don't know these people. (*Beat.*) Now I'm worried we're paying too much.

Jean   Richard –

Richard   Are we paying too much?

[handwritten: ' worrying about the house not because he wants it but because he doesn't want the crows to have it]

Jean   Okay, now you are just making things up to stress out about. Will you sit down? I'm almost done. I thought you were preparing.

Richard (*wandering back to the table*)   I can't concentrate.

Jean   I told you you need to take it easy. There's such a thing as over-preparing, you know. And you, of all people, should know that you have to keep your stress levels in check. Remember what Dr. Silverman said. / Hypertension begins with your attitude.

Richard (*going over notes, distracted*)   Hypertension begins with my attitude, Jean, yes.

Jean (*crossing with breakfast*)   I'm serious. It's real. It's a real thing! You need to listen to your body. Think of your blood pressure. I don't want you to go into that lecture hall with a nosebleed. Here. (*Presenting breakfast.*) Egg-white omelette. Turkey bacon. Sweet potato and kale hash. Freshly squeezed orange juice. Camomile tea with agave.

Richard   Look at you. Don't start getting too good at this housewife thing.

Jean   Ugh, trust me. I'm not trying to. Besides, it's somebody's big day.

Richard   Did you hear back from those people about teaching Freshman Comp next semester?

Jean   They're not going to hire someone like me.

Richard   Jean, you have a degree in writing.

Jean   And look how I used it. Ten years of freelance? They're not trying to teach these kids how to write press releases and catalogue copy.

Richard   Well, someone was telling me about an administrative opening in our department.

Jean   Richard –

Richard   What?

Jean   I don't want to be a secretary.

Richard   It's an administrative position!

Jean   It's a secretary. Besides, I don't want to be a secretary in my husband's office. Think how that would look.

Richard (*pulling her onto his lap*)   Oh come on. What? Are you afraid of a little sexual harassment?

Jean (*getting covered in kisses, enjoying it*)   Or not enough. All those co-eds coming in and out of your office, asking for extensions. I would just get too jealous. I would do something rash.

Richard (*with a kiss*)   Rash like what?

Jean   Like tell your wife.

Richard (*with another kiss*)   Tell her what?

Jean   Tell her to –

Suddenly, **Melody** *enters like a cyclone with a backpack, grumpy, pubescent, prone to shrieking maybe. She sees them and makes a very loud noise of disgust before sitting at the table and pushing her chair as far away from her parents as possible. In spite of this,* **Richard** *seems to brighten a bit in her presence. The parents disengage.*

Jean   Good morning, sweetie.

Richard   Good morning, baby!

Melody   Don't look at me!

Jean   What would you like for breakfast, honey?

Melody   I don't want anything! Stop being a parody of yourself!

Jean (*becomes more of a parody of herself*)   You're eating breakfast.

Melody   Whatever! I'll just throw it up later anyway!

Richard   Melody –

Melody   Why is everyone freaking out at me?! Why am I such a cow?

Pause, in which **Jean** *sets some breakfast down in front of* **Melody**, *who doesn't touch it.*

Jean   Your first day of school, honey. Are you nervous?

Melody   No, Mother! I am resigned! I'm resigned to my life as a social retard! Who does this!? Who transfers as a sophomore?! It's like all the hard work I did freshman year meant nothing! Now I have to start all over again in this horrible place! Why didn't you just find a time machine and go back in time and convince your younger selves to abort me while you had the chance!?

She gets up and stalks toward the door.

Richard   Where are you going?

Melody   Where do you think I'm going?

Richard   Well, let me just get the keys, at least. I'll drop you off.

Melody   No! I'm walking!

Richard   Why?

Melody (*as she's exiting*)   Because it's like eight blocks away! And being dropped off is embarrassing! Besides, my fat ass could use the exercise!

The door slams. Outside, **Melody** *takes out a pack of cigarettes and wanders off to a secluded somewhere. Meanwhile, there is a long pause, in which* **Jean** *and* **Richard** *look at each other.*

Richard   Should I go after – ?

Jean   No, no.

Richard   I think she's turning into you.

Jean   Uh, those are your genes, buddy.

Richard (*going back to work*)   I don't understand why she is being so dramatic. Kids transfer all the time.

Jean   Well, I miss California, too.

Richard   So do I, but what else were we going to do?

Jean   We could have waited.

Richard   The job wouldn't have waited, Jean.

Jean   I still think you could have held out for something at SF.

Richard (*a little annoyed by this topic*)   You didn't think five years of teaching Greek 101 was holdout enough? (*Beat, then, frustrated.*) Dammit!

Jean   What?!

Richard   Some of Rose's notes are so old you can barely read them.

Frustrated, **Richard** *gets up and goes back to the window.*

Jean   Will you stop worrying about Rose's notes? This is your class now.

Richard   She's a leading scholar in this stuff. She's been teaching this class for forever. Hell, I took this class with her. Of course, I wouldn't remember a goddamned thing about it. I don't even know why she ever thought I –

Jean *crosses to embrace him.*

Jean   Richard, stop. It's a survey course. You could teach this in your sleep. The Richard I know could stand up there and just start rambling and it would be brilliant. Rose wouldn't have fought so hard to get you hired if she didn't think think so, too. Just be yourself and you'll be great.

Beat.

Richard   I just haven't dealt with this drama crap since grad school.

Zip Coon *enters the space, carrying boxes.* **Richard**, *still in* **Jean**'s *embrace, sees him out of the corner of his eye.*

Jean (*playfully grandiose, crossing to stove*)   But it's not just drama, Richard! It's tragedy! Greek tragedy!

Richard   Which is Rose's thing. I'm just an Aristotelian. Political Aristotle. Not even aesthetic.

Jean (*fixing her own breakfast*)   It's all Greek to me!

Richard *hates that joke with a look.*

Jean   How is Rose doing, speaking of?

Richard (*out the window*)   Oh, Rose. She's hanging in there. I don't think I really understood how sick she was until yesterday. They've got her on this walker because of the bone pain, walking around in these terrible wigs. I can't stand it.

Zip *has set his boxes down to pull up his pants and tie his shoes, which takes a while. Maybe he waves his big ass in the air – in* **Richard**'s *general direction?* **Richard** *watches him, getting more distracted over the following.*

Jean (*pitying, pouty, genuine*)   Oh, Rose. But she's tough. (*Beat, suddenly exclamatory.*) 'Oh, Rose, thou art sick!' *(A real question.)* Who is that? Is that Yeats?

Richard (*unhearing, re:* **Zip**)   Are you kidding me?

Jean   Well, I don't know, Richard. I haven't read Yeats in ages.

Richard (*out the window*)   What?

Jean   I said I haven't read Yeats in ages.

Richard (*still out the window, distracted*)   Read what?

Jean (*giving up*)   Never mind. (*To herself.*) 'Oh Rose, thou art sick!' I think it's Yeats.

Jean *takes a seat at the table and starts reading something –* **Richard**'s *notes – just as* **Zip** *is jauntily crossing the stage with a box in his hands.* **Zip** *stops and sees* **Richard**, *who sees him seeing him.* **Zip** *gives a sprightly nod or wave.* **Richard**, *disgusted, not wanting to engage, abruptly closes the blinds.* **Zip** *reacts, gives a shrug, keeps walking, and immediately:*

Scene Two

Outside. **Melody**, *finishing up a quick pre-school cigarette, is finally on her way to school, just as* **Jim Crow** *enters from the other direction, his view obstructed by a box he carries full of banjos and tap shoes and stuffed chickens and thangs. When* **Melody** *has stopped to discreetly put the cigarette out,* **Jim** *bumps into her, dropping all the boxes.*

Melody   Oh my God! / I am so sor . . .

She sees **Jim** *and trails off*

Jim (*collecting his things*)   It's all right. I should watch where –

Jim *sees* **Melody** *and trails off. A super pregnant pause, before they catch themselves staring.*

Jim   Hi.

Melody   Hi.

Long beat, in which they kind of keep staring at each other.

Jim (*sensing he should explain himself*)   I'm new here. I just moved here.

Melody   Moved where?

Jim (*pointing*)   Here. Are you smoking?

Melody   Yes. (*Beat of staring.*) I live next door.

Jim   Oh. (*Beat, extending his hand.*) I'm Jim.

Melody   Melody.

Pause.

Jim   I'm sorry. You were in a hurry.

Melody   Yeah, school.

Jim   Oh, cool, there's a school around here?

Melody   Yup . . . (*Long beat of staring, then covering.*) You gonna go?

Jim   Oh, uh, I don't know. Maybe?

Melody   What do you mean, 'maybe'?

Jim   I've never been to school before so . . .

Melody   What, are you, like, homeschooled or something?

Jim   Yeah. Sort of. Well, no, actually. Just on tour, usually –

Melody   On tour?

Jim   Oh, um, my family have this sort . . . traveling act we do – I mean, not me – I'm just the stage manager. But we're actually on a hiatus right now so maybe I will go to . . . school . . . too . . .

He has noticed something on **Melody**'s *face, wants to remove it but hesitates.*

Melody   What?

Jim   Don't move.

Melody   What?! Is there something on my face? Oh my God, is it a bug?! / Oh my God!

Jim *retrieves it, showing it to her.*

Jim   Shhh! Calm down. Look: it's an eyelash. Make a wish.

Melody   What?

Jim *sticks his finger gently in her face.*

Jim   You're supposed to make a wish and blow it away.

Melody   This is weird.

Jim   Just do it.

Melody *closes her eyes, makes a wish, blows the eyelash off his finger, and opens her eyes to find him staring into her face.*

They freeze for a nanosecond, trapped in its awkward tenderness: she's just sort of standing there, leaning over, breathing softly onto his fingertips. The sound of a passing car snaps them out of it.

Melody (*seeing the car, double-take*)   Ahh, fuck!

Jim   What?

Melody   My Dad – ! (*Re: cigarette.*) Did he just see this?

Jim   Who?

Melody   Did he just – Fuck! Shit! I have to go!

She takes off, running.

Jim   Um, nice to meet you!

Melody *exits, glancing back.*

Melody   Likewise! See you around, neighbor!

Jim   See you around . . . neighbor.

Smiling, **Jim** *looks in her direction for a while then looks at the car, which slows down and stops next to him. He raises his hand to give a timid wave. The car takes off, screeching. Confused,* **Jim** *frowns slightly, but then he takes up his boxes and keeps moving, right into:*

Scene Three ✳

The Crow residence. With some struggle, **Jim** *enters his new house.*
There are cardboard boxes everywhere. **Mammy** *is hanging up some*
family portraits. **Topsy** *is making curtains in a fancy watermelon print.*
Zip *is tuning a big piano.* **Sambo** *is assembling furniture.*

Topsy   Here dis nigga is.   [handwritten: is it ok to use the "n word" within the black community]

Sambo   Damn, nigga, wut took yuh so lawng?

Jim   I ran into somebody.

Sambo   Who you runnin' into when we just got che'ah?

Topsy   Yeah, we don't know nobody yit.

Jim   This girl who lives next door.

Topsy   Aww, shucks! Jim Crow, Jr. already done founds him
a galfriend. / Ooooh!

Sambo (*humps* **Jim**)   Aw, Topsy, you know Jim Crow, Jr.
don't know the first thang to do wit a galfriend.

Jim   Shut up, you guys!

Topsy *and* **Sambo**   Ooooh!

They continue to tease and dry-hump **Jim**.

Mammy (*breaking that shit up*)   Hey! Y'all quit!

Topsy *and* **Sambo**   Yes, Mammy.

Mammy   I ain't got nerves fo y'all nappy-headed jolly nigga
games rat nah! Jimmy, you got yo' daddy's ashes witchu?

Jim   Right here, Mammy.

Jim *reaches in the box and pulls out a ceramic cookie jar fashioned into*
the shape of a black tramp biting into a huge slice of watermelon or
maybe stealing a chicken. I don't know. He hands it to **Mammy**.

Mammy   Thank you, baby. This is gonna go right che'ah.
So he can always be watching ovah us.

[handwritten: ✳ shift in language from educated Pattersons' dialogue]

She sets the cookie jar on the mantel, takes a step back, considers it. Satisfied, she clasps her hands together, looks around, takes in a whiff of her new surroundings, gets a little emotional.

Woo! Lawd! I miss y'alls daddy so much! To think he had to die for us to see this, for us to be able to own such a nice, big ole house in such a fine, fancy neighborhood? It's lak a dream. I feel laks I'se in a dream. Praise Jesus! Praise him! We made it, Jesus. Jimmy, senior, we made it! We made it, Jesus! We made it, Jim Crow! Jim Crow! Jesus! Jesus! Jim Crow! We made it, Jesus and Jim Crow!

Mammy *goes on and on with her spiritual melodrama, speaking in tongues, and swooning and stuff, talking about Jim Crow and Jesus, maybe improvising a little story about Jim Crow and Jesus hanging out together in heaven and watching cable TV or something, and the rest of the family eventually grab tambourines and add on to the backbone of her chanting with their own music, swooning, testifying, etc. Everyone except* **Jim**, *of course, who just kind of sits there, embarrassed and stunned and excluded, arms crossed, eyes rolling. This happens all the time. Eventually,* **Mammy** *catches the spirit. Everyone except* **Jim** *goes crazy with their tambourines and testifying, fanning her, helping her up. Eventually it dies down as, one by one, everyone catches* **Jim** *sort of staring into space with his arms crossed. He catches himself and sees them.*

Jim   What?

Topsy   Ain't nobody said nuthin! Shit!

Mammy   Chil'ren, why don't y'all go and heat up some uh dem collard greens and fried chicken and waffles and cornbread and candied yams with marshmallows and pigs' feet and ox tails and turkey necks and black-eyed peas and biscuits and gravy and popcorn shrimp and chitlins and peach cobbler and ice pops and red Kool-Aid fo' lunch? Mammy too tired to cook.

Topsy   But, Mammy, I wanna sing more!

Mammy   Later, girl.

Topsy   But that's what you always say! I got some new ideas for our comeback show! I wanna show everyone!

Jim   Comeback show? / What comeback show?

Mammy (*through gritted teeth*)   Girl! I said, git!

Jim   What's Topsy talking about? / A comeback show?

Mammy (*re:* **Sambo**)   And take yo nappy-headed brother witchu!

Sambo *and* **Topsy** – *with a crossing of her arms, pout of her mouth, and stomp of her feet – exit, but maybe they actually just find somewhere to eavesdrop.* **Zip** *stays at the piano, maybe underscores some of the following.*

Jim   Mammy, what's Topsy –

Mammy (*as if none of that actually just happened*)   Jimmy, we coming back!

Jim   What?!

Mammy   We booked a show at a little theater in the city!

Jim   A show?

Mammy   A comeback show!

Jim   What happened to our hiatus?! I thought we were on hiatus!

Mammy   Yes, and hi – hiya – hia – hiy – break is over, Jimmy. Nahw it's been a minute since yo' daddy died, and we can mourn all we want, but eventually we gotta get back into the swang of thangs! What? You thought we was just gonna be sittin' up in here in big ole fancy house just livin' off welfare, watching Tyler Perry movies, and doing the 'Lectric Slide all day? Nuh-uh, baby. We still gotta eat. We still got bills to pay. And this our livelihood.

Jim   But I thought we were settling down.

Mammy   Baby, we are settlin' down.

stereotype of black community

Zip   It's a sit-down show, Jimmy. If we do a good job for a coupla months, maybe we'll get sum'n regular out it.

Mammy   Then we won't have to worry about all the stress and hassle of touring no mo. Wouldn't that be nice, Jimmy?

Jim (*after a beat*)   Fine. Let me grab my binder. When are we coming back?

Mammy   This Wednesday!

Jim   What?! Mammy, that's in two days! Why didn't you give me more notice!? You know, I have to get the space measurements and hire a house manager and a run crew and – and – and we still got to put out a call for Daddy's part.

Mammy   No, you ain't gotta do that. We already found somebody.

Jim   You did? That's great, Mammy. (*Poised to write something down.*) What's his name?

Mammy   Oh! His name is Jaaaaaaaaames . . .

Jim (*writing*)   Uh-huh.

Mammy   Cuh-rooooooow.

Jim (*writing, realizing*)   Uh . . . huh . . .

Mammy   Junya.

Pause.

Jim   Mammy, what are you talking about? I already told you guys, no! I can't!

Mammy *suddenly smacks* **Jim**.

Jim   / Ow!

Mammy   Jim, nah I've have enuffa dis! Dis fambly's been doin' what we'se been doing fo' generations. Evybody's done it. Yo daddy. His daddy befo' him. His daddy's daddy. Evybody. It's in yo' blood, Jimmy. Dat ear for pitch. Dat innate rhythm. Dat natchral proclivity fo' mimicry. You can't waste those gifts, Jimmy. It's yo' destiny.

Zip   And there ain't no family act without a family in it.

Jim   But why can't we just remake the show around Daddy's part?!

Mammy *smacks* **Jim**.

Jim   / Ow, Mammy!

Mammy   Jimmy, we ain't got time for all that! And how you gonna remake the show around the frontman?

Jim   But why can't Sambo do it?

Mammy *smacks* **Jim**.

Jim   Mammy, WHY ARE YOU / SLAPPING ME?!

Mammy   Because Sambo got his own part.

Jim *removes himself from* **Mammy**'s *reach*.

Jim   Mammy, I can't do this! I'm not like Sambo and Topsy!

Mammy   Nobody sayin' you got to be like Sambo and Topsy! You could be your sweet self!

Jim   But I just don't think I'm built for this!

Mammy   Well, then, what do you think ya built fo'?

Jim (*pleading, rhapsodic*)   I don't know, Mammy. I'm built for stage managing!

Mammy   But right now we ain't got no show to stage manage, so what else ya built fo'?

Jim   I – I don't know . . . Maybe I'm – maybe I'm built for school! I heard there's a school around here. I was thinking – Maybe I can finally go to school, finally – I met this gir –

Mammy *runs up and smacks* **Jim** *really fucking hard. It's loud and painful-looking and* **Jim** *sort of falls to the floor with a shout.*

Mammy (*over-emoting*)   Not in my house!

Jim (*confused about what is happening*)   WHAT?!

Mammy (*suddenly, to the sky, eyes closed*)   Strength, Jesus! STRENGTH!

Jim   But, Mammy –

Mammy *embraces* **Jim** *so deep in her bosom that he can't talk or breathe.*

Mammy   Jimmy, shh! Calm down. You'll be great.

She holds **Jim** *there so long it's like a sleeper hold, and* **Jim** *struggles to breathe. Just before he loses consciousness, she lets him go, and he more or less collapses, gasping for air.*

Mammy   Brush up is tomorrow morning. Don't be late. (*Looks at him, getting a little verklempt.*) Oooh, my baby getting so big. (*Drops it, suddenly shouting.*) Sambo, mow the damn lawn!

Mammy *exits.* **Jim** *and* **Zip** *are alone.* **Zip** *drops a bunch of sheet music onto the floor in front of* **Jim***.* **Jim** *looks up at* **Zip** *pleadingly.*

Zip   You can't fight it, Jimmy, so just try it. See how you like it.

Jim   And what if I don't?

Zip *doesn't respond. In fact, he just stands there smiling awkwardly, as if* **Jim** *hadn't said anything, before exiting, dandily.* **Jim** *is alone. He stares at the pile of sheet music in front of him, full of dread, and immediately:*

Scene Four

A podium in a noisy college lecture hall. **Richard** *rushes in hurriedly with his briefcase and stands behind it. The lecture hall begins to quiet itself down.* **Richard** *is rifling through his briefcase, looking for his notes, realizing he's left them at home.*

Richard   Good morning, everyone. Good morning. You'll have to excuse me. I ran into a bit of traffic on the way from my daughter's . . . school . . . and I've left my notes . . . at home . . . (*Beat, as it dawns on him.*) Great. (*It seems he might have*

a meltdown.) Um, but that's okay! All right: good morning! Um.
(*He takes in the vastness of the room.*) I know many of you were
expecting Professor Wexler, but unfortunately she had to take
a last-minute leave, and I have been asked by the department
to fill in for her, though we will still go ahead and use her
syllabus. So, um, my name is Professor Patterson, Richard
Patterson, I guess, and, um, we should start off with . . . we
should start off with . . . um . . . (*Long beat, to himself.*) What the
fuck am I doing? . . . (*Recovering.*) Here – uh – you here – doing
– uh – What the fuck are we doing here? (*The class is a little
scandalized.*) Oh, come on now. We're all adults here. Sometimes
I'm just going to curse. I'm just going to keep 'real' like that.
Anyone? This is about the easiest question I'll ask you all
semester: what the . . . heck are we doing here?

Voice of a Student   Uh . . . we're here to learn?

Richard (*winging it, but finding his footing*)   Okay. Yeah . . .
that's . . . that's true, but, uh . . . how did we get here? What,
in each of our lives, has brought us where we are right now, in
this room, together? (*Beat of no response.*) No? Too deep? Okay,
well let's try something else. Tragedy! What is it? Did I scare
you guys away? Okay, well, say this: a tragedy . . . is a play –
a sad play – a play about suffering. A play about someone who
suffers – that's it – and suffering comes . . . from loss, right?
But where does loss begin? Where does tragedy begin?

Say you're having a horrible day – if you trace back every
single event, decision, or thing that took you there – where
does it take you? For instance, just as a silly example: my notes!
I forgot them! Now you all think I'm a terrible professor!
What a tragedy! Boo-hoo! But where did that moment of
forgetfulness begin? How did I forget them? Was I tired
because I didn't sleep last night? Was I nervous? Was it
because my daughter threw a little tantrum at the kitchen
table? Or maybe because we have new – neigh – new
neighbors . . . Anyway, it might be helpful for us to keep this
in mind: tragedies are somehow about something bigger than
simply the worst day or hours or even minutes of someone's

reflection of racism in America and how it was dealt with legally and socially

life. The power of tragedy lies beyond the events of the drama itself. Tragedies are about the mystery of time, about the very experience of living through it, the terror of it – of the not knowing – and how the simplest and most innocent choices we make – have made! – in the past can have such disastrous consequences. But we'll never know it until it's too late. And, in the meantime, these choices simply follow us, haunting us, deep into our very present . . . into this present even . . . and this present . . . and this present . . . and this present . . . waiting . . .

Richard *goes on, seeming more and more pleased with himself, as lights change, and immediately:*

Scene Five

The Pattersons' kitchen, which is empty. Suddenly, **Zip** *is at the door. He knocks, but there seems to be no one home. He knocks again, just as* **Jean** *comes quickly into the room, her nose buried in a big book and another book in her hand – a collected Yeats and some sort of Norton* Anthology of Poetry. *She opens the door and they are both surprised by each other's appearance.* **Zip** *carries a jar of something.*

Zip   Oh. Good morning. I'm looking for the . . . lady . . . of the house . . . ?

Jean   Yes, um. Speaking. Um –

Zip   Oh! Hi. Uh, my family and I just moved in next / next door.

Jean   Yes. Yesyesyesyesyes!

Zip   Coon Crow.

Jean   Mr Coon Crow.

Zip   The last name is just Crow.

Jean   Just Crow.

Zip   But you can call me Zip.

Jean   Zip.

Pause.

(*Almost shouting.*)   Oh! Jean! I'm Jean! Patterson!

Zip   Jean. (*Beat.*) Well, I just thought I'd come over and introduce myself and drop off a little 'howdy neighbor' gift. Pickled pigs' feet with a few intestines thrown in. Special recipe.

He hands her the jar. It's heavy.

Jean   Oh! . . . Yum. Thank you!

Zip   Oh, please. Just being neighborly.

Pause, in which they stare at each other. **Zip** *wants to be invited in.*

Jean (*embarrassed, frantic*)   Oh, I'm sorry – would you like to come in for a bit? Would you like some tea?

Zip   Why, I'd be delighted.

Jean (*rushing to make tea*)   We only have camomile right now. I hope that's okay.

Zip *enters, nosily inspecting the house.*

Zip   Girl, I only do herbal. (*Beat.* **Zip** *notices* **Jean**'s *big-ass books.*) A little light reading?

Jean   Oh, psh, no. I was just looking something up.

Zip   Ah, a poem? I love poetry.

Jean   Yes. I couldn't find it, though.

Zip (*reading the cover, sounds like*)   'Yeets?'

Jean *brings tea over.*

Jean   Uh, it's actually pronounced 'Yates'.

Zip   Are you sure? Cuz that look like 'Yeets'.

Jean   Uh, I'm sure. (*Awkward pause, then sipping.*) So! Welcome to the neighborhood!

Zip   Thank you!

Jean   Where the heck did you guys come from? I mean –

Zip   Oh, here and there. Everywhere. Nowhere, really. Been on tour for about as long as I can remember, but we thought it was time to settle down.

Jean   On tour?

Zip   Yes. My family and I – maybe you've heard of us? The Crow Family Coon-a-Palooza? (*With a crazy face and outlandish accent.*) 'Mo' Coon Than a Little Bit!' (*Breaking it.*) No?

Clown Show

Jean   No. Never.

Zip   That's weird. Though we have been on a hiatus.

Jean   Ah. What exactly is it that you guys do?

Zip (*as if he were about to explain*)   Oh, you know . . . (*Pause, in which he doesn't.*) And what do you do for a living?!

Jean   Me? Oh, I don't – I don't really work. Not right now, at least. I mean, I used to. Work, I mean. Freelance. There's just not a lot . . . freelance around these parts. But I'm looking. And I have an MFA. So, you know . . . (*Beat.*) But my husband, Richard, is a professor!

Zip   Ah?

Jean   At the college. In the Classics Department. Adjunct-soon-to-be-Assistant-Professor! Fingers crossed! His first lecture is today – was today – was now – We're actually sort of new here ourselves. We moved here the end of last spring, from San Francisco.

Zip   Oh?

Jean   Yes. Richard was just hired to fill in for this lecture class at the last minute – because the department chair, who usually teaches the class, one of his old teachers actually, from college – this incredibly sweet woman who's actually been sort of a mentor to him – she's actually the reason why he – I

mean, she convinced him to go back to school, when we –
anyway, she found out she has cancer! Which is the worst! But
also great! I'm sorry, not the cancer – the cancer's not great –
the cancer's the worst. We love Rose – but, anyway, the
opportunity – it's great for Richard, because, you know, Rose
had been planning to retire soon anyway, and she's really
pulling for him as a replacement and so – you know – this is
sort of like an audition. So this is a big day for him! For us!
And that's . . . that's why we're . . . here.

Zip   Is your husband a tall man, sort of . . .

Zip *makes a very quick, very small, not-completely-obvious gesture
meaning 'black' – like swiping his hand across his face – which* **Jean**
immediately picks up on without much thought or notice.

Jean   Yes! Have you met him?

Zip   No no. I think I just caught a glance at him through the
window or something. (*Lull, in which he slurps his tea slowly.*) But
a classics professor. Fan-cy. And Mrs. MFA.

Jean   Yes, creative writing. Kill me, right?

Zip (*gasping*)   A poet!

Jean (*shocked by* **Zip**'s *clairvoyance*)   Oh my God, how did you
know?

Zip *nods toward the big poetry volume.*

Jean   Of course. I'm such an idiot.

Zip   No, you're not! You're a poet! I love poets!

Jean   Well, used to be.

Zip   Oh, no! What happened?

Jean   Oh, nothing happened. That time in my life has
totally passed, thank God.

Zip   So what do you do instead?

Jean   Instead of what?

Zip Instead of your poetry?

Jean Oh, God. What do I do? Hopefully, I freelance. I wife. I mother.

Zip A mother?

Jean Yes! I have a daughter! Melody. She's just turned fifteen.

Zip Fifteen!

Jean I know. Just when you thought it was safe, suddenly there's a personality in there. It's great. Do you have any kids?

Zip Oh, no, no. Just two nephews and a niece, but I'm helping my sister-in-law take care of them. My brother recently passed.

Jean Oh, no. I'm sorry.

Zip Thank you, but it's been . . . it's been a while.

Jean (*easing into lighter territory*) But still . . . All teenagers? Wow.

Zip Yes.

Jean *Three* teenagers!

She sips her tea.

Zip Oh, yes. Ha ha ha ha. But you – (*Sips his tea.*) You've got the black husband!

Jean *sort of chokes on her tea.*

Zip Are you –

Jean (*clearing her throat, awkwardly*) No, no, no it's fine. It just went down the wrong way. (*Clears her throat more.*) Um. Yes. I do. I've got him. (*Recovering*) Ugh, you know, sometimes I just forget.

Zip (*skeptical*) You forget?

Jean (*self-conscious*) Yeah. Well, I mean, I don't forget. I just don't necessarily walk around being like, you know, 'Woohoo,

*balance of owning your race and your social role...
parallels "An octoroon" when Jenkins talks about
his role as a black playwright* Scene Five   245
and how he doesn't know what that means... is it

I have a black husband!' (*Small beat.*) It's more like . . . I have a *~~a quality~~* husband who happens to be black.

Beat.

Zip   Oh. Is there a difference?

Jean   Uh, you know. Like, he's my husband. But he's also black.

Zip (*confused, skeptical, but polite*)   Oh . . . okay . . .

Awkward lull. **Jean** *starts to say something before* **Zip** *interrupts.*

Zip   Well, I should really be getting back to unpacking that U-haul out front, but I hope we can do this again!

Jean   Oh, definitely!

Zip (*kind of just blurting it out*)   So glad to see I'm not the only lonely nobody in this neighborhood.

Jean   Absolu – I'm sorry, what?

Zip   I'm – Excuse me, I mean – was I – ? (*Failed recovery.*) I just meant you talk a lot – I mean – It's a sign of depression – I mean – (*Pause, in which they stare, then.*) All right, I'm gonna go! Have a good day!

Zip *exits.* **Jean** *just sort of stands there dazed for a second. She looks at the jar of pickled pig feet and intestines on her counter. Maybe she sees herself in the glass's reflection. She puts them somewhere. Lights change and immediately:*

parallels jars of body parts in the play "Appropriate"

ZIP COON'S INTERLUDE

Music plays. **Zip** *is there, arms filled with musical instruments – a tuba, a violin, a viola, a trumpet, a bugle, a tambourine, a banjo – just a ton of instruments. He has so many that for every step he takes, he drops one and has to bend over to grab it, and every time he bends over to pick up an instrument and takes another step, his pants – which are ill-fitting and held up by a rope – fall down, lower and lower, so he has to continually stop and hike up his pants in between picking up the instruments that keep falling; but the lower his pants are, the harder* parallels the struggle of the black community? Ridicules stereotypes by perpetuating them to an extreme level?

246   Neighbors

it gets to hike them up without dropping something. Quickly, it gets to the point where his pants are around his ankles and he bends down to pick them up, but he drops everything. Pissed off, he takes the pants off, holds them in his hands, picks up all the instruments – just barely, because now he has his pants in his hands. But he manages, takes a couple of steps, and then it's his underwear that starts falling down. It gets to the point where it is around his ankles, and he's just flashing the goodies to the audience. He picks up his underwear, sniffs it for no reason, recoils, holds it, but now he has so much stuff in his hands he can't pick up all the instruments. He tries anyway and fails a few times. Eventually he looks at his buttocks, which are clenched tightly, and he looks at a bugle, which is one of his largest and most ungainly instruments, and then he looks at his buttocks and gets an idea. He walks over the horn, lowers himself over the horn, inserting the skinny part of the bugle into his anus, clenches, and picks it up. It looks like he might be a success, takes a few steps, but then it slips right out. It might be too heavy for his sphincter! He tries again, lowering himself even further, rolling his eyes in an odd mixture of pleasure and pain. He has it for a second, but then he drops it again.

He tries one more time, lowering himself on the horn even further, rolling his eyes even bigger in that crazy mixture of pleasure and pain that comes with a stimulated prostate. And it sticks! He is a success! Now that he has room enough for everything, **Zip** *bends over to collect his remaining belongings and walks proudly offstage with his clothes and his instruments and the bugle sticking out of his ass, swaying back and forth like a rooster's tail. At some point, as in the beginning, a deep amber light has come up, illuminating* **Richard**, *who stands in the window, looking on with utter disgust. Music keeps playing, but it's fading, fading, fading, until it fades into a weird bugle solo, reminiscent of passing gas, and immediately:*

Scene Six

The Pattersons' kitchen, later in the day. **Richard**, *home from work, is standing there, fuming and disgusted at the sight.* **Jean** *is handling dinner business. Faintly, at some point, a small shrieking is heard in the* *background that grows and grows and grows, coming closer and closer, over the following.*

Jean   Richard, stop being so nosey. Let those people move in. Finish your story.

Richard (*shaking off what he's seen*)   What? Oh, right, well, so, anyway, I'm standing up there. My blood pressure rising. I'm on the verge of being just like 'Fuck it!' and walking out and just – I don't know. But then, Jean – you'll like this part – I heard your voice. From this morning. 'Just be yourself,' you were saying. 'Just be yourself. Just be yourself.' And suddenly, the next thing I know, I'm . . . talking. I'm like lecturing, Jean. All these things are coming out of my mouth – smart things, like from the lizard part of my brain or something – and I'm just winging it, basically, and before I know it, the hour has just flown by and we've gone over by ten minutes and no one's moved and I can't explain it, but, there was this . . . this energy in the air. You could feel it. And that's when I actually look up and out over that sea of college students and guess who I see sitting all the way in the back of the auditorium?

Jean (*a little gasp*)   Rose?!

Richard   Rose.

Jean (*heartened*)   No! She came and sat in on your first lecture? Oh my God.

Richard   I know. I mean, this is the woman who made me want to be a professor. I remember the first lecture I ever saw her give and I was just – It was so surreal. And after I've dismissed everyone, she hobbles up to me in her crazy wig and she puts her arm on my shoulder and leans into me and she says –

The kitchen door flies open and **Melody** *enters, more like a whirlwind than ever before, and just shrieking, nonstop. She bursts in, shrieking. She stalks around the room, shrieking. It's like durational performance art or something, how much she's freaking out. Her parents just watch her, dumbfounded by the display. At some point, still shrieking, she opens up her backpack and angrily empties it onto the floor, making a mess.*

Jean / Melody!

Melody *stops shrieking and zeroes in on* **Richard**.

Melody I HATE YOU! MY LIFE IS OVER!

Richard / Melody –

Jean What?

Melody This douchemonster followed me into school!

Jean What?!

Richard I was trying to make sure / she was okay!

Melody He followed me into my first-period biology class
with this huge bitch of a teacher, Mrs. Chow, who clearly
already hates me because she's like a Tiger Lady and I'm late
on the first day of school, because I'm such a fat cow, so I'm a
slow walker, and I'm not even in my chair good when Dad
stalks in, doesn't even say anything, grabs me by my arm like
I'm some sort of prostitute, and yanks me out of the classroom
where he starts yelling at me, Mom, in the hallway with this
terrible echo so the whole school can just hear him screaming
about dropping me off and rape and crack and –

Jean Rich/ard!

Richard Melody, you are exagger –

Melody Do you understand what you've done, you freak?!
You have just ruined the entire rest of high school for me!
Everyone thinks I've been raped! And that I'm on crack! And
I can't go back to that place! I can't go back ever again, because
you are a monster and I hate you and if I could I would kill
you for doing this! I would kill you and then I would kill
myself!

She runs out. **Jean**, *dumbfounded and concerned, and* **Richard** *are
left alone.*

Richard There was some boy – I saw some boy threatening
her –

Jean What?!

Richard When I left for work today, I passed her at the end of the block and he was standing there, in her face, like this. (*Demonstrates on* **Jean**, *points.*) Pointing at her like she's – I don't know. Harassing her.

Jean Harassing her?

Richard Yes! Probably propositioning her with some lewd ghetto sex act.

[handwritten: history of the word "ghetto" (misuse) assumption that Jim is a rapist and a criminal just because he's black]

Jean Richard!

Richard I couldn't hear what he was saying, but Melody had this look on her face like she was afraid for her life before she just burst into a sprint. (*Forgetting who he's talking to, reliving it.*) And of course, you know, I snap into reverse and pull right up to this little country nigger and look him dead in the face, and the son of a bitch had the nerve to give me this little wave.

He imitates.

Jean (*fighting her incredulity*)   Richard, was this boy one of our new neighbors?

Richard Yes. I mean, I don't know. He had a bunch of boxes.

Jean Well, for your information, Richard, our new neighbors are . . . a professional family of . . . performers. They are not from the ghetto, or the country, or the – They've actually been on tour for the last few years. What is wrong / with you?

Beat.

Richard What? How do you know?

Jean Know what?

Richard That they're a 'professional family of – ' What?

Jean Oh. One of them came over today and introduced himself.

Richard   Which one?

Jean   His name is Zip.

Richard   Zip?

Jean   Yes, the one with the top hat. A very well-dressed, articulate, friendly man. He lives with his sister-in-law and her three kids. He recently lost his brother. We had tea.

Richard   You mean to tell me you let one of those people in this house? He drank my tea?

Jean   Yes, Richard. Is something wrong with that? With being neighborly?

Richard   What are you – Jean, do you know who lives on this block!?

Jean   How should I know? I've never / met them.

Richard   The Dean of Faculty. And around the corner? The Academic Provost.

Jean   So?

Richard   So Jean, do you have any idea how close we are? Haven't I been busting my ass trying to publish as much as possible these past three years? My dissertation is finally about to go to press, I am struggling to make a good impression, and things are just finally starting to line up for us. They are just starting to pay off! And I just cannot – I will not stand to have a bunch of . . . bumpkins move in and fuck up my flow, okay? I'm too old to go through this again! I'm tired!

Jean   How, Richard? How are they going to 'fuck up your flow'?

Richard   People, Jean – People will see them and . . . think we're related!

Jean   What?

Richard   They're going to look at them and they're going to look at us and they're going to compare us.

Jean How are they going to compare us?!

Richard Jean, they just will! They just will!

Jean Listen. These new neighbors – I mean, they're – they're certainly a . . . you know, they're different, obviously. They're not, you know, they don't look like . . . you know, but different is good. Different is good for this stupid neighborhood. I would think you would be excited we weren't the only new faces. I mean, we weren't invited to a single barbecue all summer. And I know they're having barbecues, Richard! I can smell them! No one has paid us a single visit once! No one even says hi in the supermarket! I don't think I've even gotten so much as a phone call from a telemarketer. The only person who calls here is you!

[handwritten margin note: why won't she say "black"? Taboo?]

Richard Jean, this is exactly my point.

Jean What?

Richard These people are just not used to us. Okay? They've only been around each other for like a hundred years and they're old and wh . . . they're territorial and they just have to know that we are safe first and then they come. Then they will accept us, okay? But they will not accept us if they see us cavorting with . . . with . . .

Jean Black people?

Richard Jean, what?!

Jean I mean – I don't know!

Richard What are you – Jean, I'm black!

Jean I know, but you were calling them . . . calling them . . . n-words . . .

Richard Jean, no, I wasn't . . .

Jean You – you did. You just called the boy an 'n-word'. (*Beat.*) I heard you. And you called them that this morning.

Pause, in which they consider each other.

hard (*guiltily but defiant*)   And . . . ?

Jean (*flustered*)   And, well, I don't . . . I don't / really know.

Richard   I'm allowed to do that sometimes. I mean, so are you, if you really want.

Jean   I just – I just don't understand.

Richard (*annoyed*)   Well, Jean, I don't know how I can help you understand! You just leave it alone, please. Leave them alone. Now I have work to do, if you don't mind.

Beat, as **Richard** *goes back to work.* **Jean** *meanders back to the stove, but she's clearly preoccupied with other thoughts. Eventually* **Jean** *speaks up.*

Jean   <u>Do you see me as your white wife?</u> Or do you see me as your wife who happens to be white?

Richard (*after a beat, stopping work*)   Jean, where did that just come from?

Jean   Answer the question.

Richard (*putting down the pen, with a sigh*)   Well, is this a stupid question or a question that happens to be stupid?

Jean   Excuse me?

Richard   Jean, why you would want to reduce us to – to – I don't know – to wordplay? Don't you think we're beyond this? (*A teaching moment.*) Do you look at a green apple and think, is that a green apple or an apple that happens to be green?

Jean   So you do think of me as your white wife?!

Richard   No, that's not what I'm saying!

Jean   What are you saying?

Richard   I'm saying a green apple and a red apple are both apples but they aren't the same thing!

Jean   Why not?

[handwritten margin note:] Again, the theme of being both a me of a specific culture, and a person, society – why can't one be both sea

Richard   Because it's just not the same fucking apple, damn it, it tastes different! (*Beat, calms down.*) I don't think of you as either of those things. I look at you and I see you, my wife. Isn't that enough?

Jean   But would you agree I'm white?

Richard   Well, yes, Jean, unless there's something you're not telling me.

Jean   Okay . . . so . . . like . . . where . . . does that . . . come into the equation?

Richard   What?

Jean   Like . . . where do you . . . like . . . see that . . . when you look at me?

Richard (*incredulous*)   'Where do I see that you're white when I look at you?'

Jean *nods. A hella long beat.*

Jean   Well?

Richard *stands up and starts gathering his things.*

Jean   Wha – where are you going?

Richard   I'm going upstairs.

Jean   Why?

Richard   Because I can't focus down here.

Jean   Why not?

Richard (*calmly*)   You know, I think you're right: all this time you're spending at home all day is really taking its toll. I think you need to get a job. I know you've been having a hard time finding something that suits you, but I think you just need to get a job, any job. Take what you can get, whatever you can get, even if you have to volunteer or something, because this is . . . a little . . . embarrassing and I just think you need something to occupy yourself with.

Richard *exits, leaving* **Jean** *alone. She just stands there a while. She goes to pick up her daughter's things, puts them back in the backpack, but there's something sad about it. Is this her job? Lights change and immediately:*

Scene Seven

The Crow family's living room. **Jim** *is at the piano, poking around. His voice is all right, but also not great. A light illuminates the window and* **Melody** *is there. She is smoking a cigarette, watching him.*

Jim (*voice cracking on the last 'Crow'*)
   Come listen all you gals and guys, I'm just from Tuckyhoe;
   I'm gwine to sing a little song, my name's Jim Crow.

(*Not singing, frustrated.*) Ugh! I hate this. (*Singing, trying to hit the note.*) Crow.

Melody (*startling him*)   Boo! (*A snicker.*) What were you just singing?

Jim   Nothing.

Melody (*after a beat, exiting the window*)   Come outside.

He exits through the side door. Lights go down on his home. Lights up on the lawn between the two homes. They assess each other.

Melody   You want a cigarette?

Jim   No thanks.

Melody   Have one.

Jim   No thanks.

Melody   Come on!

Jim   I'm cool. How was school?

Melody   Ugh, it was my asshole.

Jim   Uh . . . what?

Melody   It was the worst.

Jim   Oh. Why?

Melody   I don't want to talk about it. But, just FYI, my dad thinks you're trying to rape me.

Jim   What?

Melody   I mean you were really aggressive with that eyelash.

Jim   I'm sorry – I – uh –

Beat.

Melody (*dropping some act*)   I'm kidding. It was a frickin' eyelash. My father is just an asshole. (*Beat.*) Is your father an asshole?

Jim   Uh, well, my dad is dead.

Melody   Oh! I'm so sorry.

Jim   It's fine. (*Beat, politely changing subject.*) So did your wish come true, or . . . ?

Melody   What? Oh. No. Of course not.

Jim   What did you wish for?

Melody   I can't tell you that!

Jim   Why not?

Melody   Because then it will never come true.

Jim (*surprisingly suave*)   Well, if you tell me, maybe I can make it come true.

Melody (*saccharine rebuff*)   Awww. A cornball! (*Sees his insecurity, offers a cigarette.*) You sure you don't want one?

Jim   No. Smoking's bad for you.

Melody *lights a new one.*

Melody   Not if you quit before you turn twenty-six. (*Exhaling*) Anyway, we just moved here, too.

Jim   Oh yeah? How do you like it?

Melody   Ugh, I hate it. I'm a Cali girl. This place is for the birds. There's nothing to do here.

Jim   Nothing?

Melody   Well, I mean, there's like hiking trails and shit, if you're the kind of moron who likes to hike.

Jim   Uh-huh . . .

Melody   And there's a Whole Foods.

Jim (*rapt*)   Uh-huh . . .

Melody (*noticing how strung along he is*)   And a playground, over by the hiking trail.

Jim   Uh-huh.

Melody   And sometimes, I'll hang out there long enough and this guy will drive up in a BMW and offer me twenty bucks to get in the car with him.

Jim   Wow. Twenty dollars just for that?

Melody   Well, I mean, that and a blowjob.

Jim   A what?

Melody   A blowjob. I suck his dick? I put his penis into my mouth and move it around until –

Jim   Oh my God, Melody. That's called a what?

Melody   A blowjob. And then, of course, if I feel like it, I like let him have sex with me. But I'm still a virgin, so I only let him put it in my butt . . . (*Pause, dropping another act.*) Oh my God, I'm totally kidding.

Jim   So that doesn't really happen?

Melody   Of course not! God, your sense of humor is like so off!

Jim   You're really crazy – and a good liar. You could be an actress.

Melody   Ugh, please. Not with this fugly face.

Jim   Oh, stop, you know you're very pretty.

Melody (*no one's ever said anything like this to her before*)   I'm not pretty.

Jim   Uh, yes you are. You're super-pretty. Shut up.

Pause. Check.

Melody   Well, you are like this huge corn machine. It's like you open your mouth and all this corn falls out. (*Beat, in which she studies him.*) Have you ever kissed a girl before?

Jim   No. Have you?

Melody   Yes.

She kisses him suddenly. He is at first completely taken off-guard and very uncomfortable, but eventually he relaxes into it. It's sweet. It's electric. It's a first kiss. They eventually disengage each other and share a slightly giddy pause.

Melody (*playing it off*)   All right. I'm going to go back inside now.

Jim   Okay. Uh, I hope you have a better day at school tomorrow.

Melody   I'm not going to school tomorrow.

Jim   Don't you have to?

Melody   Not if I don't want to. So watch out. (*Turning to exit, she stops herself.*) Hey, wait, did you write that song?

Jim   What song?

Melody   'Come listen all you – '

Jim   Oh. No, no, no. It's a song my dad used to sing.

Melody (*touched*)   Aww. Well, you got a decent voice.

Jim   Shut up.

Melody   No, you shut up. (*Beat, smiling.*) Good night.

Jim *waves awkwardly as she carefully sneaks back inside the house. He stands at his door, watching her, before he starts to go back inside. A small blackout, in which a screeching starts.*

Scene Eight

The Pattersons' kitchen the next morning. **Jean** *sits at the table alone, to the soundtrack of* **Melody***'s distant screeching again, to which* **Jean** *now seems immune. She is frantically searching through some poetry books for the poem. The screeching gets closer and closer and closer and closer until here's* **Melody***, walking in, trying to make a scene/pick a fight.* **Jean** *ignores her all the way to the door, when* **Melody***, confused, stops.*

Melody   I'm going to school!

Jean   Good. I'm proud of you.

Melody   What?

Jean   For being a bigger person. Your father is under a lot of stress and sometimes when your father is under a lot of stress he can be . . . insensitive and unthinking. But it's important for us to be patient with him and remember that he . . . at the end of the day, he does these things – these crazy, sometimes hurtful things – because he loves us and – and we just have to let him – have that, because love can be very difficult to express sometimes.

Melody   Whatever. He's an asshole.

Jean   No, he's not.

Melody   Yes he is, Mom. That is the definition of an asshole!

Jean   Daddy saw some boy bothering you.

Melody   Bothering me?! He was taking an eyelash off my face.

Jean   An eyelash?

Melody   Yes! An eyelash! See? He sucks. (*Beat.*) Where is that asshole anyway?

Jean   He – I don't know where your father is.

Melody   You don't know?

Jean   I woke up and he was already gone. I'm assuming he went to work.

Melody   What's wrong?

Jean   Nothing's wrong.

Melody   You seem upset.

Jean   I'm not. I just didn't sleep well.

Melody   Why not?

Jean   Melody, do we need to talk about boys?

Melody   What? No! I'm going to school!

Jean   Okay, be careful.

Melody (*starts to exit then stops*)   What are you going to do?

Jean   Um . . . a lot of stuff. I have to go to Whole Foods. I'm looking for a job.

Melody   Good.

Melody *exits.*

Jean   Wait, what?

Lights change and immediately:

Scene Nine

The Crow family's living room. Different members of the family are running in and out and about, preparing for rehearsal, except for **Jim**. **Topsy** *walks around, doing weird vocal warm-ups.* **Zip** *is at the piano tinkering around, doing scales.* **Sambo** *is going over music, doing push-ups, maybe picking his 'fro.* **Mammy** *is running around tweaking* *people's costuming or something. Suddenly the doorbell chimes to the tune of 'Dixie'. Everyone sort of stops what they're doing and looks around. They all seem mildly terrified.*

Mammy   What the hell was that?

Zip   The doorbell? You'se expecting company?

The doorbell chimes again. Everyone drops.

Mammy   Sambo, get the do'.

Sambo*'s too scared.* **Topsy** *rolls her eyes.*

Topsy   I'll gets it.

Sambo   No. I'll gets it!

They both scuffle a bit, each trying to get to the door first. They eventually open it. **Melody** *is standing there. She is kind of shocked, kind of.*

Melody   Um, hi.

Sambo   Damn, shorty. Who is you?

Melody   I, um, live next door.

Topsy   Ohhh. It's Jim's new galfriend!

Sambo *takes* **Melody***'s hand and kisses it.*

Sambo   Jim? What'cho fine self comin' ova heah lookin' fo' that chump nigga fo' when you got Sambo Crow at yo' service, gurl.

Mammy *pushes past* **Topsy** *and* **Sambo***, making her way to the door.*

Mammy   Chile, hush. (*To* **Melody**.) Well, lookit che'ah at this purty thang.

She ushers **Melody** *in.* **Jim** *has just returned from the bathroom. He freezes on the stairs.*

Zip   You must be Melody, right? Y'all, this is the neighbors' daughter.

Mammy   Ooooh! Jimmy said you was purty, but he ain't tell us we was livin' next do' to no byurty quane!

Jim *rushes past* **Mammy** *toward* **Melody** *– or tries to, but you don't rush past* **Mammy***.*

Jim (*embarrassed*)   Mammy! I never said –

He tries to rescue **Melody***.*

Mammy (*loud whisper*)   Boy, shut up. I'm tryna help you out.

Jim   Excuse us!

He takes **Melody** *into a corner, the entire family watching.*

Jim   I'm so sorry! My family is so embarrassing –

Melody   No, I'm sorry. I don't know why I thought you'd be the only / one home.

Jim   Wait, shouldn't you be at school?

Mammy   I don't mean to intuhrupt you two, but Jimmy has a rehearsal should be warming up fo'!

Melody   Warming up? I thought you were just a stage manager?

Mammy   Ackchally, Jimmy Jr. here just joint the act.

Jim   Mammy!

Melody   He did?

Mammy   He taking ova fo' his dead daddy. Is you coming to see the show?

Melody   Show? I didn't know you had a show coming up!

Mammy   Yes. It's our big comeback.

Jim   This is a nightmare.

Mammy   You mean to tells me Jim Crow ain't invited you?

Jim   I am in a nightmare.

Melody   I guess not.

Sambo   Nigga! Why ain't you invited her? (*Basically to* **Melody**.) Don't you know a purty girl always attracks in a crowd.

Jim   Okay, can we just stop please! Can we stop!

Melody   Jim, it's fine. Look, I'll go –

Jim   I'm sorry –

Mammy *takes* **Melody** *by the arm and sits her down.*

Mammy   Naw, naw, chile. You ain't got to go nowhere! We ain't got no closed rehearsals. Sit yo' skinny little behind down. Please. It's been so long since we've had an urdience. You'd be doin' us a flavor. (*Beat.*) Girl, you know, you so purty, you could be an actress.

She winks at **Jim***, who, in return, dies a little on the inside.*

Melody   Jim said the same / thing . . .

Mammy   Well, that's cuz Jimmy Jr.'s got good taste! And, besides, this is his big debutt! Maybe you'll inspire him? What's da word fuh dat, Zip? Moose? You can be his moose.

Zip   'Muse', Mammy.

Mammy   Whateva. (*Rallying the troops.*) All right, y'all, warm-up is ova!

Everyone gathers around the piano, except for **Jim***, who is just standing there in his stage-manager outfit, staring at the scene, shaking.*

Mammy   Come on, Jim.

Sambo   Come on, nigga! Shit! We'se only doin' dis fa' you.

Topsy   Yeah. We knows ourn lines.

Long pause, in which **Jim** *does not move. For a minute, it looks like he might kill everyone and run away to Alaska and live out the rest of his life canning fish or something.*

Melody (*enjoying seeing* **Jim** *like this*)   Go on, Jim.

At her encouragement, **Jim** *kind of shuffles over to the piano.*

Mammy *notices this.*

Mammy   All right, now, we all just gonna skip the overture
and go rite to da top of Scene One, from the group song.
Topsy, you wanna cue us in?

Topsy   Yes, Mammy. (*'Acting.'*) 'Whew! I thought massa
would neva leave! Everybody can come out now!'

*The playing begins. It is a rearrangement of 'We Are Family' by Sister
Sledge that feels like a jazzy Broadway number, slowed down at first and
building.*

Zip
Ev'ryone can see we're together
As we walk on by

Topsy   Fly.

Sambo
And we fly just like birds of a feather
I won't tell no lie

Topsy   All.

Jim (*terrible, meek, embarrassed*)
All of the people around us they say
Can they be that close

Mammy
Just let me state for the record
We're giving love in a family dose

*Music swells and suddenly everyone is having an incredibly fun time –
except for **Jim**, of course – doing the 'bump', etc. **Melody**'s also kind
of into it. **Jim** continues to want to die.*

Everyone
We are family!
I got all my niggas with me!
We are family!

Topsy
Living life is fun and we've just begun
To get our share of the world's delights.

Everyone   HIGH!

Sambo
High hopes we have for the future
And our goal's in sight!

Everyone   WE!

Jim *is supposed to sing his verse here, but misses it and it fucks up everyone's energy. Everyone looks at him.* **Mammy** *feeds him his line. He is fuming, maybe shaking.* **Zip** *picks up on his cue.*

Zip
Have faith in you and the things you do,
You won't go wrong. This is our fam'ly –

Jim (*throwing the sheet music to the floor*)   STOP!!!

Everything comes to a screeching halt, and everyone watches him.

Mammy   / Jimmy.

Melody   Jim.

Jim   MAMMY, WHY ARE YOU DOING THIS TO ME? I ALREADY TOLD YOU I CAN'T DO THIS! I CAN'T DO THIS AND I DON'T WANT TO! I DON'T WANT TO! I CAN'T!

There is a very long, very awkward pause, in which **Mammy** *starts breathing heavy, slowly raising her trembling slapping hand, and then suddenly takes off after* **Jim**. *It becomes a crazy commotion –* **Mammy** *swatting at the air most recently vacated by a fleeing* **Jim** *with attendant sound effects,* **Zip** *maybe providing some sort of chase-scene underscoring,* **Sambo** *and* **Topsy** *looking on, maybe shrieking and catcalling, while* **Melody** *just sits there taking the whole scene in. It's like a whole thing. Eventually,* **Jim** *somehow makes it out the front door and flees. Things get quiet.* **Zip** *is at the piano, minding his business.* **Topsy** *and* **Sambo** *are sort of giddy.* **Mammy** *is out of breath.*

Eventually, everyone sort of remembers **Melody** *is there and turns to look at her. A beat.*

[handwritten marginal note:] reoccuring theme that you are supposed to act / be / live within the confines of your culture, and if you don't, you are punished (Mammy's slap)

Mammy   I'm sorry you had to see that.

Melody   Uh, I'm sorry. I think that was probably my fault.

Topsy (*under her breath*)   Oh you thank!?

Mammy   Aw, naw, Jimmy Jr.'s just a nervous person. But maybe it was too urly for an urdience. (*To* **Zip**.) Now what are we gonna do?

Melody   Maybe I could go calm him down. I could try to bring him back. It's the least I could do.

Topsy *sucks her teeth, audibly.*

Mammy   Aww, baby, that's sweet. He does seem to listen to you. Why don't you do that?

Melody   Okay.

Mammy   But take your time. He only need to come back when he good and ready. I'm not gon' have all that negative energy fuckin' wit our shit.

Melody   OK . . . (*To everyone.*) That was totally great, you guys!

Mammy   Thank you, baby.

Melody *smiles at this and exits.*

Mammy   All right, y'all, well, I guess rehearsal's over. Come on, Zip.

Topsy *sucks her teeth, exiting with a tantrum.*

Topsy   Ugh! This is unprofeshanulllll-uh!

Sambo   Mammy –

Mammy   What, boy?

Sambo   How come you ain't ask me to sing Daddy's song?

Mammy   Is yo' name Jim Crow?

Sambo   No . . .

Mammy   Okay, then. Now mow the damn lawn like I ast you!

She walks away from **Sambo**, *exits with* **Zip**.

Sambo (*confused – wait, what are the rules?*)   Wait. What?

He stands there and looks around sadly. He looks at his daddy's ashes, crosses his arms, and pouts. Poor **Sambo**. *Lights change and immediately:*

Scene Ten

The Pattersons' kitchen. **Jean** *stares into space, thinking. The book of Yeats's poems is probably somewhere within arm's reach, but it's not open.* **Zip** *knocks on the door, snapping her out of reverie. She answers. It's a little tense.*

Zip   / Hi

Jean   Oh, hi! / How is –

Zip   I just wanted –

Jean   I'm / sorry –

Zip   No –

Jean   Go ahead –

Zip   What / were you –

Jean   Go ahead.

Zip   I wanted to come over and apologize for yesterday. I didn't mean for it to end on such an awkward note, calling you a lonely nobody –

Jean   Oh, Zip – / Don't –

Zip   – Saying you talk too mu – No, no. It was just rude and I've just been feeling completely terrible about it all day and I'm sorry – I'm so sorry.

Beat.

Jean Zip, it's fine. I mean, I do talk a lot –

Zip No! That's not what I – I meant you just talk like you've got nobody to talk to. I mean, I know that feeling – how it all comes flooding out. I mean, 'a lonely nobody'? Listen to me. It takes one to know one, right? Or maybe not – I mean, you have such – your eyes. They're – I thought I saw something in them. Something that needed a friend, needed talking to. But maybe I just saw myself. *(Beat.)* Anyway, I hope you accept my apology.

Jean *(a little stunned)* Well – yes – I mean, yes, of course I accept your apology!

Zip Really? Because I really want us to be friends.

Jean Friends?

Zip Yes. Is that – Is that weird?

Jean No, no, no. Of course – Ack, this is so awkward! No!

*Beat, as **Zip** takes in **Jean**'s bashful reaction.*

Zip Yay!

Do they jump up and down a little bit?

Okay. Now, you go.

Jean What?

Zip What were you going to –

Jean Oh, I was going to ask you how the move was going! Wait, do you want some tea or something?

Zip Well, I guess I have a little time to kill.

Jean Great!

***Zip** enters, sitting down.*

Zip Moving's done. Now it's just the show.

Jean Show? What show?

Zip   I forgot to tell you! We booked a show in town. A comeback show. A little coming out as suburbanites, so to speak. You'll have to come.

Jean   Oh, I'd love to! When is it?

Zip   It starts tomorrow.

Jean   Oh my God, that's tomorrow!

Zip   It is. Are you free?

Jean   I think so. Let me check with my husband.

Zip   Yes, please check with him. Worst-case scenario, you can come without him, right?

Jean (*a little uneasy?*)   Right.

Zip   I'll leave the comps under your name.

Jean   Oh, you don't have to do that.

Zip   Oh, please, girl. It's what neighbors do.

Jean   Well, you'll have to let me return the favor.

Zip (*slightly naughty*)   Oh, we'll figure something out. (*Super-weird beat.*) Actually, you know, I have an idea. Your poetry. I'm dying to read it. That sounds like a fair trade.

Jean   Uh . . .

Zip   Oh, don't be shy.

Jean   It's not that I'm shy – I just haven't written anything new in years.

Zip   So something old. I don't care. You must have something.

Jean   Yes, but, I –

Zip   Great. Then go get it. I'm not leaving here empty-handed.

Jean   Uh –

Theme of giving up something you love for the sake of the family's needs and confines of a culture (Jim not going to school and Jean choosing not to write)

Zip   Girl, you better go!

Jean *exits, running.* **Zip** *just kind of sits there, waiting, sipping his tea. Maybe he waves at somebody in the audience. I don't know.*

At some point the phone begins ringing. A small change takes place.

Zip (*shouting*)   Do you want me to get that?

Jean (*offstage*)   What?

Zip (*shouting*)   The phone! Do you want me to get it?

Jean (*offstage*)   Ugh, no, it's Richard. Let it go to voicemail!

The phone stops ringing. **Jean** *returns with a bunch of loose pieces of paper in her hand. She is out of breath. She puts the papers down on the table in front of* **Zip**.

Jean   Uh, this is my thesis?

Zip   What a treat! (*Reading the title.*) 'The Spirit Rapist: a Sonnet Cycle.'

Jean (*humiliated*)   I know. I don't know what I was thinking with that title. I was young.

Zip   How young?

Jean   I, jeez – how old is my daughter? Fifteen? I wrote this right after she was born. So I was twenty-three? Twenty-four? No, twenty-three.

Zip   Oh wow. And when did you marry Richard?

Jean   Twenty-four.

Zip (*doing the math*)   Oh?

Jean   Ha. Yeah.

Beat.

Zip   And how was that?

Jean   How was what?

Zip   Having a baby so –

Jean   Oh! It was totally fine. Psh. It was great. I mean, honestly, the wedding was more dramatic than the baby. Our parents were – I mean, they could have been worse, but – you know – they were reluctant. But then they came anyway and we had this beautiful ceremony on the Bay – we were in San Francisco at this point – and I remember gazing out over this crowd of all these faces, all of our friends, and seeing our parents' faces and you could see they were moved, too. They felt something. Our marriage meant something, you know. It meant something.

Beat.

Zip   Because he was black?

Jean (*taken off-guard*)   What? No!

Zip   Oh, / I'm sorry, I –

Jean   I mean, not really. Not exactly, or – (*Beat of awkward, recovering, bravely.*) Did I miss like a memo or something? Is there suddenly something wrong with thinking of someone as your husband first and then as a . . . member of their . . . race second?

Beat.

Zip   Well, Jean, that's a complicated question. I mean, I don't think so, but I also don't know what difference that makes? I mean, it's not like one day he's going to wake up and be your husband and not be black? If anything, one day he could wake up black and not be your husband, am I right? But that's a whole other conversation and certainly not something we're going to begin to answer right now, in your kitchen, over tea.

Jean (*lightly*)   Oh, of course!

Zip (*jovial*)   I mean, it's not like you have some sort of a thing for black men, right?

Jean (*laughing*)   Of course not!

[handwritten in margin: Challenge of being seamlessly a part of a culture and a member of society]

Zip (*deadly serious*)   Are you sure?

Jean *stops laughing.*

Zip (*then brightly*)   Girl, I'm just kidding.

They laugh together.

Jean   Ha ha ha ha. Yes, because, you know, it's not like Richard's really black.

Zip (*stops laughing*)   What?

Jean (*stops laughing, too*)   I mean, it's not like – ! He's not, like, you know – ! He's, you know, he's like – different! I mean, he's just very – like, even at Dartmouth, he was very different. Very strange, I mean – He was the – he was this big geeky Classics-major-debate-society-philosopher man. And he was a poet for a short while, too, you know – a much better poet than me.

It's how we met – in a poetry class, three times a week. And we even started this poetry slam spoken word society in this little coffeehouse on campus and he was – he was such an amazing performer. He had the most interesting point of view. His thoughts – they always felt so . . . dense and so new. He had all these feelings. It was so inspiring, his energy. He just felt very different to me, very unique.

Beat.

Zip   Then what happened?

Jean   What do you mean?

Zip   Girl, you just said all that in the past tense.

Jean   Oh! It was a different time. He was just feeding off the times. Things seemed to be changing. They were changing. I guess they changed.

Beat.

Zip   Wait, I just got a crazy idea.

[handwritten margin note:] classism within the heirarchy of racism – Richard isn't like "the other black people"

Jean What?

Zip Do you have a minute?

Jean Yes. Why?

Zip I want to hear you read.

Jean What?

Zip Your poetry. Come on, girl. It'll be fun! Let's go back in time! I wanna meet Miss Wildchild California Coffeehouse Poetess. (*Delivered like a choreopoem.*) I wanna see Jean / from Fifteen / Years ago / That Mr. Classics Professor got to know.

Jean Hahah, oh, no. I'm afraid you're mistaken. I wasn't some sort of – I was actually really quite shy. I mean, if anyone was the wild one, it was Richard.

Zip Then we'll deal with him when he gets here. But now I want to hear you read. Wait – (*Closes his eyes.*) Okay, go ahead. I'm ready.

Beat, as **Jean** *decides to go for it.*

Jean (*transforming*) Uh – This is the title-poem. 'The Spirit Rapist.' (*Clears her throat and begins.*) 'Dear Daddy, it's me – '

Lights change and immediately:

SAMBO'S INTERLUDE

Tribal drumming music plays and, finally, **Sambo** *comes outside with the goddamned lawnmower – a Turf Tiger 3000. He fills the lawnmower with gas. He tries over and over to start it, scratching his head like an ape when he can't figure it out. He eventually starts it. It runs for a second before stopping again. He starts it again. It runs again and stops. He starts it a third time, more comically than before, and the lawnmower runs. He tries to get behind it, but the lawnmower swivels out of his grasp. He reaches again, and it swivels out of his grasp.* **Sambo** *starts whistling and pretends to ignore the running lawnmower. Suddenly, he dives for it, but the lawnmower skids away to the other side*

(handwritten in margin:) Paralleling black people to animals, savages

of the stage. **Sambo** *begins to chase after it, lifting his knees high into the air. He chases it offstage. There is a weird crash.* **Sambo** *re-enters, being chased by the lawnmower. He exits, he re-enters, still being chased, over and over, until eventually the lawnmower steps out of the chase, waits for* **Sambo** *who still runs, ignorant to the fact he isn't being chased. The lawnmower, at the right moment, grabs him and sucks off his entire grass skirt before running offstage.* **Sambo** *stands in the middle of the stage, completely naked, holding his privates. He blushes to the audience. He sees someone in the audience. He waves, moving one of his hands, and this enormous firehose-esque phallus unravels from his groin and offstage.* **Sambo** *blushes again, tries to pull it back, but it's stuck on something.* **Sambo** *works hard to pull his penis back and whatever object it is stuck on. When he finally gets it back onstage, he realizes that it's roped a watermelon.* **Sambo** *preens. He goes up to the watermelon, tries to untie his penis from around the watermelon. He fails at the knot. Frustrated, he pouts for a bit before he gets an idea and then proceeds to chew through the shaft of his penis.*

With half of a penis and a watermelon, he is a success. He poses, pats himself on the back, preens. Then he licks his lips, looks around, to make sure no one is looking at him. He looks at the watermelon. He looks at his half of a firehose penis, which is now, I guess, the size of a semi-normal penis, and he gets an idea. He pokes a hole in the watermelon, and then inserts his penis into the watermelon, and proceeds to make wild, passionate, savage love with the watermelon. He ejaculates. He pulls out. He's exhausted, doesn't know what to do. He looks around again, to make sure no one's looking, before he breaks the watermelon over his knee. He starts eating it hungrily. He smiles the biggest smile he can at the audience. His face is dripping with watermelon juice and maybe semen, but that might be too much. Like in the first scene, the window is illuminated slowly by the stark amber light, revealing **Jean**, *who now stands in* **Richard**'*s place, with a look on her face like, 'Uhmmm.' The living lawnmower comes back onstage. The music stops. It chases* **Sambo** *offstage. Lights change, and immediately:*

What... Could this possibly be a ridiculing of a stereotype through the perpetration (self-deprecation) of it with shock value?

Scene Eleven

The Pattersons' kitchen. **Jean** *stands at the window, looking shocked and worried and aroused and compliant and distant.* **Zip** *is gone, but her thesis remains, as well as more books of poetry.* **Richard** *enters from the living room, carrying his briefcase, etc. He's just come from work.*

Richard (*sees* **Jean** *at the window, stops*) Jean?

Jean (*startled*) Richard.

They study each other across the room for a moment and the chemistry in the room seems to shift, as **Jean** *remembers that they are technically still fighting. Everything is a little passive-aggressive.*

Jean You left early this morning.

Richard (*half-covering*) Rose said it's better to have office hours as early as possible. That way you avoid all the slackers looking for excuses and extensions who can't get up before twelve.

Jean Uh-huh . . .

Richard (*trying to make conversation*) Though what she didn't tell me is that instead you get the over-achievers and there's nothing worse than over-achieving Classics students. A bunch of brainiac, contradictory punks. That's one thing that hasn't changed since college. Some nerdy kid came in today actually wanting to have a debate with me about comedy – or tragicomedy – whatever that is. I was like, 'Do you realize that you're taking a class on tragedy?' It's like, I don't have time for this. I think they come in because they have no one else to talk to – these kids. Lonely, pathetic – (*She's unimpressed.*) Did I tell you I'm reworking on my lecture for tomorrow? You inspired me to – I'm gonna abandon Rose's notes and just do my own thing from now on.

Jean (*icy*) Great.

Beat.

Richard   What's for dinner?

Jean   Oh God, dinner! Oh God, what time is it?

Richard   It's six.

Jean   Oh God. I forgot to go to Whole Foods. How is it six already?

She scrambles through the cabinets.

Richard   What have you been doing all day?

Jean (*agitated with guilt, aggressive*)   Nothing. What have you been doing all day?

They study each other across the kitchen.

Richard (*a concession, guiltily*)   Are we still fighting?

Jean   I don't know. Am I still embarrassing you?

Richard   Listen, Jean. I have been thinking a lot about last night. You're right. I didn't have to follow Melody into school, but you know I've been under a lot of stress and I saw that boy messing with her and I was already under a lot of stress and, you know me, I just freaked out, and I overreacted but I promise it was coming from a place of love and protection for my – for our daughter – and I hope that means something. I mean, isn't everything that's happening now happening for her anyway? Aren't we here for her?

Jean   The boy was removing an eyelash from her face.

Richard   What?

Jean   I asked Melody what happened this morning and she said the boy from next door was just removing an eyelash from our daughter's face. He wasn't harassing her.

Richard   Jean, he was still a stranger touching our daughter. I'm supposed to go around letting anybody just start feeling on our daughter's face? Are you out of your / mind?

Jean   She didn't seem upset. She –

Richard   She's fifteen years old. She didn't know what was going on. I know what I saw.

Jean   And how do you know what you saw is what you saw?

Richard   Because I know, Jean! I know these people. And you don't! I grew up around some of these people!

Jean   Well, I want to get to know them!

Richard (*exasperated*)   Why, Jean?! Why?!

Jean   Because – they're our neighbors?

Richard   Jean, since when has physical proximity ever meant we gotta get to know somebody?! Think of how many people you stand next to on a given day in the supermarket or – And, of all the goddamn people in this neighborhood, why do you have to get to know them?! Why them, dammit!?

Jean   Because.

Richard   Because what, Jean? Because what?

Jean   Because they . . .

Richard   Okay, see, Jean? You don't know what you're talking about so just stop – just stop right there. Please. Just stop.

Beat.

Jean   Do you think I talk too much?

Richard (*genuinely confused by her behavior*)   Jean, what is this?

Jean   Do I?

Richard (*a little off-the-cuff*)   I don't know. Sometimes?

Jean *is hurt.*

Richard   What? I still love you?

Jean   Am I a lonely nobody?

Beat.

Richard (*not getting it at all*)   I don't know . . . ? Are you?

No answer. He sees the table.

What is all this? How am I supposed to work here?

Jean (*collecting the papers*)   It's my poetry.

Richard (*with distaste, but hiding vulnerability*)   Your poetry? You're writing poetry again?

Jean   It's my thesis. I was reading my thesis.

Richard   Instead of looking for a job? What a life. I wish I could sit around all day doing that.

Jean (*pointed*)   Actually, our neighbor came over today and asked to read it.

Richard   What? (*Beat, sees the two teacups, turns one around, revealing red smears.*) You mean you let that man back in the house, after I – Wait, you mean, while I've been trapped in my office all day doing actual work, you've been sitting up in my kitchen having Def Poetry Jam with another man?!

Jean   He was interested. He asked because he was interested! In us!

Richard   Oh. Oh, shit. Okay, wow. This ⟨nigger⟩ is just coming over here to mess with me.

Jean   Oh God, what are you – He was just being nice! He was being a good neighbor! Why are you being so paranoid!?

Beat.

Richard   You know, Jean, you're only paranoid when you're wrong. But when you're right, you have good instincts.

Jean   Oh, what is that supposed to mean?

Richard   All I'm saying is, don't let me have good instincts, Jean, because this is some suspicious shit and you're blind if you don't see it.

Jean   What, Richard?! What am I not seeing?!

Richard (*pointing in her face, peak of fury*)   Okay, Jean, you know what? Just fucking keep that man out of my house! (*Something is happening.*) Whoa.

Jean   Richard? What's wrong? What's happening?

Richard (*suddenly light-headed*)   My blood pressure just – I just –

Jean (*going to him, panicking, a little shrill*)   Oh God, Richard! Oh God! Have you taken your medication? Have you taken your medication?

Richard   Yes!

Still irritated from the fight, he sort of shakes her off a little aggressively, instinctively. He realizes what he's done, just as she realizes it, and they look at each other for a beat before **Richard** *stands up and exits.*

Richard   I just need to – I think I just need to lie down. I'm going to go to bed.

Jean (*shouting after him*)   But what about dinner?!

Richard (*offstage*)   What dinner?!

Zing. **Jean** *stands there. She looks around, exhausted, somewhat despondent, somewhat angry, generally confused, but she should probably figure out dinner. She looks in the cabinets again, this time not so wholeheartedly. She sees the jar of pig intestines. She takes it down from wherever it is, opens it up, sniffs it, is a little disgusted. After a hesitation, she reaches in anyway and plucks out a pig intestine. It looks sick. She eyes it, curiously, takes a bite. She chews, almost spits it out, but she manages to swallow. It isn't half bad. It's a dinner. She takes another bite, chews, and considers the many complexities of its flavors.*

Scene Twelve

Outside. It is early, early, early the next morning, and almost completely dark – well before sunrise. Hand in hand, **Melody** *and* **Jim** *are just now coming back from their long walk. The only light is a small pool of street light that it takes a while for them to find.*

Jim   . . . It's not confidence. I just don't want to do it.

Melody   Why not?

Jim   Because . . . I don't . . . want to . . . be like Daddy? I mean, I love him, but I don't want to be like him.

Melody   Who's saying you have to be like him?

Jim   Everybody. Mammy. Uncle Zip. It feels weird just doing all the things he did. I don't feel like . . . I just don't feel like myself and I feel like I'll never feel like myself, if I'm only doing the things he did.

Melody   Yourself? What's that supposed to feel like?

Jim   I don't know. Like now. Like I feel like myself right now. With you, I feel a lot like myself. (*Beat.*) Did I just say something really corny?

Melody   Yes.

Jim (*yawning*)   I must be tired. What time is it?

Melody (*checking her phone or watch*)   Two a.m.

Jim   What? Mammy's going to kill me.

Melody   No, she won't. Just blame it on me. Tell her I kept you out.

Jim   Kept me out doing what?

Melody   I don't know. What did I keep you out doing?

*As she says this, she steps into the light, revealing her face covered in splotches of black and red, and instantly we know what they've been doing. **Jim** notices and is, for a second, really taken aback. He makes a motion to wipe it away, similar to the eyelash moment.*

Jim   Whoa, uh!

Melody   What?

Jim   You have, um –

Melody   Another eyelash?

Jim   No, um, it's –

Melody   (*touching her face*)   Oh my God, what is it?! (*Looks at her finger.*) Oh? (*Looks at* **Jim**.) Oh.

Jim   I'm sorry.

Melody   Oh, no, no. It's fine. I don't mind . . . (*Doesn't finish. Beat. Feels the black.*) You know, I used to not wash my face.

Jim   What?

Did we notice **Mammy**, *lurking in the shadows? Because she might be.*

Melody   Yeah. Like, when I was little, I didn't – my skin was like really light, like milk, and I would go into the bathroom sometimes and climb on the sink and put on my mom's make-up – Alabaster Lily – and then, you know, one day, I put it on and for the first time, it streaks. It doesn't go on like it used to. It's white. And so I think to myself, there must have been dirt on my face – days and days of dirt had accumulated on my face – so I took the make-up off and I washed my face and I reapplied and it was still streaking. And I washed my face so many times and so hard until I'd basically rubbed my face raw and finally was like whatever and put the make-up on anyway, but when I looked in the mirror, I didn't see my mother anymore. I saw this clown, basically. So I run to my mother, crying because my face is stinging because I've rubbed it raw and covered it in all these like fucked-up chemicals, and she's sort of confused for a second and then she sort of figures out what's happening and is trying to calm me down and she's like, 'Your skin is changing color!' Just like that. But, of course, I'm like five, so it doesn't occur to me that this has anything to do with my father, you know. I still think it's because I'm not like . . . washing my face . . . and I guess I was just like so traumatized that I resolved that, rather than wash my face, I was going to let it get so dirty that I was just black – like totally black. I don't think I washed my face for weeks, maybe even months. Not until I got chickenpox. Then I sort of forgot all about it.

Jim   Whoa.

Melody   I know, right? That just came back to me pretty recently. I wonder where that memory went. (*Beat.*) Ugh, but listen to me. I must sound like a total freak.

Jim   Yeah. You do.

Melody   Shut up!

Jim (*a smiley beat*)   Well, I have a choreography intensive with Mammy in four hours. (*A sweet beat.*) I had fun today.

Melody   Me, too. Maybe I'll see you tomorrow?

Jim   Ha ha ha, maybe you will. So watch out.

He waves and disappears inside. **Melody** *crosses the lawn to her home and is about to go inside when* **Mammy** *emerges from the shadows, startling* **Melody**.

Mammy   Hey, girl.

Melody (*hiding her face*)   Ah! Hi, Mammy. You scared me!

Mammy   Sorry, baby.

Melody   You're up? It's so late.

Mammy   Mammy don't sleep. Mammy don't never sleep. (*Taking* **Melody**'s *face in her hand.*) But I could ask you the same thang. Y'all was out for a minute. (*No reply, then sweetly releasing her face.*) You know you look ezzakly like one a' my aunties? Aunt Eliza Zoe Sarah Jane.

No reply, **Melody** *mortified.*

Mammy   Hey, can Mammy bum a cigarette offa you, girl? I'm all out.

Melody   Um, sure.

Melody *awkwardly gets the cigarettes out of her pocket or purse or whatever and gives one to* **Mammy**, *helps her light it.*

Mammy   What's yo' brand?

Melody Um . . . Marlboro?

Mammy Mmm, girl. Mammy need to get you into Newpo'ts. (*Beat, admiring* **Melody**.) Yes, chile. It's like lookin' at a ghost. Aunt Zoe Eliza Sarah Jane was purty just like you. Had that good hair – like you. How you get good hair like that? What you be puttin' in it?

Melody Oh. Well, my mom is actually white, so . . .

Mammy Oh! So was Auntie Zoe's!

Melody Really?

Mammy Well, no, wait, I'se sorry. It was they daddies who was white. She used to be in the show wit us, you know. I was only a little Mammy at that point, but I remember: she was such a beautiful, amazin' actress. She had all the dramatic parts – all the monologues about sufferin' and the dramatic scenes, jumping across rivers, getting chased by dogs. Ugh! Them was the days! After her scenes, the folks used to be lining up on the lip of the stage, tossing they booqwets of fla'hs, just shoutin' for her. Just shoutin'!

Melody What happened?

Mammy I don't remember. But I'd swear you was her returned from the grave. The spittin' image.

Silence, in which they finish smoking their cigarettes, sort of assessing each other out of the corner of their eyes.

Gosh them was the days. Back when we had real drama, huh? What I wouldn't give for some of that right now. Some drama. Now all we got is palooza. (*Finishing her cigarette.*) Well, Mammy better get back to warshin' these carstumes. Hope I be seein' you at dress rehearsal tomorrow.

Melody Tomorrow?

Mammy Yeah, girl. I like yo' energy. So does Jimmy. And we gotta get him over that stage fright somehow, right? (*After a beat, suddenly gruff.*) And you betta quit that smoking! 'Fo you end up looking like me. (*Drops it, guffaws.*) Night, chile.

(margin note: Reference to Uncle Tom's Cabin...)

Mammy *exits, leaving* **Melody** *alone outside. She sits there with the paint on her face. She touches it again. She studies it on her fingertips. She looks from one house to another and back again before a sudden, small blackout.*

Scene Thirteen

The Pattersons' kitchen. **Richard**, **Jean**, *and* **Melody** *are all sitting around the table, eating in perfect silence.* **Jean** *stares into* **Richard**'s *face.* **Richard** *is working. He occasionally meets her glance uncomfortably. The only one not sore is* **Melody**, *who eats her breakfast with a relish we've never seen from her. She smiles the entire time, maybe hums to herself. Maybe she gets more Cheerios. This goes on for a while. Eventually,* **Melody** *gets up, takes her time putting her dishes in the sink, grabs her bag.* **Richard** *and* **Jean** *watch her.* **Melody** *exits without a word, and* **Richard** *and* **Jean** *look at each other, a little confused, but go back to their business. Suddenly,* **Jean** *speaks up.*

Jean   Are you feeling better?

Richard   I am.

Jean   Good.

Richard   Though I've now lost an entire night of work, so I'm behind on this lecture I'm supposed to give this morning.

Jean   Hm. (*Beat.*) Can I ask you a question?

Richard   Is it about how white you are?

Jean   No.

Richard   Okay, then go ahead.

Jean   How many other white girls have you dated?

Richard (*stopping work, dying*)   Jean! Jean, please! Please! For the love of God, please!

Jean   It was just a question. I mean, I know you've had other girlfriends, but we never . . . talked about what they . . . were . . .

Beat.

Richard   No, Jean, you're the only white woman I've ever
dated. (*Pause.*) Yes, Jean, I dated exclusively white women
before you. Hundreds of them – thousands of them – millions
of them. What difference does it make?

Beat.

Jean   Which one is it?

Richard   Which one do you think it is?

Jean   I don't know! You were the only black guy I ever dated.

Richard   What do you want me to say, Jean? Good for you?

Beat.

Jean   So are you going to tell me how many white girls you
dated or not? I told you. How about black girls? Did you date
any black girls? Latino girls? Asian girls? Eskimos?

Richard (*starts packing up his stuff, angrily*)   I don't have time
for this. Don't you hear how didactic and unproductive and
labored this conversation is? Nobody wants to hear this.
Nobody!

*He exits angrily, slamming the door. Does **Jean** look out over the
audience and take in the empty seats?*

Jean (*half to herself*)   Why can't we have a mature
conversation?!

Lights change and immediately:

Scene Fourteen

*Lights come up on the Crow residence. Everyone, except **Jim**, is gathered
in the living room. **Melody** is sitting on the couch. Everyone looks
offstage in eager anticipation.*

Mammy   Jim, you betta come on and get cho behind out

che'ah! We ain't got all day!

After a moment, **Jim** *enters slowly, totally unhappily, and in costume –
straw hat, striped suit, and enormous bowtie. He kind of looks
ridiculous. He also kind of looks amazing. Also, he is humiliated.
Everyone reacts –* **Topsy** *and* **Sambo** *pejoratively. It is a moment.*

Melody   Jim, you look great!

Sambo   Like a great big ole biatch.

Mammy *smacks* **Sambo** *to the floor.*

Sambo   OW!!

Mammy (*business*)   All right, Zip, we ain't got too much
time, so let's just take it from Jim Crow's entrance.

Topsy   Ugh, Mammy!

Mammy   What, little girl?

Topsy   Me and Sambo need to practice ourn numbers, too!

Mammy   Hush up. I just said we ain't got time. Mark yo'
damn lines.

Zip   Let's take it from Topsy.

Topsy (*sucks her teef, but still 'acting full-out'*)   Sambo, you done
took my watermelon!

Sambo (*also 'acting'*)   Topsy, you stole my chicken!

Topsy   I ain't steal yo' chicken! You ain't had no chicken –

Mammy   I said mark it, girl!

Topsy *sucks her teef again, rolling her eyes, pretending to do her nails,
half-assed.*

Topsy   Chicken coon coon coon das de massa's chicken!

Sambo (*also half-assed, quick 'marking'*)   Massa coon coon coon
coon coon watermelon!

Topsy   Chicken nigga coon coon coon Jemima!

Sambo   Ooga booga ooga booga coon coon coon coon ooga booga!

Topsy   Coon coon coon coon yassah!

Sambo   No massa coon coon coon Kuntakente!

Topsy (*marking a dance, very professional*)   Dance, dance, dance. (*Stops marking dance.*) Coon nappy coon –

Sambo   Coon malt liquor coon coon –

Topsy   Jigaboo coon coon –

Sambo   Jim Crow coon –

Topsy   Coon coon coon –

Sambo   Coon coon coon –

Mammy   Coon!

Topsy   And here come Jim Crow now!

Music starts. **Jim** *is fuming, staring at* **Melody**, *humiliated, so he misses his cue.* **Zip** *plays it again.* **Jim** *misses it.*

Zip (*whispering*)   Jim.

He plays again.

Jim (*singing timidly, terribly, softly*)
    Come, listen, all you gals and boys, I'm just from Tuckyhoe;
    I'm gwine to sing a little song, my name's Jim Crow.
    I went down to de river, I didn't mean to stay,
    But there I see so many gals, I couldn't get away.

The entire family joins in the chorus.

Family
    Wheel about, an' turn about, an' do jis so!

Mammy   Wait! Cut! Cut! Stop it, Zip.

Zip *stops playing. Everyone is all bothered.*

Topsy   Come own!

Mammy (*to* **Jim**)   Where's de choreography I spent awl mo'nin teachin' you?

Jim (*through gritted teeth*)   Mammy, I told you I can't do this –

Mammy   And I told you you'se an African. Not a African't. *(To* **Zip**.) Take it from 'I went down to de river'.

Music starts again. **Jim** *heaves a big sigh. He is a little stronger, but still sucks. And there's half-assed choreo.*

Jim (*singing*)
  I went down to de river, I didn't mean to stay,
  But there I see so many gals, I couldn't get away.

Family
  Wheel about, an' turn about, an' do jis so!

Jim
  Eb'ry time I wheel about, I jump Jim Crow.

Sambo   This is ridiculous!

Jim
  I'm rorer on de fiddle, an' down in ole Virginny,

Sambo *joins in now, subtly at first but building to the point that he is kind of out-cooning* **Jim***. He also gets so bold as to start performing to* **Melody***, which upsets* **Jim***.*

Sambo *and* **Jim**
  Dey say I play de skientific, like massa Pagganninny.
  I cut so many munky shines, I dance de galloppade;
  An' w'en I done, I res' my head, on shubble, hoe or spade.

Family
  Wheel about, an' turn about, an' do jis so!

Sambo *and* **Jim**
  Eb'ry time I wheel about, I jump SAM-BO / JIM CROW.

Sambo *does the Jim Crow jig for four bars. Meanwhile,* **Jim** *is stunned. He looks to the rest of the family, who act as though nothing out of the ordinary is actually happening.*

Sambo (*amazing, at times even taunting* **Jim**)
I met Miss Dina Scrub one day, I gib her sich a buss;
An' den she turn an' slap my face, an' make a mighty fuss.
De udder gals dey 'gin to fight, I tell'd dem wait a bit;
I'd hob dem all, jis one by one, as I tourt fit.

Family (*except* **Jim**)
Wheel about, an' turn about, an' do jis so!

Sambo
Eb'ry time I wheel about, I jump Sam-bo!

Jim (*overlapping with 'Sam-bo'*)
Jim Crow!

*A hoedown happens involving everyone. Lots of hooting and hollering.
Meanwhile, something insane snaps inside of* **Jim**, *like a hurricane
unleashed as he begins to take back his song from* **Sambo**. *Progressively
but quickly, he becomes, simply put, the most incredible thing you have
ever seen in your entire life. It's a* **Jim** *we have never ever seen, almost
like a man possessed — eyes bugged out, limbs loose, moving, dancing, mo'
coon than a little bit.*

It becomes like this savage contest of manhood, and **Jim** *wins in the
end. Of course, he wins in the end.* **Sambo** *drops out halfway through,
shamed, and just stares for the last line or two. Meanwhile,* **Melody** *is
getting all heated and starry-eyed.*

Sambo *and* **Jim**
I wip de lion ob de west, I eat de alligator;

Jim
I put more water in my mouf, den boil ten load ob 'tator.
De way dey bake de hoe cake, Virginny nebber tire;
Dey put de doe upon de foot, an' stick 'em in de fire.

*Even the family is kind of stunned. It's like his father is back from the
grave.*

Family (*stunned, but working with it*)
Wheel about, an' turn about, an' do jis so!

Jim (*ending in a huge flourish, holding the last note, riffing, whatever needs to happen*)

Eb'ry time I wheel about, I jump Jim Crooooooooooooow!

Jim *holds this really incredible note for such a long fucking time that the cookie jar containing his father's ashes just kind of explodes, releasing an enormous cloud of ash, like a haze, that should remain present and perhaps spread and soak the atmosphere for the remainder of the play. When the explosion happens, everyone except* **Jim** *and* **Melody** *turns to watch it.* **Topsy** *freaks out, as she was standing too close and is now covered in her dead father's remains.* **Mammy** *immediately reaches over and covers her mouth. There is a hella long pause, in which everyone just sort of stares at* **Jim**. *Slowly, he seems to realize what has just happened. He stands up.*

Mammy   Jim?

Zip   You okay, Jimmy?

Jim *doesn't answer. The atmosphere is weird.* **Topsy** *is still screaming, or at least sobbing.*

Mammy   Maybe that's enough rehearsing for now. (*Looks at* **Zip**, *smirking, proud.*) I think we're gonna be just fine for tonight.

Sambo   But Mammy! Me and Topsy ain't even pracktus ourn sawngs!

Mammy   Y'all can practice by yo'self in yo' room. Go. And take yo' sister wit you.

Sambo *exits angrily with* **Topsy**, *who is still crying.*

Mammy   Well, I guess Imma go head and start dinnah now. (*Winks at* **Melody**, *cordially.*) Girl, I like yo' energy. I'm keep you. (*Regarding the mess.*) I'll clean this up later. (*To the ashes, darkly.*) Shame on you, Jimmy Sr. (*To* **Zip**.) Come on, Zip.

She exits with **Zip**.

Jim (*in a daze*)   What just happened – ?

Melody   Jim –

Jim   I don't know what – what just came – I felt for a second like –

Melody   Jim –

Jim   Like I was outside of myself – outside of my body – but –

Melody   Jim –

Jim   Is something on fire?

Melody   Jim –

Jim   You must think –

Melody   Jim, shut up.

Jim *shuts up.*

Melody   That was amazing. You are amazing, you – your whole family's thing, it's – it's amazing. It's wow. Wow.

Jim   What? You liked that?

Melody (*heated*)   I've never seen anything like that before, it was – I feel so – I don't know I feel so – Oh my, I feel – I didn't know you could do that – I – Can we go somewhere?

Jim   Where?

Melody   Anywhere. Outside. I need to show you something.

Jim   Well, uh, let me change.

Melody   No! Leave it on!

Melody *drags him out the door and around the corner of the house. Lights change, and immediately:*

Scene Fifteen

Richard *is at the podium. He arranges his notes as the class settles down.*

Richard   *Iphigenia at Aulis* by Euripides. What a tragedy.
(*Beat.*) So, just a quick summary for those who haven't read it –
(*Gives a look of disappointment.*) On his way to battle the Trojans,
Agamemnon and his ships are halted at Aulis by a sudden
ceasing of wind. Agamemnon seeks out the oracle Calchas,
who informs him that it is the goddess Artemis who has
stopped the wind because she's angry and that in order to
placate the goddess and continue with the war, Agamemnon
must sacrifice his daughter Iphigenia. And Agamemnon must
seriously consider this because his crazy, bloodthirsty soldiers
are stuck at the port and are getting drunk and anxious and
are about to rebel if something doesn't happen, so he's sent for
his wife to bring his daughter to Aulis under the pretense of
marrying her off to a famous soldier. And so the play, as we all
know, or as we all should know, is about Agamemnon's internal
struggle over whether or not to kill his daughter and appease
his troops and the goddess, or to not kill his daughter and
'screw everything up'. And in the end, as we all know – and
spoiler alert to those who don't – he sacrifices her. He kills her.

Beat, as he lets that sink in.

Now, echoing our first lecture, we should ask ourselves, where
does this tragedy begin? Why is the goddess so angry? Why did
she stop the wind? For our answer, we have to go back, to a
time before the start of the play, to something Agamemnon
once did that Euripides, interestingly enough, never mentions.
Apparently, many years ago, Agamemnon was hunting one
day and he killed a deer and, in a moment of pride, sort of
off-handedly boasts to his hunting buddy that he was a better
hunter than Artemis, the goddess of the hunt. Now, this whole
thing is triggered by a boast in the forest, by the fact that
Agamemnon has the gall to get 'uppity' and tell the gods,
'Hey! I am just as good as you are!' Agamemnon, as a military
man, brought up among the lowly, human 'soldiers', believed
he was and may have been just as good as the 'gods'. And he
had the nerve to believe in himself and tell them that. And, for
that, he was punished? And with what? No wind? Okay. This
was the best she could do? Is that all it takes to destroy a man?

Gradually, lights start coming up so so so slowly on two separate sides of the stage.

By the end of this lecture/tirade, we can just barely see, in one spot, **Melody** *giving* **Jim** *a blowjob, the sounds of her going at it kind of amplified, and, in the other spot,* **Jean***, sitting at her kitchen table, nibbling on her nails, sipping tea, looking crazy-eyed, occasionally glancing at her door, and looking like a total wreck. At some point, in* **Jean***'s area we hear a phone ringing faintly. She looks off absently into the direction of the noise but doesn't answer the phone.*

Richard   Not really, right? Because the real pressure isn't even coming from the gods. No, uh-uh, it's these soldiers and their base appetites – these crazy, uncouth, country-ass soldiers with no self-control, sitting in the port raping women and drinking all the time and ain't got no jobs and don't talk Greek good and it's just a mess, they're actually the ones fucking it up. Agamemnon's real mistake was giving a damn about what these people thought in the first place. And then Iphigenia, when she realizes what's going on, she has this change of heart and wants to volunteer herself to be slaughtered. Suddenly she's talking about 'honor' – the 'honor of sacrifice'. 'Honor of sacrifice'? Where she get that shit from? Because that sounds like soldier talk to me – ain't no god told her about that – and in the end Agamemnon sacrifices her because of her soldier talk and that shit is crazy. Honor?! These suckers just spent the last few weeks getting drunk and whoring and hanging out in a damn port! They aren't real soldiers! They are hooligans! And they trying to tell him how to raise – I mean, what to do with his daughter?

Beat.

It's just sad, because, Agamemnon was a new breed of Achaean. He was a god among soldiers, a soldier among gods! He was the answer! He was the change! He fucked up the whole system, and you could tell because those ignorant hooligan soldiers, them bitter gods – they was threatened! They're trying to get him to sacrifice his daughter 'cause they want to stop the change! And, really, I think Euripides is saying, Agamemnon should have trusted himself, trusted his instincts, and just been like, 'Why do they want my daughter? Why my daughter? Okay? Why won't they just leave Agamemnon and my daughter alone?' (*Beat.*) Yes, you have a question?

Voice of Student   Um, the syllabus said *Iphigenia at Tauris* and we all read that?

Richard   I – I'm sorry, what? My notes say you guys were reading *Iphigenia at Aulis*?

Voice of Student   *At Tauris. Aulis* is next week.

Lights go down suddenly on **Jim**, **Melody**, *and* **Jean**. **Richard** *shuffles his notes, really nervous. He looks like he might be on the verge of a meltdown.*

Richard   *Iphigenia at Tauris* . . . What happens in that one again? (*His nose starts bleeding*) Uh-oh. Oh. (*Dabs with his finger, sees the blood.*) Oh, I – excuse me.

Richard *rushes out, lights change, and immediately:*

Scene Sixteen

The Pattersons' kitchen. **Jean** *sits at the table, drinking tea, going through a number of poetry books, which seem to surround her. A phone rings somewhere in the house, but she doesn't notice until the last ring. She springs up to get the phone but doesn't make it in time. She sits back down, keeps thinking. She finishes her tea. She gets up to put more water in the tea kettle and then the tea kettle on the flame. She sits back down at the table. There is a knock at the door. She jumps up, rushes over to it, opens it. It's* **Zip**, *of course. He holds some mail.*

Zip   Hi, Jean!

Jean   Zip!

Zip   I just came by to drop off some of your mail. It got delivered to our place by accident.

Jean   Thank you! Our postman has a substance-abuse problem.

A beat, in which **Jean** *just sort of stares.*

Zip   Are you doing all right? You don't look so well.

Jean   Oh, I'm fine! I'm fine! (*Beat, in which that is clearly not true.*) Just thinking.

Zip   Oh? About what?

Jean   You know, actually, something came up in our conversation yesterday. You asked me this question – do, I um, do I have a quote-unquote 'thing' for black men?

Zip (*awkward, maybe a tad revealing*)   Oh, it was a joke. I didn't mean to offend –

Jean   No, no, of course! It wasn't – I wasn't offended. Unless you really think I have a thing for black men, do you?

Zip   No. Do you?

Jean   No. No, I don't.

Zip   Okay . . .

Jean   Because, like, I know that there are these like, 'supposedly', there are like these women who harbor these psychological fantasies, where they want to be – you know, fucked by like a big, muscled sort of black man with like a gigantic dick – like you know that fantasy?

Zip   Uh, I'm familiar.

Jean *takes this in, starts to shift gears. Around this time, the tea kettle starts whistling quietly. Its whistling builds with her intensity until, by the end of her monologue, it's basically screeching.*

Jean   Yeah, me, too. But I was just sitting here thinking, like, where did that even come from, you know? I mean, it didn't just come from nowhere, right? Or did it? Like I was asking myself like, where did I learn about that because – and, you know, I remembered – Okay, so there's this romance novel I read a long, a long long time ago, you know, and those things

are always trashy and don't ask me why I was reading it, my
grandmother used to read them, I was young, I was really
young – I barely remember what it was about – but there was
this plantation owner's daughter and the plantation was like
suffering during the war and her father just sort of dies and
leaves her in charge of the plantation and she's stressed out
and has all these suitors and she's really mean to this one slave,
this, you know, big Mandingo buck slave and then all this stuff
happens and then like in the penultimate scene the slave just
kind of creeps into her room and takes her, you know?

He just sort of fucks her brains out and then the like final
image of the book is her like sitting on her porch in her dress
like peacefully watching the sunset over all her slaves picking
cotton or whatever in the cotton field and for just a second
she makes eye contact with the slave – the buck Mandingo
slave who just raped her basically! – and she sort of like – she
sort of like smiles? Or something? And that recently came
back to me and I was like, 'WHAT?!'

Beat.

I mean, I just started thinking of this again, because you know
– that can't be where I got it from? Like everyone's not reading
this book, right? Or do they actually know people who want
to get fucked by black guys? And I know you were joking but
do people actually walk around thinking that about me? And
what was I doing reading that so young?! And like I'm thinking
about now, you know, like after all my feminist theory and
cultural studies classes just thinking like, like, like – those power
dynamics are just so vague! Like, you know, who's fucking who
here? I mean the slave is fucking the plantation owner's
daughter, but like maybe he's actually fucking the plantation
owner? And like she's fucking him, but like maybe she's also
like fucking her dad, because it's his property? Or like maybe
she's just fucking herself, you know? Like, you know, the power
dynamics are so vague and like I sort of realized like, what was
I doing reading that so young?! Because, you know, that's not
love! You know!

Building to a frenzy, thoughts racing.

Because I mean, my husband, I mean I love my husband, but
you know I don't think I really walk around like . . . you know,
like lusting after black men. I think. I mean to say, my husband
is the only black man I've ever slept with and since I have been
married to my husband I haven't noticed any proclivities
towards men in general, much less black men. Wait, okay:
I didn't have very many boyfriends before I dated Richard,
but I had some and they were all white, but then Richard
came along and he was just so – he was just very different.
And I don't know – I don't think that has anything to do with
his being black. And I'm not one of these women, because I
love my husband, and love is very different, right? Because love
is – you know – love is different from a 'thing'! I think! Right?
I mean, it's different from a self-conscious thing, like a fetish,
but I mean maybe those aren't real things, by which I mean to
say that they aren't real 'things', I mean, real things – real
'things' are like deep – like suppressed, right? And so, it's like,
how can you ever even know what your 'things' are, you know?
Are you supposed to care? And that's really scary, because how
do you even know who you are, much less what your 'things'
are, you know? And if you can't even figure that stuff out
about yourself, how are you expected to even get to know
other people, you know? I mean, or does it even matter?

Pause. The kettle is screeching. **Zip** *just sort of looks at her.*

Zip   I think your tea's ready.

Jean (*springs to take the tea off the boil*)   Oh yes, the tea. (*Beat.*)
I'm sorry if that came across as a bit manic.

Zip   Oh, do not apologize. I didn't mean to make you go
so deep.

Beat.

Jean   Ugh, it's not just you. This all just started with this
stupid fight I got into with my husband last night, you know.
It's just so weird that – that this hasn't been an issue for us
ever, until now.

Zip   Until now? Has something happened?

Jean (*lying, then not lying*)   No! No. He's just – his job's – it's something at his job. Or maybe it's me, or I don't know. Maybe he's right. Maybe I do need a job. Maybe I just need a job. I don't know. But would a job make it go away? I don't know.

A beat of consideration.

Zip   Do you . . . need a job, Jean?

Jean   Sort of.

Zip   Well, you know, we actually need help with our show – like run crew. We need a house manager. It's not like a lot of money, but it's something, if you think it will help.

Jean   Oh, Zip, you don't have to –

Zip   This isn't about you, honey. We really need the help. Though neighbors are there for each other. Neighbors help each other out.

Jean   Well, thank you. I have . . . to check with my husband first.

Zip (*taking her hand, kind of too tenderly*)   Of course. But just let me know if there's anything – anything I can ever do for you.

Small pause in which **Jean** *looks at her hand in his, gets kind of nervous.*

Jean   Zip, can I ask you a personal question?

Zip *removes his hand.*

Zip   Absolutely.

Jean (*wants to know if he's gay*)   You're . . . you're . . . right?

Zip   I'm what?

Jean   You're . . .

Beat.

Zip (*super-ambiguous*)   Oh! Yes! Yes, of course. Girl, yes.

Jean   Great! I mean, great. I mean, that's great.

At some point, **Richard** *enters, crossing toward the doorway. His nostrils are stuffed with bloody tissues, and he looks panicked.* **Jean** *and* **Zip** *don't see him at first. He stands some distance away glowering.*

Zip   Yes. (*Beat.*) Well, I must get going. Just let me know about tonight, okay?

Jean (*noticing* **Richard**)   Richard!

Zip   Richard?

Jean   What happened to you?

Richard *approaches slowly, glowering. He looks from* **Zip** *to* **Jean**, *angrily.*

Jean   Oh, this is – this is our new neighbor. Zip!

Zip *stands, extending his hand.*

Zip   Zip . . . Coon.

Richard (*not taking his hand*)   What?!

Zip   I actually think we might have seen each other the other morning. I waved, but you probably didn't see –

Richard   Yes, I probably didn't. If you'll excuse me, I need to have a talk with my wife.

Zip   Oh certainly. (*Beat, to* **Jean**.) Well, I hope to see you tonight!

He winks at **Jean**. **Richard** *sees this and seethes.*

Jean (*conflicted about what to show*)   Yes!

Zip   And, Richard, it's a pleasure to finally –

Richard *slams the door in* **Zip**'*s face and turns to his wife.*

Jean (*concerned*)   What happened? Is that blood?

Richard *sits at the table, puts his head on the table or in his hand, defeated.*

Richard I THOUGHT I TOLD YOU I DID NOT
WANT TO SEE THAT MAN IN MY HOUSE.

Jean He wasn't in our house.

Richard Excuse me?

Jean He was standing outside the door, dropping off our
mail. He offered me a job.

Richard What kind of a job?!

Jean House . . . managing his family's show!

Richard What – / Oh hell no –

Jean (*building to a snap*)   I thought you said I needed a job.
I thought you said I should take what I can get!

Richard I told you about a job in the department – !

Jean I need something that's mine! Something for me! And,
also! Are you actually forbidding me from making a friend –

Richard Friend?

Jean When all I do is sit around the fucking house all day
waiting for you and Melody to come back to make me useful
again?! Sit around this fucking house we don't even own, this
fucking house you basically dragged me by my hair across the
country to live in, to go crazy all day in this neighborhood full
of old . . . bitches thinking God Knows What about me and
who won't even look me in the eye because I'm married to
you – because I married you?

There is a long pause, in which **Jean** *tries to regain her composure. It
takes a while.* **Richard** *watches her and tries to calm himself down.*

Richard What is that supposed to mean? Do you think this
is easy for me too, Jean? We're on our way – trying to get
somewhere, and it's hard, Jean, but we struggle now so the
struggling will stop. Right? Right? Isn't that how it works?
So I'm sorry you're unhappy! I'm sorry you're lonely! But,
goddammit, when I'm sitting in that office doing all this shit

I never thought I would be doing, I'm feeling unhappy and lonely, too! I, too, am wishing I could go back to that crappy Mission loft and live off our granola and our coffee grounds, our 'poetry' and our 'good intentions', but we can't because everything is different! We're different! We can't live on my Greek instructor salary and your freelance and no health insurance! That's not what we want, right? So we just have to keep moving, Jean! We have to move forward. Keep moving –

Jean   But, Richard, what does this have to do with our neighbors?! What did they ever do?

Richard   Jean, this has nothing to do with them!

Jean   Yes it does! You are having these issues with your neighbors!

Richard   No, I am having issues with the kind of people they are and where they came from and how that will reflect upon us, in the eyes of people who aren't us, because of those other people's own issues. And, if I could, Jean, I would change everything!

If I could, I'd get rid of those other people's issues, but I can't, Jean. We can't. We can only hold on to what we've got and keep my head down and keep moving because, some day, if we're lucky, we will look up and those people and those issues and those neighbors, they will be gone! And that has nothing to do with the fact that they are black. But you wouldn't understand that, Jean.

Jean   Why couldn't I? (*Beat.*) Because I'm white? Because I'm your white wife?

Richard (*changing the subject*)   Where is our daughter?

Jean   What?

Richard   Melody. Where is she?

Jean   At school.

Richard (*getting up, suddenly upset*)   No. She's not.

(margin handwriting) How do you move forward in a healthy way without shutting a part of yourself?

Jean   How do you know?

Richard   Because I got a call from her school telling me she's not, and they only called me because no one has been picking up here. And what exactly were you doing all day when they've been calling? Sitting around reading poetry? Meditating on the race problem in America?

He is leaving.

Jean   What are you doing?

Richard (*exiting, slamming doors*)   I'm going out to find her. What are you doing?

Jean *is alone. Again. Lights change and immediately:*

MAMMY'S INTERLUDE

A brassy big-band sort of music starts playing and builds with the scene. **Mammy** *is outside, cleaning clothes on a washboard. She looks exhausted. She lights a cigarette and begins to smoke. It relaxes her. She leans back against the door frame, nods off a little, but then catches herself. She takes another drag of the cigarette and nods off halfway into the drag. She drops the cigarette onto her ample, ample, ample bosom, where it gets lost. Her breasts start smoking.* **Mammy** *snaps up, half awake, goes for the cigarette, which she thinks is in her fingers. She doesn't know where it is. Has she dropped it? She looks around on the ground around her, can't seem to find it. All the while her breasts are smoking more and more. Eventually she stands up straight. She smells smoke. She sniffs around comically, before she realizes that the smoke is coming from her breasts. She goes bug-eyed. She runs around, miming like she's screaming. She starts pushing her breasts together, trying to get the cigarette out. Eventually it pops out and flies all the way across the stage into a pile of leaves, which immediately goes up in flames. She stares at the growing flames, goes bug-eyed again, starts running around again, mimes like she's screaming again. Eventually, she gets an idea. She opens up her shirt, takes out her behemoth breasts— which are probably not real breasts — and proceeds to put out the fire with an ungodly amount of breast milk. It works. She turns to the audience, breasts hanging out —*

maybe the music turns to that of an African folk documentary – and then wipes her brow. Boy, is she tired. And thirsty too. She takes one of her huge breasts and proceeds to drink her own breast milk. Yum!

A white woman, played by **Melody**, *runs onstage. She is pregnant. She is freaking out. She runs up to* **Mammy**, *who is still suckling on her own breasts, and gestures to her stomach.* **Mammy** *shakes her head. The woman gestures again.* **Mammy** *shakes her head. 'No.' The pregnant white woman slaps* **Mammy** *across the face.* **Mammy** *nods her head. 'Yes.' The pregnant white woman gets down on the ground, spreads her legs. Lots of fake blood and silly string fly out from between her legs, yet* **Mammy** *pushes through it like some sort of Eskimo pushing through an ice storm or something. Eventually, she births two babies. Twins. She holds them both, one on each arm, and holds them out to the pregnant lady. The pregnant lady jumps up and runs offstage, abandoning* **Mammy** *with the two children.* **Mammy** *goes bug-eyed. She runs around in circles, as before, miming like she's screaming. Eventually, as before, she stops. She notices her breasts hanging out. She takes her huge breasts and attaches one baby to each nipple. They suckle. They start to hurt her. She tries to pry them off, but they're stuck. She lets go and they sort of hang there. She tries to shake them off, but they hang there. This shaking gets more and more extreme until eventually she is doing a Mata Hari-esque belly dance, putting her hands behind her head and twirling the babies clamped to her nipples like tassels on a bra. She does jazz hands. Deep amber lighting, as before, comes up on* **Melody**, *now at the window, a look of total confusion on her face. The music is at its loudest.* **Mammy** *dances around in stage, shimmying, twirling, maybe she pops into a split, and then she dances right offstage as the music fades into recorded applause and immediately:*

Scene Seventeen

Lights come up dim on the Pattersons' kitchen. It is dusk. **Melody** *has just sneaked home from her rendezvous with* **Jim**. *There is a silhouette figure huddled at the dinner table.* **Melody** *shakes off the shock of seeing* **Mammy** *do whatever* **Mammy** *was doing on the lawn and quietly closes the door, which is just barely ajar. It closes with a small* *click. She turns and tries to sneak toward the doorway that leads to the living room. The silhouetted figure rustles a bit and then speaks. It is* **Richard.** *He is pissed. No one turns on a light just yet.*

Richard   Do you know your principal called me at work? But I was in class, so she left me a message. Said you haven't been to school in two days, wanted to know if you were ill. And, I thought to myself, now, I saw my daughter this morning. At breakfast. Has something happened to her on her walk between here and school? Because we both know what happened last time. Maybe she got sick or something and came home? Call your cell. No answer. I come home. Not here. I drove around for three hours looking for you, peered up every little asscrack that stupid town's got and: nothing. So, of course, I'm starting to freak out. I'm starting to imagine the worst, like that stupid nigger boy next door and that look of his that I saw him give you. I've seen that look. That is the look a predator gives before he preys. And I knew that's what that boy was doing to you, just as I was circling the block in my old Honda – I could see his mouth dripping with blood, your belly torn open, and he's preying on you. And at that point, my only option is to head to the police, to file a missing person's report, but they don't let you do that until somebody's been missing for forty-eight hours. But! Then! I remembered your principal's voicemail to me. Two days, she said. She's been missing for two days. Which means you didn't go to school the day before either, but you came on home, though, didn't you? You were home for breakfast. But two days of missing school. So, I thought to myself, just let me come home and wait and see what decides to show up.

Melody   I'm going upstairs.

Richard   No, you are not! Not before you tell me where the hell you've been!

Melody   None of your business! Why can't you just leave me alone!

In the darkness, **Richard** *jumps up from the table and grabs her arm before she can exit.*

Richard   Nuh-uh, girl, 'cause when I leave you alone, when I don't drive your little ass to school every morning, you get lost.

Melody   Stop grabbing me! Who do you think you are!

Richard   You're not going to talk to me like that in my house!

Melody   Then I'm going to leave this stupid house!

Richard   Oh yeah and do what?

Melody   Be an actress!

Richard (*scoffing*)   Oh, okay! Like that's going to happen!

Melody   Oh, okay! Like I'm going to take life advice from a bastard like you! You nothing! You nobody! You joke!

Pause, before **Richard** *starts shaking her violently.*

Richard   Who do you think you are talking to! Don't you know I could snap your little-ass neck!

Melody (*shrieking*)   Get off of me! Get off of me!

Jean *enters from the living room.*

Jean   What is going on!? Why is everyone screaming?!

She flips on a light switch, and everything is revealed, and most importantly the fact that **Melody** *is smeared all over with black and maybe a little white, especially on the palm of her right hand and around her mouth. There's kind of, you know, some penis-shaped smears here and there.* **Richard** *stops, stunned. He stares at her, but the stare transforms quickly into something else, into a tremor, which in turn blossoms into anger, shock, and disbelief, and* **Melody** *is ashamed.* **Jean** *is also shocked.*

Richard   What the fu –

Melody (*trying to pull away*)   I'm going upstairs!

Richard (*stopping her*)   No, you are not!

He tries to lift up **Melody**'s *shirt.*

Melody Stop it!

Jean Richard!

He successfully lifts up her shirt. Her entire body is smeared with black paint. Handprints, mouthprints, faceprints disappear into the waist of her jeans.

Richard (*raising his hand*) You little – !

Jean (*shouting, going to pull him away*) RICHARD!

She pulls him away. He is restrained. Only because something is happening to him. He is weakened. His nose starts bleeding again.

Richard (*discombobulated, under attack*) You – Jean, get off of me – / Jean – I –

Melody You don't know anything about me!

Richard JEAN, GET THE HELL OFF OF ME!

Melody *spits in his face before fleeing the house, causing* **Richard** *to flip his shit.* **Melody** *exits running, slamming the door.* **Jean** *is still restraining* **Richard**, *who looks like he might be having a borderline stroke.*

Richard (*almost crying*) JEAN, WHAT ARE YOU DOING?!

Jean Richard, your blood pressure! Your / blood pressure!

Richard She just – Jean, fuck my blood pressure – Go after her!

Jean Richard, you have to calm down! You're bleeding everywhere –

Richard *breaks free. He kind of stumbles to the door. The rage in him is stronger than himself. He opens the door, he looks out.*

Richard (*out of breath*) Come. Back here. Come. You – (*Sinks down to the floor.*) Oh my God. Oh my God.

Jean *brings him pills and some water.*

Jean Take these pills. Take these.

Richard (*in shock*)   Oh my God.

Jean (*very scared, but trying to be responsible*)   Drink, drink, Richard. Please, drink! I hate this! I hate this!

Richard *drinks. He gets a little of his strength back. Long pause.*

Richard (*out of it*)   Something has happened. Something is wrong. I wasn't even thinking –

Jean   Richard, keep –

Richard   Go after her –

Jean   She'll come back! She's coming back! I need to – I'm calling an ambulance!

Richard   JEAN, SHUT UP! SHE IS NOT COMING BACK AND SHE'S NOT COMING BACK BECAUSE YOU FUCKED UP! YOU SAT AROUND ALL DAY WITH YOUR FUCKING POETRY BEING SELF-INVOLVED WHEN YOU SHOULD HAVE BEEN STOPPING THIS – WHAT DID I TELL YOU?! NOW LOOK! NOW LOOK WHAT IS HAPPENING! WILL YOU PLEASE JUST GO AFTER HER?!

Jean *is stunned. She stands up. She backs away, pretends to be clearing up some sort of a mess.*

Richard   I knew – I knew it – They're trying to take you, but why me? Why me? What did I do? What did I do?

Jean   It wasn't Yeats, Richard.

Richard   What?

Jean   'Oh Rose, thou art sick!' It was Blake. William Blake. Not William Butler Yeats. I was such an idiot. How could I have been so stupid? William Butler Yeats. '

> O Rose, thou art sick!
> The invisible worm
> That flies in the night,
> In the howling storm

Has found out thy bed
Of crimson joy;
And his dark secret love
Does thy life destroy –

Richard   What the hell are you talking about?

Jean   What a shame. How could I have forgotten? There
was a time I could identify a poet within the first two lines,
isn't that crazy? I used to have so many poems memorized. You
did, too. Don't you remember? In those early days together –
after we'd made love – we would roll over and I could – I could
start reciting a poem and you would finish it. Remember?
Like that Carl Sandburg one, 'Bricklayer Love'. 'I thought of
killing myself / because I am only a bricklayer . . . ' That's
one of my favorite poems – our favorite poems. Can you
finish that one? We used to surrounded ourselves, our lives,
with verse and beauty and feelings, Richard. I was actually
trying to remember what I imagined my future would look
like back then – back when all I wanted was to be a part of
something big and fall in love. What happened? This isn't my
life. This isn't what my life is supposed to look like. I don't
even know – I don't even know how I got here. Is that funny?
But now look at this. I'm in my bathrobe. My daughter is
roaming the streets, covered in . . . And you – look at you –
you – huddled in a corner, bleeding. What was that? I just
don't get why suddenly – suddenly everything is so hard. I
mean, it was hard in the beginning. My parents – even they
were calling me saying, 'It's going to be so hard, Jean,' but I
didn't care. I thought – we could figure it out. And we would.
And it would all be so easy, right? And we'd be happy! And
we would show them! And I thought that we had! But now
it's . . . it's still hard? But it's a different hard? Or maybe it's
just harder? And I don't understand –

Richard   Jean, this is no time for you to start soliloquizing –

Jean (*really angry*)   No, Richard, I don't understand! Or at
least that's what you keep telling me. Jean, you don't

[handwritten annotation: she doesn't understand because there hasn't been a real discussion about race, and unless you lived it, there is no real exposure to the issue]

understand! Jean, you don't get it! Because you're white! Jean you're white, white, white, white, white. WHAT, RICHARD?!

WHEN DID I SUDDENLY BECOME THIS WHITE? I thought it didn't matter! I thought that was the whole point! I don't understand how suddenly this is a problem.

Richard   Your fucking fixation is the only problem. It's an illusion! If you ignore it, it will go away! This is not about race!

Jean   Yes, this is about race. Somehow. That's why I don't get it. I don't get race. But how come I can't get it? How come you won't help me get it?

Richard   Jean, what am I supposed to help you get?!

Jean   Why can't you just tell me things, Richard? Why can't I know what you're thinking and feeling?

Richard   Jean, I have been telling you! And you haven't been listening!

Jean   No, you haven't! – Not what you really feel!

Richard   JEAN, HOW THE FUCK WOULD YOU KNOW THAT?

Beat.

Jean   WHY DON'T YOU TRUST ME?!

Richard   WHY DON'T YOU TRUST ME?!

Jean   WHAT?

Richard   WHAT?

Jean   STOP ACTING LIKE A CHILD!

Richard   STOP ACTING LIKE A CHILD!

A very long pause, in which they stare deeply into each other's eyes, having hit a brick wall. They hold this stare for an impossibly long time, struggling to connect without words, but ultimately, somehow, failing – a failure which frustrates, a frustration which turns to anger.

Jean (*with a reluctant, sad venom*)   You're a . . . you're a . . . a . . . a beast.

Richard (*with a reluctant, sad venom*)   And you're a bitch. A stupid white bitch.

Jean *gasps, then a long pause.*

Richard   Is that what / you wanted to hear?

Jean   Well, the only nigger in this neighborhood is you, Richard! Nigger! NIGGER!

Pause, nothing happens. Nothing is resolved. They both seem confused and angry and out of breath. **Jean** *goes over and slaps* **Richard**, *lightly.*

Richard   Jean, I was –

Jean *slaps him again.*

Richard   JEAN!

Jean *tries again, he grabs her hand.*

Richard   Jean, I swear to God –

Jean *slaps him again with her free hand.* **Richard** *grabs* **Jean** *by the neck, almost like he's about to strangle her, but then he doesn't. Instead, he punches her. He punches her square in the face. She falls backward. She holds her eye. She scrambles to get up.* **Richard** *is just sort of standing there. Fuming, breathing hard, like he's about to explode.*

He can barely catch his breath. Suddenly, he kind of half collapses, grabbing his head. **Jean** *takes a long look at him, looks at him bent over, before exiting through the kitchen door.*

Richard   Oh my God. Jean –

He collapses and starts to seize as lights change and immediately:

TOPSY'S INTERLUDE/INTERRUPTION

A spot comes up on a bare space and we can hear **Topsy** *entering before we ever see her. She makes her way calmly to the center of the spot, decked out in an obvious Josephine Baker knock-off – a revealing halter studded with diamonds and a banana skirt. Around her ankles, neck, and*

[handwritten margin note: parallels the explosion in Jenkins' play "Appropriate"... issue of race is suppressed until someone loses it... Bo explodes, Richard explodes]

*wrists are strings of gypsy bells and a shit ton of other jewelry that
makes a lot of noise when she moves. Stage hands wheel a big standing
harp out on stage.* **Topsy** *addresses the audience.*

Topsy   Um, hey y'all. Um, so – Topsy. Hi. Hi! How y'all
doing? Y'all doin' all right? Y'all enjoying the show? Yes? No?
No, you not? Okay, yikes. Well, anyway: I'm sure y'all have
noticed that all throughout this evening, members of my
family have been coming out here from time to time and
delighting y'all with some of ourn classics antics, and I wuz
lak watchin' Sambo's wawtamellon bit and Mammy's *Gone
with the Wind* tribute, and lak, kindsa feeling emburrassed cuz,
you know, I'm supposed to come out here and do a tap dance
and masturbate with a banana, but I don't think that really
represents me as uh artist. You see, during the intamission,
I was having a talk wit Massa (*Last Name of the Artistic Director*),
and I convinced him ta let me come out cheah and take this
opportunity or whatever to show y'all that I'm not, you know,
like the rest of my family. I mean, as an artist. It's not that I
don't respect what we be doin' or whateva, but lak, I think
the work I really want to be doing maybe isn't exactly as
commercial as all this. I'm really tryna make work about the
shared human experiamentience, because, ta me, das de real
definition of Art. So, uh, because y'all have really just been an
amazing audience and because I thank we're running just a
little bit under, I just wawnted to show y'all summa the stuff
I been warkin on. I hope that's okay? Is that okay? Great.
Hope y'alls likes it.

Topsy *gets in place behind the harp and holds the pose, as the music
cues up. What follows is the most insane and brilliant spectacle anyone
can dream up, during which she doesn't play the harp once but crams the
history of African Americans onstage into three minutes. Music, video
projections everywhere, dance, lasers, disco balls, fog, backup dancers,
whatever might be totally unexpected, and it is absolutely nothing less
than utter, utter transcendence. And maybe it ends with her masturbating
with a banana. In front of a strobe light.*

*She continues to do so, even as everything fades up and it is just her on
the stage, completely exhausted. Recorded applause, even if the real*

audience is applauding, which it probably isn't. Dozens of roses begin to people the stage. A stage hand comes out to drape **Topsy** *in a robe. She is weak, but she loves the audience and the audience loves her.*

Topsy (*blowing kisses and exiting*)   Thank y'alls! Thank y'alls fo' believin' in me!

Of course, at some point, as before, an amber light has come up somewhere on the stage, illuminating the Pattersons' window, but this time the window is empty.

Lights change and immediately:

Scene Eighteen

The Pattersons' kitchen. **Richard** *is alone, drinking water and just shoveling handfuls of pills into his mouth. He is covered in blood, but he is alert. He looks like he's been stripped to a core, and you can't tell whether he's recovering or dying. He looks like complete, complete shit. He shudders and struggles to speak and breathe, slurring his words.*

Richard (*exhausted, almost unaware of himself*)
    O Rose, thou art sick
    The invisible worm,
    That flies in the night,
    In the howling storm,
    Has found out thy bed
    Of crimson joy;
    And his dark secret love
    Does thy life destroy.

Beat.

    I thought of killing myself . . . because I am only a
    bricklayer and you . . . and you a woman who loves the
    man who runs a drug store . . .

    I don't care like I used to; I lay bricks . . . straighter than
    I used to . . . and I sing slower handling the trowel
    afternoons . . .

When the sun is in my eyes . . . and the ladders are shaky . . .
and the mortar boards go wrong . . . I think of you.

Beat.

Of course I remember. I gave you that poem. But I didn't
write it. Some dead man wrote it, Jean. Some dead white man.
(*Beat, really upset. Beat, straightens up.*) No, I do. I do. I do I do I
do I do I do. (*Beat.*) I don't. (*Beat.*) I do. (*Beat.*) I thought of
killing myself. . . because I am only a bricklayer and you . . . a
woman who loved the man who runs the drug store . . . I don't
care like I used to . . . I don't care like I used to . . . Like I used
to . . . (*Beat.*) Jean, where are you? Where am I?

The door opens. He half staggers, half jumps up.

(*Almost shouting*)   Jean, baby, I'm sorr –

It's **Zip** *at the door.*

Richard   Wha?

Zip   Jean told me the door would be open.

Richard   Where is she?

Zip   She's with me. She's –

Richard   What the FUCK?

Zip   Richard.

Richard   Don't say my name! You don't know me! (*Beat, he
half collects himself.*) Where is my wife?

Zip   Your wife is with me. She's fine. She's calming down.

Richard   She what? What?

Zip   She sent me over here to see if you were okay.

Richard   Oh.

Zip   And get her stuff.

Richard   For what?

Zip   You know, I'm not sure. She just wants me to get a suitcase.

Richard   And do what with it?

Zip   Well, I think she –

Richard   What?

Zip   I think Jean needs a bit of time to herself. I –

Richard   And where is she going to go?

Zip *shrugs.*

Richard   Oh. Okay. Okay. Okay okay okay okay okay okay. I see what's happening. I see what's going on!

Zip   Listen, brother –

Richard *picks up a chair and flings it. Almost suddenly his strength is almost back.*

Richard   NIGGA, I AM NOT YOUR BROTHER!

Zip   Listen, Mister . . . You look like shit. I am going to call / an ambulance.

Richard   I DON'T NEED YOUR MOTHERFUCKING HELP MOTHERFUCKER!

Zip   I really don't think there is any need for any sort of altercation. I gotta show I'm supposed to be at –

Richard (*mocking*)   Yo' muthafuckin' show! Oooh, my little show, my little show.

Zip   But I didn't go 'cause I got a woman running into my house telling me her husband has gone berserk, all right? This is a favor, man. I am doing this as a favor to Jean, who we both know, and both love –

Richard   Love? Motherfucker, you just moved in three days ago!

Zip   Jean is a good friend –

Richard   Friend, my black ass. You. Just. Got. Here. (*Beat.*)
Man, why don't you just say it? Why don't you just come out
and fucking saying it?

Zip   Say what?

Richard   You just want to fuck my wife. You just want to
fuck my pretty white wife, because you're jealous. Jealous like
all the rest of you stupid niggers who couldn't get it together
enough to change your own life!

Pause. **Zip** *smirks a bit. He has been taking a kind of pleasure in seeing*
Richard *like this, subtle but sinister.*

Zip   Suppose I did.

Richard (*wasn't really expecting that*)   What?

Zip   Suppose I did want to fuck your wife, as you say. Then
what?

Richard *doesn't respond.*

Zip   Suppose I did notice you not wave back that morning.
Suppose I saw your snarl that said, Don't Come Here. I
recognize that snarl, Richard. I've seen it before. And suppose
I did come over in spite of that, to meet your lovely, beautiful,
sexy, intelligent, lonely, frustrated, insecure little white snowflake
of a wife and your sweet, pretty little girl. Your family, who
you've always taken for granted. And suppose I saw something
in Jean that you did, too, at least at one point, and suppose I
knew I could take it. Suppose I knew how to take it. Suppose
I've been wanting to take it ever since I saw her – no, ever
since I saw you.

Richard (*another spell coming on*)   You shut up!

Zip   And suppose I've been sitting in your house every
minute you haven't been here, listening to her poetry, stroking
her hair, charming her, whispering all kind of nice things into
her ear, telling her to lie to you, telling her she can trust me,
and she knows she can trust me, because she sees something
in me that's not in you. Anymore. And suppose I been doing

this for the past few days, before I even moved in, building something up inside of her, inside of both of you, something so intricate and crazy that I knew it could come to this.

Richard (*fainter*)   You shut your fucking mouth!

Zip   And suppose I've been waiting. Suppose I've been sitting in my house waiting, waiting for her to come across and bang on my door, screaming, yelling, HE HIT ME! HE HIT ME!

Richard (*weak*)   Fuck! You!

Zip   And suppose the first arms she runs into are mine, and suppose I grin and suppose I whisper to her, Yes, it's fine, baby girl. Zip Coon here now. Zip Coon here. And suppose I take her, and she stays wit me. (*A different* **Zip***, or maybe the same* **Zip***, or maybe a different* **Zip***.*) So what then, nigga? So what then?

Richard (*so weak*)   Shut −

Zip (*taunting*)   I know you, nigga. I seen you before. I grew up around some − a' you. I ain't even have to talk to you, before I knew you.

Richard   You don't know me.

Zip   Oh, but I do, son. I do.

Richard   You don't know me!

Zip   No, baby, I do, because, guess what? We'se da same!

Richard   No, I'm not! I'm nothing like you, you coon. You're just a fucking nigger whose clothes don't fit! A fuckin' − a fuckin' wannabe . . . no good . . . nigger . . .

Zip   Like you?

Richard   Like me . . . Not like . . . me . . . You are not like me! You are not me!

Zip   Nigga! Who is this 'me' you keep talking about? This 'you'. Who is 'you'? Where is he?

Richard   He's me.

Zip   Is he? Tell me, nigga. Have your 'you' tell 'me': where does this 'you' that is 'you' even begin to be 'you'?! Is he you?

Richard *can't find the answer, but he's trying, he's trying, he's trying.*

Zip   Or. Is. He. (*Starting to point to himself.*) Me?

Before **Zip** *can point to himself, something rushes into* **Richard***, adrenaline maybe, the dying man's last fight. He springs up and onto* **Zip***, grabbing his throat. At first,* **Zip** *is startled, but then he starts to return the fire. It's really not clear who has the upper hand, but it is violent. Things are getting overturned. Cups and saucers and plates are breaking. Glass is breaking.* **Richard** *periodically shouts 'Nigger!' at the top of his lungs, almost to God. We hear canned sounds of an auditorium in waiting, whispers, murmurs, an orchestra. Lights go to half on the brawl, which is so scary in its violence. Lights come up on the Crow family, except for* **Zip***, in the 'backstage' area.* **Jim** *looks nervous. The following happens over the cacophony of noises – the sounds of the kitchen being destroyed, the noisy auditorium.*

Mammy   Is everybody ready?

Topsy   Yes, ma'am.

Sambo   Yep.

Mammy   Jimmy?

Jim   Where's Uncle Zip?

Mammy   He's on his way.

Jim   Should we wait?

Mammy   Naw, baby. It's okay. He ain't in the overture anyway.

Jim (*nervous*)   Okay.

He goes into a corner and tries to shake off his nerves. **Sambo** *notices.*

Sambo   Don't be nervous.

Topsy   Don't be nervous, Jimmy.

Mammy   Yeah. Whatchu gots to be nervous about?

Jim   What if they don't like me? What if they don't laugh? What if they don't think I'm interesting? What if they boo?

Mammy   Oh, please. Is that all you're nervous about? Boy, don't you know they luvs us. They luvs evathang we does.

Topsy   They luvs when we dance.

Sambo   When we shucks.

Mammy   When we jives.

Topsy   When we chuckles lak dis.

Sambo   When we guffaws and slaps our thighs lak dis.

Topsy   They luvs it when we talk crazy-like.

Mammy   And we smacks our lips.

Topsy   And sucks our teefeses.

/ **Sambo**   When we be misprunoudenencing wards wrongs en stuff.

Topsy   When we make our eyes big and rolls em lak dis.

Mammy   And roll our necks and be lak, 'I know you di-in't!'

Sambo   And when we acts all gay and vogue.

Topsy   And snap like this!

Sambo   And be like 'You go, gurl.'

/ **Mammy**   When we be hummin' in church and wear big hats and be like, 'Mmmm! Testify!'

Topsy   When we ax all sad and be like, 'Dat's de bluez.'

Sambo   When we say stuff lak, 'My baby mama!'

Topsy   When we ax like we on crack lak dis.

Sambo   (*doing a stomp routine*) When we stomps our feet lak dis.

Topsy   When we drop it lak it's hot lak dis.

Sambo   When we be singin' like lak dis.

Mammy   They luvs it when we be like, 'Black people like this. White people like that.'

Sambo   They luvs it when we soliloquizing like, 'The white maaann!'

Mammy   'The white man done done me wrong!'

Sambo   'The white man put me in jail!'

Mammy   'The white man has done took my home!'

Sambo   'The white man has emasculated me!'

Topsy   'The white man made me wanna be white!'

Sambo   'I can't get out the ghettooooo!'

Mammy   'I hates myself!'

Sambo   'I hates the white man!'

Mammy   'I hates the world!'

Topsy   'But I can't break these chains!'

Mammy   'These white man chains!'

Sambo   'Even though I'm a human, dammit! I am human!'

Topsy   'Respect me, white maaaaan!'

Sambo   ''Cause I'm so angrrryyyy!'

Mammy   They luvs when we be lak dat.

Topsy   So if you get nervus, just do dat.

Sambo   Do any uh dat.

Mammy   And you be fine, baby. Be yo'self. It's just a show.

Jim   You right. Okay. Okay. I can do this. Okay.

Mammy   Good. So you ready, Jimmy?

Jim   Yes. I think so. I'm ready.

Everyone prepares. The fighting in the kitchen is still happening.

Announcer's Voice   Now presenting . . . THE CROW
FAMILY MINSTRELS!

*Recorded applause. The kitchen continues to be destroyed. The atmosphere
is soaked in the ash cloud that is Jim Crow Sr. The Crow family
without* **Zip** *take their place on 'stage', standing in a straight line.
'Dixie' plays, but they don't move. Instead, they simply look into every
face in the room, as the song slowly fades.* **Zip** *and* **Richard** *are still
fighting in half-light, and this is the only sound we hear, as the entire
family looks the entire audience over. Just before 'Dixie' is gone and
silence arrives, the entire theater, house and all, is ever so slowly and
completely washed in amber light. We watch them. They watch us. We
watch each other.*

*Occasionally, the family point to people in the audience and whisper
together, sometimes mockingly, sometimes out of concern. Maybe they
giggle.*

Sudden blackout.

*Silence before lights come back up for curtain call. Only the Crow family
takes a bow, and we see in the front row of the audience* **Melody***, who
gives the most exuberant standing ovation you have ever seen. There are
even tears of joy in her eyes. She's there for her boyfriend. The Crow
family bows and exits the empty stage.*

There is no 'real' curtain call, and **Melody** *leaves with the audience.
She goes outside and has a cigarette. She doesn't talk to anyone, waiting
at the stage door, maybe with her mother. She looks different now, maybe,
less like herself. Her mother house manages.*

Eventually **Jim** *comes out of the stage door to greet her. They hug and
kiss. Maybe she gives him a cigarette, which he smokes. Maybe people
catch this, maybe they don't.*

Melody   How do you feel?

*'We Are Family' is heard blasting away over the speakers back in the
empty theater, as the actor playing Jim Crow starts to tell her how he
really feels.*